MW00580791

## ACKNOWLEDGMENT

The patent rights in the Montessori apparatus and material are controlled, in the United States and Canada, by The House of Childhood, Inc., 16 Horatio Street, New York. The publishers are indebted to them for the photographs showing the Grammar Boxes.

# TRANSLATOR'S NOTE

So far as Dr. Montessori's experiments contain the affirmation of a new doctrine and the illustration of a new method in regard to the teaching of Grammar, Reading and Metrics, the following pages are, we hope, a faithful rendition of her work. But it is only in these respects that the chapters devoted to these subjects are to be considered a translation. It will be observed that Dr. Montessori's text is not only a theoretical treatise but also an actual text-book for the teaching of Italian grammar, Italian reading and Italian metrics to young pupils. Her exercises constitute a rigidly "tested" material: her Italian word lists are lists which, in actual practise, have accomplished their purpose; her grammatical categories with their relative illustration are those actually mastered by her Italian students; her reading selections and her metrical analyses are those which, from an offering doubtless far more extensive, actually survived the experiment of use in class.

It is obvious that no such value can be claimed for any "translation" of the original material. The categories of Italian grammar are not exactly the categories of English grammar. The morphology and, to a certain extent, the syntax of the various parts of speech differ in the two languages. The immediate result is that the Montessori material offers much that is inapplicable and fails to touch on much that is essential to the teaching of English grammar. The nature and extent of the difficulties thus arising are more fully set forth in connection with specific cases in our text. Suffice it here to indicate that the English material offered below is but approximately "experimental," approximately scientific. The constitution of a definitive Montessori material for English grammar and the definitive manner and order of its presentment must await the results of experiments in actual use. For the clearer orientation of such eventual experiments we offer, even for those parts of Italian grammar which bear no relation to English, a virtually complete translation of the original text; venturing meanwhile the suggestion that such studies as Dr. Montessori's treatise on the teaching of Italian noun and adjective inflections — entirely foreign to English — may prove valuable to all teachers of modern languages. While it might seem desirable to isolate such superfluous material from the "English grammar" given below, we decided to retain the relative paragraphs in their actual position in the Italian work, in order to preserve the literal integrity of the original method. Among our additions to the text we may cite the exercises on the possessive pronouns — identified by Dr. Montessori with the possessive adjectives — the interrogatives and the comparison of adjectives and adverbs.

Even where, as regards morphology, a reasonably close adaptation of the Italian material to English uses has been possible, it by no means follows that the pedagogical problems involved remain the same. The teaching of the relative pronoun, for instance, is far more complicated in English than in Italian; in the sense that the steps to be taken by the child are for English more numerous and of a higher order. Likewise for the verb, if Italian is more difficult as regards variety of forms, it is much more simple as regards negation, interrogation and progressive action. We have made no attempt to be consistent in adapting the

translation to such difficulties. In general we have treated
the parts of speech in the order in which they appear in
the Italian text, though actual experiment may prove that
some other order is desirable for the teaching of English
grammar. The English material given below is thus in
part a translation of the original exercises in Italian, in
part new. In cases where it proved impossible to utilize
any of the Italian material, an attempt has been made to
find sentences illustrating the same pedagogical principle
and involving the same number and character of mental
processes as are required by the original text.

The special emphasis laid by Dr. Montessori upon selections from Manzoni is due simply to the peculiar conditions
surrounding the teaching of language in Italy, where general concepts of the national language are affected by the
existence of powerful dialects and the unstable nature of
the grammar, vocabulary and syntax of the national literature. We have made no effort to find a writer worthy of
being set up as a like authority, since no such problem
exists for the American and English public. Our citations
are drawn to a large extent from the " Book of Knowledge " and from a number of classics. Occasionally for
special reasons we have translated the Italian original.
The chapter on Italian metrics has been translated entire
as an illustration of method ; whereas the portion relating
to English is, as explained below, entirely of speculative
character.

To Miss Helen Parkhurst and Miss Emily H. Green-
man thanks are due for the translation of the chapters on
Arithmetic, Geometry, and Drawing.

# CONTENTS

## PART I

### GRAMMAR

# CONTENTS

## PART II

### READING

## PART III

### ARITHMETIC

# CONTENTS

# PART IV

## GEOMETRY

# PART V

## DRAWING

# CONTENTS

## PART VI

### MUSIC

## PART VII

### METRICS

# ILLUSTRATIONS

# PART I

# GRAMMAR

# MONTESSORI ELEMENTARY
# MATERIAL

## I

## THE TRANSITION FROM THE MECHANICAL TO THE INTELLECTUAL DEVELOPMENT OF LANGUAGE

In the " Children's Houses " we had reached a stage of development where the children could write words and even sentences. They read little slips on which were written different actions which they were to execute, thus demonstrating that they had understood them. The material for the development of writing and reading consisted of two alphabets: a larger one with vowels and consonants in different colors, and a smaller one with all the letters in one color.

(In English, to diminish the phonetic difficulties of the language, combinations of vowels and consonants, known as phonograms, are used. The phonograms with few exceptions have constant sounds and little attention is paid to the teaching of the separate values of the different letters: not until the child has built up his rules inductively does he realize the meaning of separate vowel symbols.)

However, the actual amount of progress made was not very precisely ascertained. We could be sure only that the children had acquired the mechanical technique of

3

writing and reading and were on the way to a greater intellectual development along these lines. Their progress, however extensive it may have been, could be called little more than a foundation for their next step in advance, the elementary school. What beyond all question was accomplished with the little child in the first steps of our method was to establish the psycho-motor mechanism of the written word by a slow process of maturation such as takes place in the natural growth of articulate speech; in other words, by methodically exercising the psycho-motor paths.

Later on the child's mind is able to make use of the successive operations performed with the written language which has been thus built up by the child as a matter of mechanical execution (writing) and to a certain extent of intelligent interpretation (reading). Normally this is an established fact at the age of five. When the child begins to think and to make use of the written language to express his rudimentary thinking, he is ready for elementary work; and this fitness is a question not of age or other incidental circumstance but of mental maturity.

We have said, of course, that the children stayed in the "Children's House" up to the age of seven; nevertheless they learned to write, to count, to read, and even to do a certain amount of simple composition. It is clear, accordingly, that they had gone some distance in the elementary grade as regards both age and educational development. However, what they had actually accomplished beyond the mechanical technique of writing was more or less difficult to estimate. We can now say that our later experiments have not only clarified this situation, but enabled us to take the children much farther along than before.

This only proves, however, that on beginning elementary grade work we did not depart from the "Children's House" idea; on the contrary we returned to it to give distinct realization to the nebulous hopes with which our first course concluded. Hence the "Children's House" and the lower grades are not two distinct things as is the case with the Fröbel Kindergarten and the ordinary primary school — in fact, they are one and the same thing, the continuation of an identical process.

Let us return then to the "Children's House" and consider the child of five and one-half years. To-day in those "Children's Houses" which have kept up with the improvements in our method the child is actually started on his elementary education. From the second alphabet of the "Children's House" we go on to a third alphabet. Here the movable letters are a great deal smaller and are executed in model hand-writing. There are twenty specimens of each letter, whereas formerly there were but four; furthermore, there are three complete alphabets, one white, one black, and one red. There are, therefore, sixty copies of each letter of the alphabet. We include also all the punctuation marks: period, comma, accents (for Italian), apostrophe, interrogation and exclamation points. The letters are made of plain glazed paper.

The uses of this alphabet are many; so before we stop to examine them let us look somewhat ahead. Everybody has recognized the naturalness of the exercise, used in the "Children's House," where the children placed a card bearing the name of an object on the object referred to. This was the first lesson in reading. We could see that the child knew how to read as soon as he was able to identify the object indicated on the card. In schools all over the world a similar procedure would, I imagine, be considered logical.  I suppose that in all the schools where the objective method is used much the same thing is done; and this is found to be not a hindrance but a help to the child in learning the names of objects.  As regards the teaching of the noun, accordingly, we have been using methods already in use — the objective method, with practical exercises.  But why should we restrict such methods to the noun?  Is the noun not just as truly a *part of speech* as the adjective, or the verb?  If there is a method by which the knowledge of a noun is made easy, may there not be similar ways of facilitating the learning of all the other parts of speech (article, adjective, verb, pronoun, adverb, interjection, conjunction, and preposition)?

When a slip with the interpreted word is placed on the object corresponding to it, the children are actually distinguishing the noun from all the other parts of speech. They are learning intuitively to define it.  The first step has thus been taken into the realm of grammar.  But if this "reading" has brought the child directly into word *classification,* the transition has not been for him so abrupt as might at first appear.  The child has built *all* his words with the movable alphabet, and he has, in addition, *written* them.  He has thus traversed a two-fold preparatory exercise involving, first, the analysis of the sounds and, second, the analysis of the words in their meaning.  In fact, we have seen that, as the child reads, it is his discovery of the tonic accent that brings him to recognize the word. The child has begun to analyze not only the sounds and accent but also the form of the word.[1]

[1] The process of learning to read has been more fully set forth in *The Montessori Method:* the child at first pronounces the sounds represented by the individual letters (phonograms), without under-

How absurd it would seem to suggest a study of phonology and morphology in a nursery with four-year-old children as investigators! Yet our children have accomplished this very thing! The analysis was the means of attaining the word. It was what made the child able to write without effort. Why should such a procedure be useful for single words and not so for connected discourse? Proceeding to the classification of words by distinguishing the noun from all other words, we have really advanced into the analysis of connected speech, just as truly as, by having the sand-papered letters "touched" and the word pronounced, we took the first step into the analysis of words. We have only to carry the process farther and perhaps we shall succeed in getting the analysis of whole sentences, just as we succeeded in getting at the composition of words — discovering meanwhile a method which will prove efficacious in leading the child to write his thoughts more perfectly than would seem possible at such a tender age.

For some time, then, we have been actually in the field of grammar. It is a question simply of continuing along the same path. The undertaking may indeed seem hazardous. Never mind! That "awful grammar," that horrible bugaboo, no less terrible than the frightful method, once in use, of learning to read and write, may perhaps become a delightful exercise, a loving guide to lead the child along pleasant pathways to the *discovery* of things he has *actually performed*. Yes, the child will suddenly find himself, one day, in possession of a little composition, a little "work of art," that has issued from

standing what they mean. As he repeats the word several times he comes to read more rapidly. Eventually he discovers the tonic accent of the word, which is then immediately identified.

his own pen! And he will be as happy over it as he was when for the first time words were formed by his tiny hands!

How different grammar will seem to the young pupil, if, instead of being the cruel assassin that tears the sentence to pieces so that nothing can be understood, it becomes the amiable and indispensable help to "the construction of connected discourse"! It used to be so easy to say: "The sentence is written! Please leave it alone!" Why put asunder what God has joined? Why take away from a sentence its meaning, the very thing which gave it life? Why make of it a mere mass of senseless words? Why spoil something already perfect just for the annoyance of plunging into an analysis which has no apparent purpose? Indeed, to impose upon people who can already read the task of reducing every word to its primal sounds, would be to demand of them an effort of will so gigantic that only a professional philologist could apply himself to it with the necessary diligence, and then only because he has his own particular interests and aims involved in such work. Yet the four-year-old child, when he passes from those meaningless sounds to the composition of a whole, which corresponds to an idea and represents a useful and wonderful conquest, is just as attentive as the philologist and perhaps even more enthusiastic. He will find the same joy in grammar, if, starting from analyses, it gains progressively in significance, acquiring, step by step, a greater interest, working finally up to a climax, up to the moment, that is, when the finished sentence is before him, its meaning clear and *felt* in its subtlest essences. The child has created something beautiful, full grown and perfect at its birth, not now to be tampered with by anybody!

The analysis of sounds which, in our method, leads to spontaneous writing, is not, to be sure, adapted to all ages. It is when the child is four or four and a half, that he shows the characteristically childlike passion for such work, which keeps him at it longer than at any other age, and leads him to develop perfection in the mechanical aspect of writing. Similarly the analytical study of parts of speech, the passionate lingering over words, is not for children of all ages. It is the children between five and seven who are the *word-lovers*. It is they who show a predisposition toward such study. Their undeveloped minds can not yet grasp a complete idea with distinctness. They do, however, understand *words*. And they may be entirely carried away by their ecstatic, their tireless interest in the *parts* of speech.

It is true that our whole method was born of heresy. The first departure from orthodoxy was in holding that the child can best learn to write between the ages of four and five. We are now constrained to advance another heretical proposition: children should begin the study of grammar between the ages of five and a half and seven and a half, or eight!

The idea that analysis must be preceded by construction was a matter of mere prejudice. Only things produced by nature must be analyzed before they can be understood. The violet, for instance, is found perfect in nature. We have to tear off the petals, cut the flower into sections, to see how it grew. But in making an artificial violet we do just the opposite. We prepare the stems piece by piece; then we work out the petals, cutting, coloring, and ironing them one by one. The preparation of the stamens, even of the glue with which we put the whole together, is a distinct process. A few simple-minded peo-

ple, with a gift for light manual labor, take unbounded
delight in these single operations, these wonderfully varied steps which all converge to the creation of a pretty
flower; the beauty of which depends on the amount of
patience and skill applied to the work on the individual
parts.

Analysis, furthermore, is involved quite as much in
building as in taking to pieces. The building of a house
is an analytical process. The stones are treated one by
one from cellar to roof. The person who puts the house
together knows it in its minutest details and has a far
more accurate idea of its construction than the man who
tears it down. This is true, first, because the process of
construction lasts much longer than that of demolition:
more time is spent on the study of the different parts.
But besides this, the builder has a point of view different
from that of the man who is destroying. The sensation of
seeing a harmonious whole fall into meaningless bits has
nothing in common with the alternating impulses of hope,
surprise or satisfaction which come to a workman as he
sees his edifice slowly assuming its destined form.

For these and still other reasons, the child, when interested in words at a certain age, can utilize grammar
to good purpose, dwelling analytically upon the various
parts of speech according as the processes of his inner
spiritual growth determine. In this way he comes to own
his language perfectly, and to acquire some appreciation
of its qualities and power.

Our grammar is not a book. The nouns (names),
which the child was to place on the objects they referred
to as soon as he understood their meaning, were written
on cards. Similarly the words, belonging to all the other
parts of speech, are written on cards. These cards are all

of the same dimensions: oblongs (5 × 3½ cmm.) of different colors: black for the noun; tan for the article; brown for the adjective; red for the verb; pink for the adverb; violet for the preposition; yellow for the conjunction; blue for the interjection.

These cards go in special boxes, eight in number. The first box has two compartments simply; the second, however, three; the third, four; and so on down to the eighth, which is divided into nine. One wall in each section is somewhat higher than the others. This is to provide space for a card with a title describing the contents of the section. It bears, that is, the name of the relative part of speech. The title-card, furthermore, is of the same color as that used for the part of speech to which it refers. The teacher is expected to arrange these boxes so as to provide for the study of two or more parts of speech. However, our experiments have enabled us to make the exercises very specific in character; so that the teacher has at her disposal not only a thoroughly prepared material but also something to facilitate her work and to check up the accuracy of it.

## II

## WORD STUDY

When a little child begins to read he shows a keen desire to learn words, words, words! Indeed in the " Children's House " we had that impressive phenomenon of the children's tireless reading of the little slips of paper upon which were written the names of objects.

The child must acquire his word-store for himself. The peculiar characteristic of the child's vocabulary is its meagerness. But he is nearing the age when he will need to express his thoughts and he must now acquire the material necessary for that time. Many people must have noticed the intense attention given by children to the conversation of grown-ups when they cannot possibly be understanding a word of what they hear. They are trying to get hold of *words,* and they often demonstrate this fact by repeating joyously some word which they have been able to grasp. We should second this tendency in the child by giving him an abundant material and by organizing for him such exercises as his reactions clearly show us are suitable for him.

The material used in our system not only is very abundant, but it has been dictated to us by rigid experimentation on every detail. However, the same successive choices of material do not appear among the children as a whole. Indeed their individual differences begin to assert themselves progressively at this point in their education. The exercises are easy for some children and very hard for others, nor is the order of selection the same among all the children. The teacher should know this material thoroughly. She should be able to recognize the favorable moment for presenting the material to the child. . As a matter of fact, a little experience with the material is sufficient to show the teacher that the educational facts develop spontaneously and in such a way as to simplify the teacher's task in a most surprising manner.

### Suffixes and Prefixes

Here we use charts with printed lists of words which may be hung on the wall. The children can look at them and also take them in their hands.

### List I

#### SUFFIXES: AUGMENTATIVES, DIMINUTIVES, PEGGIORA- TIVES, ETC.

*buono (good):* buonuccio, buonino, buonissimo

*casa (house):* casona, casetta, casettina, casuccia, casaccia, casettaccia

*formica (ant):* formicona, formicuccia, formicola, formichetta

*ragazzo (boy):* ragazzone, ragazzino, ragazaccio, ragazzetto

*lettera (letter):* letterina, letterona, letteruccia, letteraccia

*campana (bell):* campanone, campanello, campanellino, campanino, campanaccio

*giovane (youth):* giovanetto, giovincello, giovinastro

*fiore (flower):* fioretto, fiorellino, fioraccio, fiorone

*tavolo (board):* tavolino, tavoletta, tavolone, tavolaccio

*seggiola (chair):* seggiolone, seggiolina, seggiolaccia

*pietra (stone):* pietruzza, pietrina, pietrone, pietraccio

*sasso (rock):* sassetto, sassolino, sassettino, sassone, sassaccio

*cesto (basket):* cestino, cestone, cestello, cestellino

*piatto (plate):* piattino, piattello, piattone

*pianta (plant* or *tree):* piantina, pianticella, pianticina, pianterella, piantona, piantaccia *fuoco (fire):* fuochetto, fuochino, fuocherello, fuocone, fuochettino

*festa (festival):* festicciola, festona, festaccia

*piede (foot):* piedino, piedone, pieduccio, piedaccio

*mano (hand):* manina, manona, manaccia, manuccia

*seme (seed):* semino, semetto, semone, semaccio, semettino

*semplice (simple person):* semplicino, semplicetto, sempliciotto, ·
  semplicione

*ghiotto (" sweet-tooth "):* ghiottone, ghiottoncello, ghiottaccio,
  ghiottissimo

*vecchio (old man):* vecchietto, vecchione, vecchiaccio, vecchissimo

*cieco (blind):* ciechino, ciechetto, ciecolino, ciecone, ciecaccio

Note: — The rôle of augmentative and diminutive suffixes in English is vastly less important than in Italian. Here are a few specimens:

| | |
|---|---|
| *lamb* — lambkin | *mouse* — mousie |
| *duck* — duckling | *girl* — girlie |
| *bird* — birdling | *book* — booklet |
| *nest* — nestling | *brook* — brooklet |
| *goose* — gosling | *stream* — streamlet |
| | *poet* — poetaster |

The child's exercise is as follows: he composes the first word in any line with the alphabet of a single color (e.g., black). Next underneath and using the alphabet of the same color, he repeats the letters in the second word which he sees also in the first. But just as soon as a letter changes he uses the alphabet of another color (e.g., red). In this way the root is always shown by one color, the suffixes by another; for example: —

buono
buon*uccio*
buon*ino*
buon*issimo*

*For English:*

stream
stream*let*
lamb
lamb*kin*

Then the child chooses another word and repeats the same exercise. Often he finds for himself words not included in the list which is given him.

In the following chart the suffixes are constant while the root varies. Here the suffix changes the meaning of the word. From the original meaning is derived the word for a trade, a place of business, an action, a collective or an abstract idea. Naturally, the child does not realize all this at first but limits himself merely to building the words mechanically with the two alphabets. Later on, however, as grammar is developed, he may return to the reading of these charts, which are always at his disposal, and begin to realize the value of the differences.

## LIST II

macello (slaughter) — macellaio (butcher)
sella (saddle) — sellaio (saddler)
forno (oven) — fornaio (baker)
cappello (hat) — cappellaio (hatter)
vetro (glass) — vetreria (glaziery)
calzolaio (shoe-maker) — calzoleria (shoe-shop)
libro (book) — libreria (book-store)
oste (host) — osteria (inn)
pane (bread) — panetteria (bakery)
cera (wax) — cereria (chandler's shop)
dente (tooth) — dentista (dentist)
farmacia (pharmacy) — farmacista (druggist)
elettricità (electricity) — elettricista (electrician)
telefono (telephone) — telefonista (telephone operator)
arte (art) — artista (artist)
bestia (beast) — bestiame (cattle)
osso (bone) — ossame (bones, *collective*)
corda (string) — cordame (strings, *collective*)
foglia (leaf) — fogliame (foliage)

pollo (chicken)       pollame (poultry)
grato (grateful)      gratitudine (gratitude)
beato (blessed)       beatitudine (blessedness)
inquieto (uneasy)     inquietudine (uneasiness)
grano (grain)         granaio (barn)
colombo (dove)        colombaio (dove-cote)
paglia (straw)        pagliaio (hay-stack)
frutto (fruit)        frutteto (orchard)
canna (reed)          canneto (brake)
oliva (olive)         oliveto (olive-grove)
quercia (oak)         querceto (oak-grove)

### ENGLISH EXAMPLES

teach         teacher
sing          singer
work          worker
cater         caterer
wring         wringer
conduct       conductor
direct        director
launder       laundry
seam          seamstress
song          songstress
priest        priestess
mister        mistress
cow           cowherd
piano         pianist
art           artist
pharmacy      pharmacist
drug          druggist
physic        physician
prison        prisoner
house         household
earl          earldom
king          kingdom
count         county
real          reality
modern        modernness
good          goodness
sad           sadness
aloof         aloofness

The child's exercise with the two alphabets will be as follows:

| | | | |
|---|---|---|---|
| frutto | frutt*eto* | oliva | oliv*eto* |
| canna | cann*eto* | quercia | querc*eto* |

*For English:*

| | | | |
|---|---|---|---|
| song | song*ster* | song*stress* | |
| art | art*ist* | art*less* | art*ful* |

## List III

### PREFIXES

*nodo (knot):* annodare, snodare, risnodare
*scrivere (write):* riscrivere, trascrivere, sottoscrivere, descrivere
*coprire (cover):* scoprire, riscoprire
*gancio (hook):* agganciare, sganciare, riagganciare
*legare (bind):* collegare, rilegare, allegare, slegare
*bottone (button):* abbottonare, sbottonare, riabbottonare
*macchiare (spot):* smacchiare, rismacchiare
*chiudere (close):* socchiudere, schiudere, richiudere, rinchiudere
*guardare (look at):* riguardare, traguardare, sogguardare
*vedere (see):* travedere, rivedere, intravedere
*perdere (lose):* disperdere, sperdere, riperdere
*mettere (put, place):* smettere, emettere, rimettere, permettere, commettere, promettere, sottomettere
*vincere (overcome):* rivincere, avvincere, convincere, stravincere

*For English:*

*cover:* uncover, discover, recover
*pose:* impose, compose, dispose, repose, transpose
*do:* undo, overdo
*place:* displace, replace, misplace
*submit:* remit, commit, omit, permit
*close:* disclose, foreclose, reclose
*arrange:* rearrange, disarrange

The child's exercise with the two alphabets will be as follows:

coprire
*s*coprire
*ri*coprire

*For English:*

place
*dis*place
*re*place

## LIST IV

### COMPOUND WORDS

cartapecora (parchment)
cartapesta (papier maché)
falsariga (guide)
madreperla (mother-of-pearl)
melagrana (pomegranate)
melarancia (orange)
biancospino (hawthorn)
ficcanaso (busybody)
lavamano (wash-stand)
mezzogiorno (noon)
passatempo (pastime)
ragnatela (cobweb)
madrevite (vine)
guardaportone (doorkeeper)
capoluogo (capital)
capomaestro ("boss")
capofila (pivot-soldier)
capopopolo (demagogue)
caposquadra (commodore)
capogiro (dizziness)
capolavoro (masterpiece)
giravolta (whirl)

mezzaluna (half moon)
mezzanotte (midnight)
palcoscenico (stage)
acchiappacani (dog-catcher)
cantastorie (story-teller)
guardaboschi (forester)
lustrascarpe (boot-black)
portalettere (letter-carrier)
portamonete (pocketbook)
portasigari (cigar-case)
portalapis (pencil-case)
portabandiera (standard bearer)
guardaroba (wardrobe)
asciugamano (towel)
cassapanca (wooden bench)
arcobaleno (rainbow)
terrapieno (rampart, terrace)
bassorilievo (bas-relief)
granduca (grand-duke)
pianoforte (piano)
spazzacamino (chimney-sweep)
pettorosso (redbreast).

*For English:*

sheepskin
cardboard
shoestring
midnight
midday
noontime

redbreast
appletree
afternoon
moonlight
starlight
doorknob

| | |
|---|---|
| bedtime | bathroom |
| daytime | streetcar |
| springtime | lifelike |
| flagstaff | pocketbook |
| rainbow | inkwell |
| workman | tablecloth |
| housekeeper | courtyard |
| pastime | honeycomb |
| chimneysweep | beehive |
| sheepfold | flowerpot |
| barnyard | buttonhole |
| sidewalk | hallway |
| snowshoe | midway |
| shoeblack | storekeeper |
| firefly | horseman |
| steamboat | masterpiece |
| milkman | bookcase |

The children read one word at a time and try to reproduce it from memory, distinguishing through the two alphabets the two words of which each one is composed:

| | |
|---|---|
| carta *pecora* | spazza *camino* |
| bianco *spino* | lava *mano* |
| piano *forte* | |

*For English:*

moon *light*
work *man*

In the following chart the words are grouped in families. This chart may be used by children who are already well advanced in the identification of the parts of speech. All the words are derived from some other more simple word which is a root and of which the other words, either by suffix or prefix, are made up. All these roots are primitive words which some day the child may look for in a group of derivatives; and when he finds them he will realize that the primitive word is a noun, adjective, or a verb, as the case may be, that it is the word which contains the simplest idea, and so the derivatives may be nouns, adjectives, verbs or adverbs.

On these charts appear various word-families. The teacher is thus spared the trouble of looking them up. Furthermore the child will some day be able to use them by himself. The exercises based on these are still performed with two different alphabets of different color so that the child can tell at a glance which is the root word.

### WORD-FAMILIES

*terra (earth):* terrazzo, terremoto, terrapieno, atterrare, terreno, terriccio, terricciola, territorio, conterraneo, terreo, terroso, dissotterrare

*ferro (iron):* ferraio, ferriera, ferrata, ferrigno, ferrugginoso, ferrare, sferrare, inferriata

*soldo (penny):* assoldare, soldato, soldatesca, soldatescamente

*grande (great):* ingrandire, grandiosità, grandioso, grandiosamente, grandeggiare

*scrivere (write):* scrittura, scritto, scritturare, scrittore, inscrizione, trascrivere, sottoscrivere, riscrivere

*beneficio (benefit):* beneficare, benefattore, beneficato, beneficenza, beneficamente

*benedizione (benediction):* benedire, benedicente, benedetto, ribenedire

*felicità (happiness):* felice, felicemente, felicitare, felicitazione

*fiamma (flame):* fiammante, fiammeggiante, fiammeggiare, fiammelle, fiammiferi, infiammare

*bagno (bath):* bagnante, bagnino, bagnarola, bagnatura, bagnare, ribagnare

*freddo (cold):* freddolose, infreddatura, freddamente, raffreddore, raffreddare, sfreddare

*polvere (dust):* spolverare, impolverare, polverino, polverizzare, polverone, polveroso, polveriera, polverizzatore

*pesce (fish):* pescare, pescatore, ripescare, pescabile, ripescabile *opera (work):* operaio, operare, operazione, operoso, operosamente, cooperare, cooperazione, inoperare

*canto (song):* cantore, cantante, cantare, cantarellare, canticchiare, ricantare

*gioco (game):* giocare, giocattolo, giocarellare, giocatore, giocoso, giocosamente

*dolore (pain):* doloroso, dolorosamente, dolente, addolorare, dolersi, condolersi, condoglianza, addolorato

*pietra (stone):* pietrificare, pietrificazione, pietroso, impietrire, pietraio

*sole (sun):* assolato, soleggiante, soleggiare

*festa (festival):* festeggiare, festino, festeggiatore, festeggiato, festaiolo, festante, festevole, festevolmente, festosamente

*allegro (happy):* allegria, allegramente, rallegrare, rallegramento

*seme (seed):* semina, semenze, seminare, semenzaio, seminatore, riseminare, seminazione, disseminare, seminatrice

*For English:*

*wood:* wooden, woodworker, woody, woodsman, woodland

*earth:* earthen, earthy, earthly, earthborn, earthward, earthquake, earthling

*fish:* fishing, fisherman, fishery, fishy, fishmonger, fishnet

*well:* welcome, wellmeaning, wellknit

*war:* warrior, warlike, warship, warhorse, war-whoop, warsong, war-cry

*play:* player, playful, playhouse, playmate

*politic:* politics, politician, political, polity, politically

*hard:* hardly, harden, hardness, hardship, hardy, hardihood, hardware

*turn:* return, turner, turnstile

*close:* disclose, closet, unclose, closure, foreclose

The child sees that the mother word is always the shortest. The *root* remains in one color.

# III

## ARTICLE AND NOUN

[Note: — The English language presents a far simpler situation than the Italian as regards the agreement of article and adjectives. Gender itself being, in the case of English nouns, more a matter of logical theory than of word-ending, adjectival agreement in the formal sense is practically unknown to English grammar. Likewise the formation of the plural is much simpler in English than in Italian, where the singular and plural word-endings are closely associated with gender. It is a question, in fact, whether the whole subject of the gender of English nouns should not be taken up somewhat later in connection with the pronouns, where English shows three singular forms masculine, feminine, neuter (him, her, it) as against the Italian two, masculine and feminine (*lo, la,* plural *li, le,* etc.). Signora Montessori's discussion of the situation in Italian still remains instructive to the teacher of English as an illustration of method. We retain her text, accordingly, in its entirety.— Tr.]

As we have already said, the words chosen for grammatical study are all printed on small rectangular pieces of cardboard. The little cards are held together in packages by an elastic band and are kept in their respective boxes. The first box which we present has two compartments. In the holders at the back of each compartment are placed the cards which show the part of speech to be studied, in this case *article* and *noun.* The article cards are placed in the article compartment and the nouns in the noun compartment. When the children have finished their exercise they replace the cards — the nouns in the place for the nouns and the articles in the place for the articles. If the words *article* and *noun* are not a sufficient guide for the child, the color at least will make the task easy. In fact the child will place the black cards for the noun in the compartment indicated by the black guide-card (marked *noun*); the tan cards for the article with the tan guide-card (marked *article*). This exercise recalls the child's experience with the alphabet boxes, where one copy of each letter is pasted to the bottom of the box as a guide for the child in replacing the other letters. The child begins to speak of the *article-section,* the *noun-section,* and *article-cards* and *noun-cards.* In so doing he begins to *distinguish* between the parts of speech. The material must be prepared very accurately and in a definitely determined quantity. For the first exercise, the children are given boxes with the articles and nouns shuffled together in their respective compartments. But there must be just enough articles of each gender to go with the respective nouns. The child's task is to put the right article in front of the right noun — a long and patient research, which, however, is singularly fascinating to him.

We have prepared the following words. We should recall, however, that the cards are not found in the boxes in this order, but are mixed together — the articles shuffled in their box-section and the nouns in theirs.

il fazzoletto (the handkerchief)    i colori (the colors)
il libro (the book)    i fiori (the flowers)
il vestito (the dress)    i disegni (the drawings)
il tavolino (the *little* table)    i compagni (the companions)
lo specchio (the mirror)    gli zoccoli (the *wooden* shoes)
lo zucchero (the sugar)    gli uomini (the men)
lo zio (the uncle)    gli articoli (the articles)
lo stivale (the boot)    le sedie (the chairs)

la stoffa (the cloth)                le scarpe (the shoes)
la perla (the pearl)                 le addizioni (the sums)
la piramide (the pyramid)            le piante (the plants, the trees)
la finestra (the window)

l'occhio (the eye)
l'amico (the friend)
l'acqua (the water)
l'albero (the tree)
gl'invitati (the guests)
gl'incastri (the insets)
gl'italiani (the Italians)
gl'insetti (the insects)

(We suggest as a corresponding English exercise the
introduction of the *indefinite* article. This substitution
involves four processes against the eight of the Italian
exercise. The use of *an* before a vowel is quite analogous to the problem of the Italian *l'* and *gl'*. However,
the theoretical distinction between the definite and indefinite article, as regards meaning, is reserved by Signora Montessori to a much later period, though the practical distinctions appear in the earliest *Lessons and Commands.*— Tr.)

the handkerchief              the colors
the book                      the flowers
the dress                     the drawings
the table                     the children
the mirror                    the shoes
the sugar                     the men

a man                         an orange
a pearl                       an apple
a prism                       an uncle
a card                        an eye
a window                      an insect
a chair                       an American
a tree                        an aunt

The child tries to combine article and noun and puts
them side by side on his little table. In this exercise he is

One of the first steps in grammar. The children are deeply interested in placing the correct articles and nouns together. (*A Montessori School in Italy.*)

Grammar Boxes. The one on the left is for articles and nouns only; the one on the right, for articles, nouns, and adjectives.

guided by sound just as he was in building words with the movable alphabet. There the child's first step was to find relationships between real objects and the linguistic sounds corresponding to them. Now he sees suddenly revealed to him hitherto unsuspected relationships between these sounds, these words. To have an empirical way of demonstrating and testing these relationships, to practise very thoroughly on two kinds of words, suddenly brought forth into systematic distinctness from the chaos of words in his mind, offers the child not only a necessary exercise but the sensation of relief which comes from satisfying an inner spiritual need. With the most intense attention he persists to the very end of the exercise and takes great pride in his success. The teacher as she passes may glance about to see if all the cards are properly placed, but the child, doubtless, will call her to admire or verify the work that he has done, before he begins to gather together, first, all the articles, then, all the nouns, to return them to their boxes.

This is the first step; but he proceeds with increasing enthusiasm to set the words in his mind "in order," thereby enriching his vocabulary by placing new acquisitions in an already determined place. Thus he continues to construct, with respect to exterior objects, an inner spiritual system, which had already been begun by his sensory exercises.

### SINGULAR AND PLURAL

The exercises on the number and gender of nouns are done without the help of the boxes. The child already knows that those words are articles and nouns, so we give him now small groups of forty cards (nouns and articles) held together by an elastic band. In each one, the group (tied separately) of the ten singular nouns serves as the guide for the exercise. These nouns are arranged in a column on the table, one beneath the other, and the other cards, which are shuffled, must be placed around this first group in the right order. There are two more cards of different colors on which the words *singular* and *plural* respectively are written; and these are placed at the top of the respective columns. We have prepared four series of ten nouns in alphabetical order. In this way four children may do the exercise at the same time and by exchanging material they come in contact with a very considerable number of words.

This is the way the cards should finally be arranged in the four different exercises:

| Singolare | Plurale | Singular | Plural |
|---|---|---|---|
| il bambino | i bambini | the child | the children, |
| il berretto | i berretti | the cap | etc. |
| la bocca | le bocche | the mouth | |
| il calamaio | i calamai | the inkstand | |
| la calza | le calze | the stocking | |
| la casa | le case | the house | |
| il cappello | i cappelli | the hat | |

| Singolare | Plurale | Singular | Plural |
|---|---|---|---|
| la maestra | le maestre | the teacher | the teachers, |
| la mano | le mani | the hand | etc. |
| la matita | le matite | the pencil | |
| il naso | i nasi | the nose | |
| il nastro | i nastri | the ribbon | |
| l'occhio | gli occhi | the eye | |
| l'orologio | gli orologi | the clock (watch) | |
| il panchetto | i panchetti | the bench | |

| Singolare | Plurale | Singular | Plural |
|---|---|---|---|
| il dente | i denti | the tooth | the teeth, |
| l'elastico | gli elastici | the elastic | etc. |
| il fagiolo | i fagioli | the bean | |
| la fava | le fave | the bean | |
| la gamba | le gambe | the leg | |
| il gesso | i gessi | the plaster | |
| la giacca | le giacche | the coat | |
| il grembiale | i grembiali | the apron | |

| Singolare | Plurale | Singular | Plural |
|-----------|---------|----------|--------|
| il piede | i piedi | the foot | the feet, |
| il quaderno | i quaderni | the copy book | etc. |
| la rapa | le rape | the turnip | |
| la scarpa | le scarpe | the shoe | |
| la tasca | le tasche | the pocket | |
| il tavolino | i tavolini | the table | |
| la testa | le teste | the head | |
| l'unghia | le unghie | the nail (finger) | |

Like material has been prepared for the masculine and feminine forms: The masculine group is kept by itself, while the feminines are shuffled.

| Maschile | Femminile | Masculine | Feminine |
|----------|-----------|-----------|----------|
| il conte | la contessa | the count | the countess, |
| l'amico | l'amica | the friend | etc. |
| l'asino | l'asina | the donkey | |
| il babbo | la mamma | the father | |
| il benefattore | la benefattrice | the benefactor | |
| il bottegaio | la bottegaia | the shop-keeper | |
| il cugino | la cugina | the cousin | |
| il cuoco | la cuoca | the cook | |
| il cacciatore | la cacciatrice | the hunter | |
| il cavallo | la cavalla | the horse | |

| Maschile | Femminile | Masculine | Feminine |
|----------|-----------|-----------|----------|
| il duca | la duchessa | the duke | the duchess, |
| il canarino | la canarina | the canary | etc. |
| il dottore | la dottoressa | the doctor | |
| il dattilografo | la dattilografa | the stenographer | |
| l'elefante | l'elefantessa | the elephant | |
| il figlio | la figlia | the son | |
| il fratello | la sorella | the brother | |
| il gallo | la gallina | the cock | |
| il gatto | la gatta | the cat | |

| Maschile | Femminile | Masculine | Feminine |
|----------|-----------|-----------|----------|
| il leone | la leonessa | the lion | the lioness, |
| l'ispettore | l'ispettrice | the inspector | etc. |
| il lupo | la lupa | the wolf | |
| il lettore | la lettrice | the reader | |
| il maestro | la maestra | the schoolmaster | |
| il marchese | la marchesa | the marquis | |
| il mulo | la mula | the mule | |
| il nonno | la nonna | the grandfather | |
| il nemico | la nemica | the enemy | |

| Maschile | Femminile | Masculine | Feminine |
|---|---|---|---|
| l'oste | l'ostessa | the host | the hostess, |
| l'orologiaio | l'orologiaia | the watch-maker | etc. |
| il poeta | la poetessa | the poet | |
| il pellicciaio | la pellicciaia | the furrier | |
| il padre | la madre | the father | |
| il re | la regina | the king | |
| il ranocchio | la ranocchia | the frog | |
| lo sposo | la sposa | the husband | |
| il servo | la serva | the man-servant | |
| il somaro | la somara | the ass | |

Finally there are three series of nouns in four forms: Singular and Plural, Masculine and Feminine. Each group has eighty cards counting both nouns and articles, and the ten singular masculines in the guiding group are kept together, apart from the others. The title cards (twelve in number) are *singular* and *plural* and for each of them is a card marked *masculine* and a card marked *feminine*. The following is the order of the material when properly arranged by the child:

| SINGOLARE | | SINGULAR | |
|---|---|---|---|
| *Maschile* | *Femminile* | *Masculine* | *Feminine* |
| l'amico | l'amica | the friend | the friend, |
| il bambino | la bambina | the child | etc. |
| il burattinaio | la burattinaia | the puppet-player | |
| il contadino | la contadina | the peasant | |
| il cavallo | la cavalla | the horse | |
| il compagno | la compagna | the companion | |
| il disegnatore | la disegnatrice | the designer | |
| il dattilografo | la dattilografa | the stenographer | |
| l'ebreo | l'ebrea | the Jew | |
| il fanciullo | la fanciulla | the boy | |

| PLURALE | | PLURAL | |
|---|---|---|---|
| *Maschile* | *Femminile* | *Masculine* | *Feminine* |
| gli amici | le amiche | the friends | the friends, |
| i bambini | le bambine | the children | etc. |
| i burattinai | le burattinaie | the puppet-players | |
| i contadini | le contadine | the peasants | |
| i cavalli | le cavalle | the horses | |
| i compagni | le compagne | the companions | |

| PLURALE | | PLURAL | |
| --- | --- | --- | --- |
| *Maschile* | *Femminile* | *Masculine* | *Feminine* |
| i disegnatori | le disegnatrici | the designers | |
| i dattilografi | le dattilografe | the stenographers | |
| gli ebrei | l'ebree | the Jews | |
| i fanciulli | le fanciulle | the boys | |

| SINGOLARE | | SINGULAR | |
| --- | --- | --- | --- |
| *Maschile* | *Femminile* | *Masculine* | *Feminine* |
| il gatto | la gatta | the cat | the cat, |
| il giardiniere | la giardiniera | the gardener | etc. |
| il giovinetto | la giovinetta | the youth | |
| l'infermiere | l'infermiera | the nurse | |
| l'italiano | l'italiana | the worker | |
| il lavoratore | la lavoratrice | the Italian | |
| il medico | la medichessa | the physician | |
| il materassaio | la materassaia | the mattress-maker | |
| l'operaio | l'operaia | the workman | |
| il pittore | la pittrice | the painter | |

| PLURALE | | PLURAL | |
| --- | --- | --- | --- |
| *Maschile* | *Femminile* | *Masculine* | *Feminine* |
| i gatti | le gatte | the cats | the cats, |
| i giardinieri | le giardiniere | the gardeners | etc. |
| i giovinetti | le giovinette | the youths | |
| gl'infermieri | le infermiere | the nurses | |
| gl'italiani | le italiane | the Italians | |
| i lavoratori | le lavoratrici | the workers | |
| i medici | le medichesse | the physicians | |
| i materassai | le materassaie | the mattress-makers | |
| gli operai | le operaie | the workmen | |
| i pittori | le pittrici | the painters | |

| SINGOLARE | | SINGULAR | |
| --- | --- | --- | --- |
| *Maschile* | *Femminile* | *Masculine* | *Feminine* |
| il ragazzo | la ragazza | the boy | the girl, |
| il romano | la romana | the Roman | etc. |
| lo scolare | la scolara | the scholar | |
| il sarto | la sarta | the tailor | |
| il santo | la tagliatrice | the saint | |
| il tagliatore | la donna | the cutter | |
| l'uomo | la vecchia | the man | |
| il vecchio | la visitatrice | the old man | |
| il visitatore | la zia | the visitor | |
| lo zio | la santa | the uncle | |

| PLURALE | | PLURAL | |
|---|---|---|---|
| *Maschile* | *Femminile* | *Masculine* | *Feminine* |
| i ragazzi | le ragazze | the boys | the girls, |
| i romani | le romane | the Romans | etc. |
| gli scolari | le scolare | the scholars | |
| i sarti | le sarte | the tailors | |
| i santi | le sante | the saints | |
| i tagliatori | le tagliatrici | the cutters | |
| gli uomini | le donne | the men | |
| i vecchi | le vecchie | the old men | |
| i visitatori | le visitatrici | the visitor | |
| gli zii | le zie | the uncles | |

Occasionally class exercises are used in our schools for the four forms of the Italian noun, masculine and feminine, singular and plural. They take the form almost of a game, which the children find amusing. A child for instance distributes around the class all the plural nouns. Then he reads aloud a noun in the singular. The child who holds the corresponding plural answers immediately. The same thing is next done for masculine and feminine, and, finally, for all four forms at once.

When these exercises have become familiar to the child, others somewhat more difficult may be presented. These new ones comprise: nouns which change form completely as they change gender and of which, so far, only the most familiar examples (*babbo,* "father," *mamma,* "mother," etc.) have been given (Series A); nouns in which the form is the same in the singular of both genders (Series B); those in which both genders have a common form in the singular and a common form in the plural (Series C); nouns which have only one form for both singular and plural (Series D); nouns where the same form appears in both genders but with a different meaning (Series E); finally, nouns which change gender as they pass from the singular to the plural (Series F).

## SERIES A

| Singolare | | Singular | |
|---|---|---|---|
| *Maschile* | *Femminile* | *Masculine* | *Feminine* |
| il babbo | la mamma | the father | the mother |
| il becco | la capra | the he-goat | the she-goat |
| il frate | la suora | the friar | the nun |
| il fratello | la sorella | the brother | the sister |
| il genero | la nuora | the son-in-law | the daughter-in-law |
| il montone | la pecora | the ram | the ewe |
| il maschio | la femmina | the male | the female |
| il marito | la móglie | the husband | the wife |
| il padre | la madre | the father | the mother |
| il padrino | la madrina | the godfather | the godmother |
| il porco | la scrofa . | the hog | the sow |
| il toro | la vacca | the bull | the cow |
| l'uomo | la donna | the man | the woman |
| il re | la regina | the king | the queen |

| Plurale | | Plural | |
|---|---|---|---|
| *Maschile* | *Femminile* | *Masculine* | *Feminine* |
| i babbi | le mamme | the fathers | the mothers, etc. |
| i becchi | le capre | the he-goats | |
| i frati | le suore | the friars | |
| i fratelli | le sorelle | the brothers , | |
| i generi | le nuore | the sons-in-law | |
| i montoni | le pecore | the rams | |
| i maschi | le femmine | the males | |
| i mariti | le mogli | the husbands | |
| i padri | le madri | the fathers | |
| i padrini | le madrine | the godfathers | |
| i porci | le scrofe | the hogs | |
| i tori | le vacche | the bulls | |
| gli uomini | le donne | the men . | |
| i re | le regine | the kings | |

## SERIES B

| Singolare | | Singular | |
|---|---|---|---|
| *Maschile* | *Femminile* | *Masculine* | *Feminine* |
| l'artista | l'artista | the artist | the artist, etc. |
| il collega | la collega | the colleague | |
| il dentista | la dentista | the dentist | |
| il pianista | la pianista | the pianist | |
| il telefonista | la telefonista | the telephone operator | |
| il telegrafista | la telegrafista | the telegraph operator | |
| il violinista | la violinista | the violinist | |

| PLURALE | | PLURAL | |
|---------|---|--------|---|
| *Maschile* | *Femminile* | *Masculine* | *Feminine* |
| gli artisti | le artiste | the artists | the artists, |
| i colleghi | le colleghe | the colleagues | etc. |
| i dentisti | le dentiste | the dentists | |
| i pianisti | le pianiste | the pianists | |
| i telefonisti | le telefoniste | the telephone operators | |
| i telegrafisti | le telegrafiste | the telegraph operators | |
| i violinisti | le violiniste | the violinists | |

## SERIES C

| SINGOLARE | | SINGULAR | |
|-----------|---|----------|---|
| *Maschile* | *Femminile* | *Masculine* | *Feminine* |
| il consorte | la consorte | the husband | the wife, |
| il custode | la custode | the keeper | etc. |
| il cantante | la cantante | the singer | |
| l'erede | l'erede | the heir | |
| il giovane | la giovane | the youth | |
| l'inglese | l'inglese | the Englishman | |
| il nipote | la nipote | the nephew (grandson) | |

| PLURALE | | PLURAL | |
|---------|---|--------|---|
| *Maschile* | *Femminile* | *Masculine* | *Feminine* |
| i consorti | le consorti | the husbands | the wives, |
| i custodi | le custodi | the guards | etc. |
| i cantanti | le cantanti | the singers | |
| gli eredi | l'eredi | the heirs | |
| i giovani | le giovani | the youths | |
| gl'inglesi | le inglesi | the Englishmen | |
| i nipoti | le nipoti | the nephews (grandsons) | |

## SERIES D

| *Singolare* | *Plurale* | *Singular* | *Plural* |
|-------------|-----------|------------|----------|
| il bazar | i bazar | the bazaar | the bazaars, |
| il caffè | i caffè | the coffee | etc. |
| il gas | i gas | the gas | |
| la gru | le gru | the crane | |
| il lapis | i lapis | the pencil | |
| la libertà | le libertà | the liberty | |
| l'omnibus | gli omnibus | the omnibus | |
| la virtù | le virtù | the virtue | |

## SERIES E

| SINGOLARE | | SINGULAR | |
|---|---|---|---|
| *Maschile* | *Femminile* | *Masculine* | *Feminine* |
| il melo | la mela | the apple tree | the apple |
| il pesco | la pesca | the peach tree | the peach |
| l'ulivo | l'uliva | the olive tree | the olive |
| il pugno | la pugna | the blow (punch) | the battle |
| il manico | la manica | the handle | the sleeve |
| il suolo | la suola | the floor | the sole |

| PLURALE | | PLURAL | |
|---|---|---|---|
| *Maschile* | *Femminile* | *Masculine* | *Feminine* |
| i meli | le mele | the apple trees | the apples |
| i peschi | le pesche | the peach trees | the peaches |
| gli ulivi | le ulive | the olive trees | the olives |
| i pugni | le pugne | the blows (punches) | the battles |
| i manichi | le maniche | the handles | the sleeves |
| i suoli | le suole | the floors | the soles |

## SERIES F

| *Singolare* | *Plurale* | *Singular* | *Plural* |
|---|---|---|---|
| il centinaio | le centinaia | the hundred | the hundreds, |
| il dito | le dita | the finger | etc. |
| la eco | gli echi | the echo | |
| il paio | le paia | the pair | |
| il riso | le risa | the smile (laugh) | |
| l'uovo | le uova | the egg | |

### THE SINGULAR AND PLURAL IN ENGLISH

TRANSLATOR'S NOTE: — While the formation of the English plural does not present the complications of gender that appear in Italian, the phonetic adaptations required by the plural ending -s along with certain orthographical caprices and historical survivals of the language, result in a situation somewhat more complex than that treated by Signora Montessori. In fact, her analysis of the Italian plural requires eight word-lists, while English requires at least fourteen, not including the question of foreign nouns. The special stress on the article is hardly necessary in English. An analogous treatment for English would be somewhat as follows:

## SERIES I
### (Simple plurals in -s)

| Singular | Plural | Singular | Plural |
|----------|--------|----------|--------|
| book | books | train | trains |
| bed | beds | ticket | tickets |
| desk | desks | car | cars |
| street | streets | floor | floors |
| tree | trees | chair | chairs |
| card | cards | pin | pins |
| prism | prisms | shoe | shoes |
| lamp | lamps | wagon | wagons |
| cow | cows | bean | beans |
| cat | cats | counter | counters |

## SERIES II
### (Plurals in -es, including -s pronounced like -es)
#### LIST A

| Singular | Plural | Singular | Plural |
|----------|--------|----------|--------|
| house | houses | case | cases |
| horse | horses | sausage | sausages |
| prize | prizes | wedge | wedges |
| judge | judges | edge | edges |
| cage | cages | ledge | ledges |

#### LIST B

| Singular | Plural | Singular | Plural |
|----------|--------|----------|--------|
| bush | bushes | watch | watches |
| church | churches | topaz | topazes |
| box | boxes | class | classes |
| fox | foxes | wretch | wretches |
| glass | glasses | | |

## SERIES III
### (Plurals of Nouns in -o)
#### LIST A

| Singular | Plural | Singular | Plural |
|----------|--------|----------|--------|
| potato | potatoes | volcano | volcanoes |
| negro | negroes | tomato | tomatoes |

SERIES III

(Plurals of Nouns in -o)

LIST A

| hero | heroes | motto | mottoes |
| mosquito | mosquitoes | domino | dominoes |

LIST B

| Singular | Plural | Singular | Plural |
| --- | --- | --- | --- |
| piano | pianos | dynamo | dynamos |
| soprano | sopranos | canto | cantos |
| zero | zeros | solo | solos |
| banjo | banjos | memento | mementos |
| halo | halos | chromo | chromos |

SERIES IV

(Nouns in -f or -fe)

LIST A

| Singular | Plural | Singular | Plural |
| --- | --- | --- | --- |
| calf | calves | shelf | shelves |
| elf | elves | thief | thieves |
| half | halves | leaf | leaves |
| loaf | loaves | self | selves |
| wolf | wolves | | |

LIST B

| Singular | Plural | Singular | Plural |
| --- | --- | --- | --- |
| knife | knives | life | lives |
| wife | wives | | |

LIST C

| Singular | Plural | Singular | Plural |
| --- | --- | --- | --- |
| staff | staffs | scarf | scarfs |
| wharf | wharfs | chief | chiefs |
| puff | puffs | fife | fifes |
| cliff | cliffs | | |

## SERIES V
### (Nouns in -*y*)
#### LIST A

| Singular | Plural | Singular | Plural |
|----------|--------|----------|--------|
| body | bodies | soliloquy | soliloquies |
| sky | skies | sty | sties |
| gipsy | gipsies | Mary | Maries |
| berry | berries | ferry | ferries |
| penny | pennies | country | countries |

#### LIST B

| Singular | Plural | Singular | Plural |
|----------|--------|----------|--------|
| boy | boys | day | days |
| valley | valleys | derby | derbys |

## SERIES VI
### (Plurals in -*en*)

| Singular | Plural | Singular | Plural |
|----------|--------|----------|--------|
| child | children | brother | brethren |
| ox | oxen | | (brothers) |

## SERIES VII
### (Plurals with internal change (umlaut))

| Singular | Plural | Singular | Plural |
|----------|--------|----------|--------|
| foot | feet | mouse | mice |
| tooth | teeth | man | men |
| goose | geese | woman | women |
| louse | lice | | |

## SERIES VIII
### (Singular and Plural identical)

| Singular | Plural | Singular | Plural |
|----------|--------|----------|--------|
| sheep | sheep | deer | deer |
| fish | fish | swine | swine |

## SERIES IX
### (Compound words)
#### LIST A

| *Singular* | *Plural* |
|---|---|
| black-bird | black-birds |
| steamboat | steamboats |
| redcoat | redcoats |
| redbreast | redbreasts |
| forget-me-not | forget-me-nots |
| spoonful | spoonfuls |
| mouthful | mouthfuls |

#### LIST B

| *Singular* | *Plural* |
|---|---|
| brother-in-law | brothers-in-law |
| mother-in-law | mothers-in-law |
| court-martial | courts-martial |
| attorney-general | attorneys-generals |
| general-in-chief | generals-in-chief |
| Knight-Templar | Knights-Templar |

All these groups of words in their order are reproduced in special booklets which the children may take home and read. In actual practise such books have proved both convenient and necessary. The children generally spend much time on them and delight in reading the words over and over in the order in which they themselves have discovered them in the card exercise. This recalls and fixes their own ideas, inducing a sort of inner maturation which is often followed by the spontaneous discovery of grammatical laws on the relations of nouns, or by a lively interest which throws the children into exclamations or laughter as they observe what great differences of meaning are sometimes caused by a very slight change in the word. At the same time these simple exercises, so fruitful in results, may be used for work at home and well meet the demands for something to do with which children are continually assailing their parents. For homework we have prepared alphabets where the letters are printed in type-writing order. With them the child can compose words, or later, sentences, at the same time becoming familiar with the alphabet arrangement of standard typewriters.

# IV

## LESSONS — COMMANDS

The first lessons in grammar which I gave to children go back fully sixteen years. I first attempted the education of defectives in the "Scuola Magistrale Ortofrenica" in Rome in the year 1899 following a course of lectures I had given to teachers in the normal school of our capital. In this experiment I went far enough with primary work to prepare some of the defective children for successful examinations in the public schools. A very brief and incomplete summary of my pedagogical studies delivered in the teacher's courses is given in the appendix to this volume.

The teaching of grammar was not at that time so complete as it has since been made in my work with normal children; even so it was a marked success. Grammar was actually *lived* by the children, who became deeply interested in it. Even those wretched children who came, like rubbish thrown out of the public schools, directly off the street or from the insane asylums, passed delightful half hours of joyous laughter over their exercises in grammar. Here are some excerpts from the old pamphlet of 1900 giving an idea of the didactic material which was then used and some notion of a lesson on nouns. "As each word is read or written for every object-lesson, for every action, printed cards are being assembled which will later be used to make clauses and sentences with words that may be moved about just as the individual letters were moved about in making the words themselves. The simple clauses or sentences should refer to actions performed by the children. The first step should be to bring two or more words together: e.g., *red-wool, sweet-candy, four-footed dog,* etc. Then we may go on to the sentence itself: *The wool is red; the soup is hot; the dog has four feet; Mary eats the candy,* etc. The children first compose the sentences with their cards; then they copy them in their writing books. To facilitate the choice of the cards, they may be arranged in special boxes: for instance, one box may be labeled *noun:* or the boxes may be distinguished thus: *food, clothing, animals, people,* etc. There should be a box for *adjectives* with compartments for colors, shapes, qualities, etc. There should be another for *particles,* with compartments for articles, conjunctions, prepositions, etc. A box should be reserved for *actions,* with the label *verbs* above it, and containing compartments for the infinitive, present, past and future. The children gradually learn by practise to take their cards from the boxes and put them back in their proper places. They soon learn to know their "word boxes" and they readily find the cards they want among the *colors, shapes, qualities,* etc., or among *animals, foods,* etc. Ultimately the teacher will find occasion to explain the meaning of the big words written at the top of the drawers, *noun, adjective, verb,* etc., and this will be the first step into the subject of *grammar.*

NOUNS

We may call persons and objects by their *name,* their *noun.* People answer if we call them, so do animals.

Inanimate objects, however, never answer, because they cannot; but if they could they would. For example, if I say *Mary,* Mary answers; if I say *peas,* the peas do not answer, because they cannot. You children *do* understand when I call an object and you *bring* it to me. I say, for example, *book, beans, peas.* If I don't tell you the name of the object, you don't understand what I am talking about; because every object has a different name. This *name* is the word that stands for the object. This name is a *noun.*

Whenever I mention a noun to you, you understand immediately the object which the noun represents: tree, chair, pen, book, lamb, etc. If I do not give this noun, you don't know what I am talking about; for, if I say simply *bring me* .... *at once, I want it,* you do not know what I want, unless I tell you the name of the object. Unless I give you the *noun,* you do not understand. Thus every object is represented by a word which is its *name;* and this name is a *noun.* To understand whether a word is a noun or not, you simply ask: *Is it a thing? Would it answer if I spoke to it?* or *Could I carry it to the teacher?* For instance, *bread:* yes, bread is an object; *table:* yes, it is an obejct; *conductor:* yes, the conductor would answer, if I were to speak to him.

Let us look through our cards now. I take several cards from different boxes and shuffle them. Here is the word *sweet.* Bring me *sweet!* Is there anything to answer when I call *sweet?* But you are bringing me a piece of candy! I didn't say *candy:* I said *sweet.* And now you have given me *sugar!* I said *sweet! Sweet,* you see, is not an object. You cannot guess what I have in mind when I say *sweet.* If I say *candy, sugar,* then you understand what I want, what object I am thinking about, because the words *candy, sugar,* stand for objects. Those words are *nouns*." [1]

This summary, however, fails to give a real idea of the success of these lessons. When I said with a tone of decision, as if I could not think of the necessary word, " Bring me — bring me — bring me —," the children would gather round me, looking fixedly at my lips, like so many little dogs, waiting for me to throw something for them to fetch. They were in fact ready to run and get what I wanted. But the word refused to come. " Bring me —, bring me —." Finally in great impatience I cried, " But bring it to me quick — I want it." Then their faces lit up and they would laughingly cry, " But bring you what? What is it you want? What shall we bring you? "

This was the real lesson on the noun, and when, after great difficulty, the word " *sweet* " came out, the children would run and bring me every possible object that was sweet. I would refuse each one in turn. " No, I didn't ask for candy! No, I didn't ask for sugar! " The children would look at the object they had in their hands, half laughing, half puzzled and beginning to realize that *sweet* was not a *name,* that it was not a *noun.* These first lessons, which seemed something like commands that needed the help of the children to express themselves, brought the children to understand some part of speech, while evoking, at the same time, vivid and interesting scenes. They furnished the original impulse to the development we have reached to-day in our lessons on grammar. For such lessons we have adopted the term " commands." But with normal children these " commands " were gradually multiplied and evolved. They are no longer entrusted to the

1 See pp. 446–448.

teacher's ingenuity; nor are they dependent solely upon her dramatic sense — something essential if she is to stimulate the weak nervous reactions of little defectives and so gain and hold their attention. The "commands" to-day are written and may be read. They are combined with the card-exercises where the cards are read in silence and interpreted through actions — a method which grew spontaneously and with such great success from the work in the "Children's House." That is why, to-day, we speak in the elementary courses of "reading commands" or even of "writing commands."

The study of grammar has finally been arranged in a methodical series of exercises and the material has been prepared after careful and rigid experiment. Those who read this method will get a clear idea of the teacher's task. She has a material ready for use. She need not bother to compose a single sentence nor to consult a single program. The objects at her disposal contain all that is necessary. She need know simply what they are and how they are to be used. The lessons which she must give are so simple, and require so few words, that they become lessons rather of gesture and action than of words. It must be borne in mind, further, that the work is not as uninteresting as would appear from this arid summary. The actual school is a real intellectual laboratory, where the children work all the time and by themselves. After the material has been presented to them, they *recognize* it and like to hunt for it. They know how to find for themselves the precious objects which they want to use. They often exchange materials and even lessons with other children. The few lessons the teacher gives connect, as it were, a system of live wires, which set in motion activities quite disproportionate to the energy expended in the simple act she performs. She pushes, so to speak, a button and here a bell rings, there a light goes on, there a machine begins to buzz. Very often the teacher sees a whole week go by without any need of intervention on her part. .

And yet what delicacy and tact are necessary properly to "offer" this material, to give in an interesting way a lesson calculated to exert a direct action upon the child's spiritual activity! How skilful we must be to leave all the child's spontaneous impulses free to develop themselves, to keep careful watch over so many different individual impulses! This we must do if we are to "keep the lamp burning"! When, for example, on passing a table where the child has analyzed a sentence with the colored cards, the teacher shifts about, as if in play, one of the little slips, not only must she be possessed of the psychological insight necessary for intervening in this child's work at the proper time, but she must also have in mind the grammatical rule of which she wishes to give the child his first intuition. It follows that every single act of the teacher, however insignificant apparently, is, like the acts of the priest in the service, of the greatest importance, and should come from a consciousness thoroughly awake, and full of potentiality. Instead of giving out what she has in herself, the teacher must bring out the full possibilities of the children.

The teacher's extrinsic preparation is a matter of thorough acquaintance with the material. It should be so much a part of her that she knows at once what is needed for each individual case as soon as it arises. Actual practise soon develops this skill.

The exercises are performed with these little packages of specially prepared cards. The most important problem (for Italian grammar) is in the *agreements;* the agree-

ment of article and noun, as we have already shown, the
agreement of noun and adjective, and later on of pronoun
and verb, and pronoun and noun. There are two kinds
of exercises, which we have termed respectively " analyses " and " commands."

The *commands* involve both work done by the teacher
and exercises performed by the children. The purpose
here is to clarify the meanings of words and often to suggest a *practical* interpretation of them. This *explanation* is followed by an exercise of the children themselves,
who in turn practically interpret the meaning of one or
more sentences written on a card which they read just as
they did in the first exercises of reading in the " Children's House." On this card are the words which the
teacher has just explained. In our experiments we gave
these lessons immediately after " silence " just as we did
for reading in the " Children's House." All the children, however, do not necessarily take part in these executions — oftenest it is only a group of children, sometimes
one child alone, again, at other times, almost all of them.
If possible the commands are given in another room, while
the other children continue their work in the large hall.
If this is not possible it takes place in the same room.
These commands might be called " an introduction to
dramatic art," for right there little dramatic scenes full
of vivacity and interest are " acted out." The children
are singularly delighted in working for the one exact " interpretation " which a given word requires.

The *analyses,* on the other hand, are of quite different
character. " Analysis " is done at the table. It is work
which requires quiet and concentration. While the command gives the *intuition,* the analysis provides for the
*maturation* of the idea. The grammar boxes are used in

these exercises. In a larger compartment which each box contains, are placed several slips bearing a printed sentence; for example, *Throw down your handkerchief.* The child draws a slip and places it to one side on the table. Then he takes from the different boxes the colored slips corresponding to the different words in the sentence and places them side by side one after the other. In this way he composes the entire sentence: *Throw down your handkerchief.* The child is actually doing here a very simple thing: he is merely translating into colored cards the sentence which is printed on his slip. He composes this sentence in the same way in which he has already composed words with the moveable alphabet. But here the exercise is even more simple because the child need not remember the sentence, for it is there right before his eyes. His attention must be concentrated on other facts, so that all intellectual effort in the composition of the sentence itself is eliminated. The child has to note the colors and the position of the cards in the different boxes, since he must take the cards now from the noun box, now from the adverb box, now from that of the preposition, etc.; and the colors together with the position (each section has a title, as we have already seen) strengthen his consciousness of a *classification* of words according to *grammar.*

But what really makes this exercise in analysis so interesting is the teacher's repeated permutation of the different cards. As she goes by a table she changes, as though in fun, the position of a card, and in this way provokes the intuition of grammatical rules and definitions. Indeed, when she takes out the card, which refers to some new part of the exercise, the remaining sentence with its changed meaning emphasizes the function of the part of speech which has been moved. The effect shows a distant analogy to the light that pathology and vivisection throw on physiology. An organ which fails in its function illustrates exactly that function, for never does one realize the precise use of an organ more clearly than when it has lost its power of functioning. Furthermore the removal of the words demonstrates that the meaning of the sentence is not given by the word alone but by the *order* of the word in the sentence, and this makes a great impression on the child. He sees the same cards first in a chaotic mass and then in an orderly arrangement. What was first a collection of meaningless words has suddenly become the expression of a *thought*.

From now on the child begins to experience a keen interest in the *order* of words. The meaning, the only thing the child is after, is no longer hidden in confusion. He begins to enjoy subtle permutations, changes which, without destroying the expression of a thought, obscure its clarity, complicate it, or make it " sound wrong." It is here that the teacher must have at her fingertips the rules governing the position of the various parts of speech. This will give her the necessary " lightness of touch," perhaps even the opportunity of making some brilliant little explanation, some casual observation, which may suddenly develop in the child a profound " grammatical insight." When the child has understood this he will become a deep " strategist " in mobilizing, disposing and moving about these cards which express *thought;* and if he really succeeds in mastering this secret, he will not be easily satiated with so fascinating an exercise. No one but a child would ever have the patience to study grammar so profoundly and at such length. This subtle work is, after all, not so easy for the teacher. That is why the material must be such as to suggest each step in detail. The

teacher should be relieved as much as possible of the labor
of preparation and research: for her delicate work of *intervention* is a task hard enough in itself.   In preparing
this material we have worked for her: we have acted as
the workmen who produce the various objects necessary
to life; she has but to "live" and "make live."   This
will show still more clearly how far from truth is the
modern conception of pedagogy which attempts to realize
its desire for freedom in the school by saying to the
teacher, "Try to respond to the needs of the pupils without being conscious of your authority over them."   When
we ask a teacher to respond to the needs of the inner life
of man, we are asking a great deal of her.   She will never
be able to accomplish it, unless we have first done something for her by giving her all that is necessary to that
end.   Here is our material: —

### COMMANDS ON NOUNS
#### "CALLING"

Call loudly:

Mary! Lucy! Ethel!

Later call again:

Blonde! Beautiful! Good!

Call:

Peter! bring a chair.
George! bring a cube.
Louis! get a frame.
Charles! Charles! quick! bring me the . . . bring it to me,
  quick, quick.

Call slowly this way:

Come! Come! give me a kiss — please, come!

Then say:

Mary! come! give me a kiss!

These commands lend themselves to a little dramatic
scene.   It is really a sort of play, which the children recite.

The tendency to recitation and to imitation is very
strong and often well developed at the age of five years.
Little children experience a singular fascination in pronouncing the words with sentiment and in accompanying
them with gestures.   One can hardly imagine the simplicity of the little dramatic acts which interest the five
year old child.   Nothing but actual experiment could possibly have revealed it to us.   One day, in fact, our little
children were invited to be present at a dramatic enter-
tainment given by the older children of the Public Schools.
They followed it with really surprising interest.   However, they remembered only three words of the play they
had heard; but with these three words they made up a
little dramatic action of their own, which they repeated
over and over again the following day.

The commands of these " call " cards are, accordingly,
real plays for our little ones.   The child calls, pronouncing the name with a sort of sustained drawl; the child who
is called comes forward; then the same thing is done with
the other names, and each child obeys as he is called.
Then the incomplete calls begin: *blonde! blonde! beautiful!*   And no one moves!   This makes a great impression on the children.   Imperative commands, like re-
quests, lend themselves to active dramatic action.   Peter
has been called and has brought his chair; George has
brought the cube; Louis has taken out a frame; but
Charles sits there intent, expectant, while the child calls
out,— *But bring it to me, bring it to me quickly!*   And
how expressive we found the vain request,— *Come, come!
please give me a kiss,— come, come!*   At last the cry,—

*Mary! come!* brings the resulting action and Mary runs to give the kiss which has been so long invoked!

These little " plays " require a real study of the parts, and the children rehearse their different rôles over and over again.

# V

## ADJECTIVES

MATERIAL: *Grammar box.*
*Various objects already familiar to the children.*
*New objects.*

The material for word analysis consists of small cards for articles (tan), nouns (black) and adjectives (brown). There is one box with three compartments, each section marked with a card bearing the respective title: *article, noun, adjective.* At the front of the box is a space for other cards containing printed sentences to be analyzed.

### DESCRIPTIVE ADJECTIVES

The child is to read the sentences, find the objects described in them, and finally build the sentences with his cards as follows: suppose the card reads:

| | |
|---|---|
| il colore verde | the green color |
| il colore turchino | the blue color |
| il colore rosso | the red color |

The child finds the three colored tablets used in the familiar exercise of the " Children's House " for the education of the sense of color. He places these tablets on his table. Then he builds the phrases out of his word cards:

| il | colore | verde | the | green | color |
|----|--------|-------|-----|-------|-------|

Beside the completed expression he places the green
color-tablet.  Passing to the next phrase, he does not disturb the words *the* and *color*.  He removes only the word
*green* and substitutes for it the adjective *blue,* at the same
time removing the green tablet and substituting for it the
blue.  Similarly, for the third phrase, he changes the adjective, putting the red tablet at the end.  Thus the *three
different objects* were distinguished *only* by the adjective:

$$il\ colore \begin{cases} \text{verde} \\ \text{turchino} \\ \text{rosso} \end{cases} \quad the \begin{cases} \text{green} \\ \text{blue} \\ \text{red} \end{cases} color$$

All the phrases and sentences refer to objects used in
the previous educational material.  Occasionally the
teacher will have to prepare something herself (e.g., hot,
cold, warm, or iced water; clear water; colored water).
For this exercise on *water,* the box contains six slips with
the six printed phrases.  In the box-sections, the child
finds the corresponding word-cards which are exactly in
the number needed for the exercise (not corresponding,
that is, to the number of words in the phrases, since the
articles and nouns are not repeated).  There are five
groups of such exercises, dealing with various kinds of
sensation.

| A. SENSO CROMATICO | SENSE OF COLOR |
|---|---|
| il colore rosa | the pink color |
| il colore rosa scuro | the dark pink color |
| il colore rosa chiaro | the light pink color |
| | |
| il prisma azzurro | the blue prism |
| il prisma marrone | the brown prism |

| A. Senso Cromatico | Sense of Color |
|---|---|
| il colore verde | the green color |
| il colore turchino | the blue color |
| il colore rosso | the red color |
| | |
| i lapis neri | the black pencils |
| i lapis colorati | the colored pencils |
| | |
| l'acqua colorata | the colored water |
| l'acqua incolora | the clear water |
| | |
| il colore giallo | the yellow color |
| il colore arancione | the orange color |

| B. Senso Visivo: Dimensioni | Sense of Sight: Size |
|---|---|
| l'asta lunga | the long staff |
| l'asta corta | the short staff |
| | |
| il cubo grande | the large cube |
| il cubo piccolo | the small cube |
| | |
| il cilindro alto | the tall cylinder |
| il cilindro basso | the short cylinder |
| | |
| il prisma marrone grosso | the thick brown prism |
| il prisma marrone fino | the thin brown prism |
| | |
| il rettangolo largo | the broad rectangle |
| il rettangolo stretto | the narrow rectangle |
| | |
| l'incastro solido | the solid inset |
| l'incastro piano | the plane inset |

| C. Senso Visivo: Forma | Sense of Sight: Shape |
|---|---|
| il triangolo equilatero | the equilateral triangle |
| il triangolo isocele | the isoceles triangle |
| il triangolo scaleno | the scalene triangle |
| | |
| il triangolo acutangolo | the acute-angled triangle |
| il triangolo ottusangolo | the obtuse-angled triangle |
| il triangolo rettangolo | the right-angled triangle |
| | |
| l'incastro circolare | the circular inset |
| l'incastro quadrato | the square inset |
| l'incastro rettangolare | the rectangular inset |
| | |
| la piramide quadrangolare | the quadrangular pyramid |
| la piramide triangolare | the triangular pyramid |

| C. Senso Visivo: Forma | Sense of Sight: Shape |
|---|---|
| il prisma azzurro rettangolare | the blue rectangular prism |
| il prisma azzurro quadrangolare | the blue quadrangular prism |
| | |
| la scatola cilindrica | the cylindrical box |
| la scatola prismatica | the prismatic box |

| D.  Senso Tattile: Muscolare | Sense of Touch: Muscular Sense |
|---|---|
| la superfice piana | the flat surface |
| la superfice curva | the curved surface |
| | |
| la stoffa ruvida | the rough cloth |
| la stoffa liscia | the smooth cloth |
| | |
| l'acqua calda | the hot water |
| l'acqua fredda | the cold water |
| l'acqua tiepida | the warm water |
| | |
| l'acqua fredda | the cold water |
| l'acqua ghiacciata | the  iced water |
| | |
| la tavoletta pesante | the heavy black-board |
| la tavoletta leggera | the light black-board |
| | |
| la stoffa morbida | the soft cloth |
| la stoffa dura | the hard cloth |

| E.  Senso Uditivo; Olfattivo; Gustativo | Senses of Hearing; Smell; Taste |
|---|---|
| il rumore forte | the loud noise |
| il rumore leggero | the faint noise |
| | |
| il suono acuto | the sharp sound |
| il suono basso | the deep sound |
| | |
| l'acqua odorosa | the fragrant water |
| l'acqua inodora | the odorless water |
| | |
| l'odore buono | the good smell |
| l'odore cattivo | the bad smell |
| | |
| il sapore amaro | the bitter taste |
| il sapore dolce | the sweet taste |
| | |
| il sapore acido | the sour taste |
| il sapore salso | the salty taste |

The teacher who is observing notices whether the child has taken the right objects; if so, she proceeds to the permutations.

## PERMUTATIONS

At this point, the teacher should recall (in dealing with Italian) the grammatical rules for the position of adjectives, some of which (the fundamental ones) will certainly be very useful to her in executing these first permutations: —

I. In general, the adjective follows the noun. If placed before the noun, it is less conspicuous; if placed after, it assumes more importance and has a different force.

II. When the adjective is used to signify the exclusive superlative of a quality, it is not only placed after the noun, but is preceded by the article. (*Umberto il buono,* " Humbert the Good.")

Example: — The child has composed the following phrase with his cards: *il triangolo rettangolo* " the right-angled triangle." The teacher can interchange the words thus: *il rettangolo triangolo,* " the triangle right-angled." Similarly also, for other phrases: —

| | |
|---|---|
| il prisma rettangolare azzurro | the rectangular blue prism |
| il rettangolare azzurro prisma | the prism, rectangular, blue |
| i lapis neri | the black pencils |
| i neri lapis | the pencils black |
| il colore rosso | the red color |
| il rosso colore | the color red |

Both the meaning and the child's habits show him the normal position of the adjective. In some phrases, such as,

| | |
|---|---|
| il rumore leggero | the faint sound |
| il sapore dolce | the sweet taste |

the placing of the adjective before the noun renders the meaning vague, figurative, emotional, or generic, whereas it would be clearly descriptive and precise were the adjective in its normal position:

| | |
|---|---|
| il dolce sapore | the taste sweet |
| il leggero rumore | the noise faint |

(In English the normal position of the adjective is before the noun. The permutation develops a strong rhetorical flavor, of which the child will become conscious later in his studies on poetic inversions.— Tr.)

After the teacher has made these changes, if they have interested the child, she may say for example: " The adjective comes after its noun " (for Italian) ; " The adjective comes before its noun " (for English). In this way she will have given a lesson in *theoretical* grammar.

### INFLECTION OF ADJECTIVES
### (Exclusively for the Italian language)

Another exercise to be done at the table deals with the formation of the singular and plural of adjectives in the two genders. This exercise brings the child in contact with a great many adjectives of quality. Two series, one of twenty masculine, the other of twenty feminine adjectives (in the two numbers) and two other series, twenty singulars and twenty plurals (in the two genders), form four groups of cards, one-half of which (tied separately) serves to direct the placing of the other half. Here are the words in their groups:

| *Singolare* | *Plurale* | |
|---|---|---|
| acuto | acuti | sharp |
| allegro | allegri | joyous |
| attenta | attente | careful, attentive |

| *Singolare* | *Plurale* | |
|---|---|---|
| basso | bassi | low |
| buona | buone | good |
| caldo | caldi | hot |
| cattiva | cattive | bad |
| dolce | dolci | sweet |
| duro | duri | hard |
| educata | educate | educated, well mannered |
| felice | felici | happy |
| fredda | fredde | cold |
| grande | grandi | large |
| grazioso | graziosi | graceful, pretty |
| gioiosa | gioiose | merry |
| gentile | gentili | kind |
| italiano | italiani | Italian |
| rabbioso | rabbiosi | angry |
| largo | larghi | broad |
| lento | lenti | slow |
| malata | malate | ill |
| odorosa | odorose | fragrant |
| arioso | ariose | airy |
| prezioso | preziosi | precious |
| piena | piene | full |
| pesante | pesanti | heavy |
| pulito | puliti | clean |
| rozza | rozze | rough, uncouth |
| rosso | rossi | red |
| robusta | robuste | robust |
| sincero | sinceri | sincere |
| studioso | studiosi | studious |
| stretto | stretti | narrow |
| stupida | stupide | stupid |
| vecchia | vecchie | old |
| morbido | morbide | soft |
| leggiera | leggiere | light (weight) |
| lunga | lunghe | long |
| grosso | grossi | thick |
| colorita | colorite | colored |

| *Maschile* | *Femminile* | |
|---|---|---|
| alti | alte | tall |
| bello | bella | beautiful |
| brevi | brevi | short, brief |
| biondo | bionda | blonde |
| chiaro | chiara | clear, light (of color) |
| corto | corta | short |
| coraggiosi | coraggiose | courageous |
| disordinato | disordinata | disorderly |
| dolce | dolce | sweet |
| debole | debole | feeble |
| esatto | esatta | accurate |
| freddo | fredda | cold |
| grazioso | graziosa | graceful |
| grande | grande | large |
| garbati | garbate | polite |
| gentili | gentili | kind |
| italiani | italiane | Italian |
| inglese | inglese | English |
| lento | lenta | slow |
| svelto | svelta | lithe |
| ottimo | ottima | best, excellent |
| ordinato | ordinata | orderly |
| pigri | pigre | lazy |
| pallido | pallida | pale |
| piccolo | piccola | small |
| ruvidi | ruvide | rough |
| serio | seria | serious, honest |
| suo | sua | his, her, your |
| sgarbato | sgarbata | rude |
| tuo | tua | thy |
| timido | timida | timid |
| ultimo | ultima | last |
| vostro | vostra | yours |
| zoppi | zoppe | lame |
| zitto | zitta | silent |
| carino | carina | dear |
| liscio | liscia | smooth |

| *Maschile* | *Femminile* | |
|---|---|---|
| obbediente | obbediente | obedient |
| contenti | contente | content, happy |
| allegro | allegra | joyous |

Here, just as with the four noun forms (masculine,
feminine, singular and plural), class games may be found
useful. The plural forms may be dealt out to the class,
while one child reads aloud the singulars, one after the
other. The child, who, in a given case, has the proper
plural, reads his card in answer. Similarly, for masculine
and feminine.

LOGICAL AND GRAMMATICAL AGREEMENT OF NOUNS AND
ADJECTIVES

(For Italian Exclusively)

Another table exercise consists in arranging two groups
of fifty cards, of which twenty-five are nouns (constituting the directing group), while the other twenty-five are
adjectives. The nouns are put in a row and the child
looks among the adjectives (which have been thoroughly
shuffled) for those which are best suited to the different
nouns. As he finds them he places them by the nouns
with which they belong. Sometimes the nouns and adjectives placed together cause a great deal of merriment by
the amusing contrasts that arise. The children try to
put as many adjectives as possible with the same noun
and develop in this way the most interesting combinations. Here are two groups which come prepared with
the material:

| Nome | Aggettivo | Adjective | Noun |
|------|-----------|-----------|------|
| contadina | allegra | happy | peasant-girl |
| casa | bella | beautiful | house |
| zia | brava | good | aunt |
| mamma | cara | dear | mother |
| professore | alto | tall | professor |
| maestra | magra | thin (lean) | teacher |
| lavandaia | pulita | neat | washerwoman |
| marinaio | robusto | strong | sailor |
| carrettiere | abbronzato | sunburnt | wagon-driver |
| bambino | buono | good | child |
| lavagnetta | rettangolare | square | slate |
| foglio | bianco | white | paper (sheet of) |
| panchetto | basso | low | bench |
| prisma | grosso | thick | prism |
| vaso | largo | broad | vase |
| foglia | verde | green | leaf |
| circolo | perfetto | perfect | circle |
| pizzicagnolo | grosso | fat | butcher |
| testa | unta | oily (dirty) | head |
| gomma | densa | hard, dense | rubber |
| fanciullo | stizzito | cross, angry | child |
| figlio | obbediente | obedient | son |
| pietra | nera | black | rock, stone |
| latte | bianco | white | milk |
| formaggio | tenero | soft, tender | cheese |
| carne | fresca | fresh | meat |
| vino | rosso | red | wine |
| disegno | grazioso | pretty | drawing |
| perla | lucente | shining | pearl |
| vetro | trasparente | transparent | glass |
| ragazzina | impertinente | impertinent | lass |
| asino | paziente | patient | donkey |
| gallina | grassa | fat | hen |
| topo | agile | quick, nimble | mouse |
| acqua | limpida | clear | water |
| saponetta | odorosa | perfumed, fragrant | soap |
| medico | bravo | good | doctor |
| giardiniere | bizzarro | surly | gardener |
| cane | arrabbiato | mad | dog |
| manicotto | morbido | soft | muff |
| gatto | arruffato | ruffled | cat |
| colombo | viaggiatore | traveling (carrier) | pigeon |
| uomo | brontolone | grumbling | man |
| ragno | pericoloso | dangerous | spider |
| serpente | velenoso | poisonous | snake |

| Nome | Aggettivo | Adjective | Noun |
|------|-----------|-----------|------|
| medicina | amara | bitter | medicine |
| nonna | indulgente | indulgent, kind | grandmother |
| babbo | severo | strict | father |
| vespa | maligna | cruel | wasp |
| cassetto | ordinato | orderly | box |

For a class game with these lists, the nouns may be placed on one table and the adjectives on another. Moving as during the " silence " lesson, each child selects first a noun, and then an adjective. When the selections have all been made, the pairs are read one after the other amid general enthusiasm.

### DESCRIPTIVE ADJECTIVES
#### COMMANDS (*Individual Lessons*)

The study of the adjective may furnish occasion for giving the child a knowledge of physical properties (of substances) so far unknown to him. For example, the teacher may present a piece of transparent glass; a piece of black glass (or any opaque screen); a sheet of white paper with an oil stain. The child will see that through the *transparent* glass objects may be seen distinctly; that through the oil stain only the light is visible; that nothing at all can be seen through the *opaque* screen. Or she may take a small glass funnel and put into it a piece of filter paper, then a sponge, then a piece of waterproof cloth. The child observes that the water passes through the filter paper, that the sponge absorbs water, and that the water clings to the surface of the waterproof. Or take two glass graduators and fill them with water to different heights. In the case of the graduator filled to the very top, the surface of the water is *convex;* in the other, it is *concave.*

The commands are printed on little slips of paper which

are folded and all held together by an elastic band with a
series of brown cards containing the adjectives used in the
commands.   Here is the material prepared:

— Fill one graduator with water to the point of over-flowing,
and another not so full.  Notice the form assumed by the surface of the water in each case and apply the proper adjective:
*convex, concave.*

— Take various objects such as filter paper, cloth, a sponge,
and see whether water can pass through them, applying the
adjectives: *permeable, impermeable, porous.*

— Take a piece of clear glass, a sheet of black paper, a sheet
of oiled paper; look at the light through them, applying the
adjectives: *transparent, opaque, translucent.*

Object lessons demonstrating comparative weights may
also be given by putting successively into a glass of water,
oil, alcohol colored with aniline, a piece of cork, a little
leaden ball (to be dropped).   Then the command would
be:

— Compare the weights of water and of colored alcohol;
water and oil; water and cork; and water and lead.  Then tell
which is *heavier* and which is *lighter* than the other.

As an answer the child should give a little written exercise something like the following: *Water is heavier
than oil,* etc.   The children actually perform these little
experiments, learning to handle graduators, funnels, fil-
ters, etc., and to pour the last drops of water very carefully so as to obtain the concave and convex surfaces.
They acquire a very delicate touch in pouring the colored
alcohol and oil on the water.   Thus they take the first
step into the field of practical science.

To continue the study of adjectives of quality, there is a
series of commands relating to the comparative and superlative.   An example of the comparative crept into these

experiments on weight. Here are additional commands where the little slip and the brown cards are kept together.

— Take the blue stairs or any other objects and put with each object the proper adjectives from the following list: *thick, thin, thickest* (Ital. grossissimo), *thinnest* (Ital. finissimo).

— Take the eight tablets of the color you like best, arrange them according to shades and apply the proper adjectives of quality from the following: *light, lightest, dark, darkest*.

— Take the series of circles in the plane insets, and pick out the circles which correspond to these adjectives: *large, small, intermediate*.

— Take the cloths or other objects adapted to these adjectives: *smooth, smoothest, rough, roughest, soft, softest*.

— Take the cubes of the pink tower or any other objects adapted to these adjectives: *large, largest, small, smallest*.

— Grade a number of objects according to weight so as to fit these adjectives to them: *heavy, heaviest, light, lightest*.

### Adjectives of Quantity
#### commands (*Individual Lessons*)

Just as above, the slip is tied with the series of brown cards by an elastic band. Thus a group is formed. In our material the following three groups are available.:

— Take the counters and make little piles which correspond in quantity to these adjectives: *one, two, three, four, five, six,* etc.

— Take the beads and make little piles of them to fit these adjectives: *few, none, many, some*.

— Decide first of all on some definite number of beads (two) and then make other little piles to fit these adjectives: *double, triple, quadruple, quintuple, sextuple, tenfold, half, equal*.

### ORDINALS

#### (*Individual Commands*)

— Build the blue stair and on each step place the proper adjective from the following: *first, second, third, fourth, fifth, sixth, seventh, eighth, ninth, tenth.*

— Place the following adjectives on the different drawers of the cabinet, beginning with the top drawer: *first, second, third, fourth, fifth.*

— Differentiate between the drawers of the cabinet by the following adjectives, beginning with the lowest: *first, second, third, fourth, fifth.*

### DEMONSTRATIVE ADJECTIVES

#### (*Class Lessons*)

As occasion may offer, the teacher may assemble a group of children and give them a few simple explanations on the meaning of certain words: *questo,* " this " (near us) ; *cotesto,* " that " (near you) ; *quello,* " that " (over there away from both of us). (Note: English lacks the demonstrative of the second person.)

Then she can distribute these commands which require collective actions of the class : —

— Gather in *that* (codesto) corner of the room near you; then all of you come over to *this* (questo) corner near me; then all of you run over to that (*quello*) corner over there.

— Choose one of your school-mates and tell him to put a box on *this* (questo) table; a small plate on *that* (quello) table over there.

— Tell one of your companions, pointing at the place, to put a green bead in *this* (questo) vase; a blue one in *that* (codesto) vase; a white one in *that* (quello) vase over there.

Arrange the children in groups in three different places in the room, and then give this command:

— Let *that* (quello) group over there take the place of *this* (questo) group. Let *that* (codesto) group break up, the children going back to their tables.

## POSSESSIVE ADJECTIVES

### (*Class Lessons*)

In like manner the teacher explains the meaning of the words *my, your, his, her,* etc. She may do this with a simple gesture. Here are the commands:

— Point out various objects saying: This is *my* slate; that is *your* slate; that (over there) is *her* slate.

— Point at the different seats, saying: That (over there) is *his* place, that is *your* place, and this is *my* place.

— Pass around the little baskets, saying: This is *my* basket. Whose is that other basket? Is it *your* basket? And this one? Ah, this one is *his* basket.

— Let us take a turn around the room and then return to *our* seats. *You* go to *your* seat and *they* will go to *their* seats. Then we will divide up our things. Let us put *our* things here and *their* things there. We will go to *your* seats and you go to *their* seats. Meanwhile they will get up and then come over here to take *our* places.

[Signora Montessori does not differentiate between the possessive *adjective* and the possessive *pronoun;* perhaps because there is in Italian no characteristic pronominal form. Strictly speaking the Italian predicate form *mio* (e.g., *Questo libro è mio*) is adjectival, while the form *il mio* (i.e., with the definite article) is pronominal (e.g., *Questo è il mio*). English has, however, the pronominal possessives: *mine, yours* (thine), *his, hers, ours, yours, theirs,* used also as predicate adjectives. The above exercise should therefore be repeated later under the subject of pronouns in a slightly different form.— Tr.]

# VI

## VERBS

When I gave the first grammar lessons to defective children I put special emphasis on nouns and verbs. The noun (= object), and the verb (= action) were distinguished with the greatest clearness, much as we distinguish matter from energy, chemistry from physics. *Condition* and *motion,* as potential and kinetic energy, are both expressed by verbs. Whereas formerly the child took the objects in his hands and studied their name and attributes, here he must *perform* actions. In the execution of actions he must necessarily receive some help, for he is not always capable of interpreting the word with the precise action which corresponds to it. On the contrary, the study of the verb is necessary to initiate him into a series of " object lessons " upon the different actions he must perform. The teacher therefore must give individual lessons teaching the child to interpret the verb.

### ANALYSES

In the usual manner we present a box which has four compartments, for the article, the noun, the adjective, and the verb. The sections are designated by the usual title cards: tan, black, brown, and red. In the compartment at the back of the box there are six slips for each exercise, and for every written word there is a card, except for such words as are repeated in successive sentences.

For example: if the following sentences are written on the cards:

Close the door!
Lock the door!

on the corresponding cards will be found the words:

$$\left.\begin{array}{l} \text{Lock} \\ \text{Close} \end{array}\right\} \text{ the door.}$$

And so the child after he has composed his first sentence needs to change only one card (*lock* for *close*) for the second sentence. This brings out the force of the verb, showing that one sentence may be changed into another by indicating an entirely different action. The child performs the action and then on his table he builds the sentences with the cards. In the series we have prepared, the verbs are either synonyms or antonyms. Here is the material:

### SERIES A

— Close the door      — Fold the paper
   Lock the door        Unfold the paper

— Tie a knot      — Open the book
   Untie a knot        Shut the book

— Spread your beads      — Speak a word
   Collect your beads        Whisper a word

### SERIES B

— Raise your hands      — Touch the velvet
   Lower your hands        Feel the velvet

— Toss the ball      — Write a short word
   Throw the ball        Erase a short word

— Show your right hand      — Draw a circle
   Hide your right hand        Fill a circle

### SERIES C

— Bring a chair      — Lace a frame
   Drag a chair        Unlace a frame

— Raise your head
Bow your head

— Arrange the brown cards
Mix the brown cards

— Fill a glass
Empty a glass

— Roll the white handkerchief
Twist the white handkerchief

### SERIES D

— Embrace your nearest schoolmate
Kiss your nearest schoolmate

— Cover your face
Uncover your face

— Gather your prisms
Separate your prisms

— Lift the red counter
Drop the red counter

— Borrow a black pencil
Lend a black pencil

— Smooth the white paper
Crumple the white paper

### SERIES E

— Clench your two hands
Open your two hands

— Rub the table
Scratch the table

— Spread the large carpet
Fold the large carpet

— Pour the water
Spill the water

— Bend your left arm
Straighten your left arm

— Comb your hair
Part your hair

### PERMUTATIONS

The teacher should have in mind the grammatical rules for the position of the verb in the sentence, to give the child a clear idea of its normal location before the direct object: "first the verb, then the object upon which it acts."

Example:

Smooth the white paper.

The verb should, for the first permutation, be transferred to the end:

the white paper smooth.

Or, if you wish,

Arrange the brown cards.
the brown cards arrange.

When the verb is taken away entirely the action vanishes:

Lift
Drop } the red counter.
the red counter.

Making all possible permutations, the child sees that only one order of words is capable of bringing a meaning out of the confusion:

Roll the white handkerchief.
the white handkerchief roll.
white the handkerchief roll.
white roll handkerchief the.

### LESSONS AND COMMANDS ON THE VERB

The children take considerable delight in our verb lessons which develop through interpretations of actions. We use packs of red cards, tied with an elastic, each pack containing ten cards. The child executes the actions indicated on each card, one after the other. He may afterward copy the cards — an exercise specially attractive to very young children.

Examples:

— walk, sing, jump, dance, bow, sit, sleep, wake, pray, sigh.
— write, erase, weep, laugh, hide, draw, read, speak, listen, run.
— arrange, clean, dust, sweep, button, lace, tie, hook, greet, brush.
— comb, wash, wipe, embrace, kiss, smile, yawn, scowl, stare, breathe.

These are fairly common words, representing actions more or less familiar to the pupils. But this exercise is only an introduction to the real verb-lessons. For these the teacher selects, as subject for a lesson, a series of synonymous verbs. Their shades of meaning are taught

to the children by translating them into action, the teacher
executing the action herself. She then distributes around
the class commands making use of the verbs in question.
There may be several copies of a given command if the
pupils are very numerous. The child reads by himself
the card he has received, executing the action from memory of what he has seen the teacher do. We have tested
experimentally the Italian material (*i.e.,* the verbs in
parentheses), as follows:

Subject:

lay, throw, toss, hurl (posare, gettare, lanciare, scagliare).

Commands: —

— Take a counter and *lay* it on the floor. Pick it up again
and *throw* it on the floor.

— Roll your handkerchief into a ball. *Toss* it into the air.
Pick it up again and *hurl* it against the wall.

— *Lay* your handkerchief carefully, very carefully, on the
floor. Pick it up again and *throw* it on the floor. Make a
ball of it and *hurl* it across the room. Pick it up and *toss* it
into the air.

Subject:

lie, crouch, sit, rise (sollevare, alzare, levare).

Commands: —

— Go to the sofa and *lie* with your face to the wall. Now
*rise,* go to your table and *sit* with head erect.

— *Rise* from your chair and *crouch* behind the table, as
though you were playing hide-and-seek. *Rise* and go back to
the sofa.

Subject:

open, close, lock, unlock (aprire, spalancare, chiudere, socchiudere, serrare, disserrare).

Commands: —

— Go to a window and *open* it a little; wait a moment and

then *close* it again. *Open* the window as wide as you can and *close* it immediately.

— Go to the door and *open* it wide. Then *close* the door gently. If the key is in the key-hole *lock* the door; but before you go away, *unlock* it again, so that everything is left just as you found it.

Subject:

breathe, inhale, exhale (respirare, sospirare, inspirare, espirare).

Commands: —

— Go to the window, open it, and *inhale* and *exhale* the fresh air five times. Then after a moment *inhale* once and hold your breath as long as you can. When you can hold your breath no longer, *exhale* as slowly as you can.

— Take a hand mirror and *breathe* upon the glass. What happens?

Subject:

hang, attach (appendere, affiggere, sospendere).

Commands: —

— *Hang* one of your best drawings on a hook in the room.

— *Attach* the drawing you like best with two pins to the wall near the door.

Subject:

cover, wrap, tie, undo (avvolgere, involgere, svolgere).

Commands: —

— Take a book, a string and a large piece of cloth. Lay the book on your table and *cover* it with the cloth.

— Take the cloth and *wrap* it around the book so that the book cannot be seen.

— *Tie* a string around the cloth so that the book will not fall out.

— *Undo* the bundle, and return each object to the place where you found it.

Subject:

turn, invert, revolve, whirl, reverse (volgere, capovolgere, rovesciare).

Commands: —

— *Turn* a picture toward one of your school-mates so that he can see it clearly.

— *Invert* the picture, so that it will be upside down.

— *Reverse* the picture so that the back only can be seen by your school mate.

— *Revolve* the seat of the piano-stool as rapidly as you can.

— Stand with your back to the window and *turn* slowly on your heel till you face the window. *Whirl* on your heel completely around till you again face the window.

Subject:

breathe, blow, puff, pant (sbuffare, soffiare, alitare).

Commands: —

— Tear a large piece of paper into tiny bits on your table. *Blow* steadily upon the table till the pieces of paper are all on the floor.

— Pick up the pieces of paper and place them on the table. *Puff* three times upon them and see if they all fall to the floor. Gather up the pieces and throw them into the waste-basket.

— *Breathe* softly upon the back of your hand. What do you feel?

— *Blow* upon the back of your hand. What do you feel?

— *Puff* upon the back of your hand. What do you feel?

— *Pant* noisily as though you had been running a long way.

Subject:

murmur, mutter, whisper, speak, grumble (mormorare, sussurrare, brontolare).

Commands: —

— Ask one of your school-mates to listen carefully to what you say; then *murmur* a short sentence as though you were speaking to yourself.

— *Mutter* the same words in a louder voice and see whether he understands.

— *Whisper* the same words in the ear of one of two children. Then ask the other whether he has heard.

— *Grumble* the same words and watch how the two children look at you.

— *Speak* the same words aloud and as distinctly as you can. Do the children understand?

Subject:
touch, rub, graze (toccare, tastare, palpare, sfiorare).

Commands: —

— Go to your table and with your eyes shut *touch* it as though to recognize it.

— *Rub* the table with the tips of your fingers, bearing down as hard as you can. What do you feel?

— *Graze* the table with the tips of your fingers, trying not to touch it.

Subject:
spread, sprinkle, collect, scatter (spargere, spruzzare, aspergere).

Commands: —

— Take a box full of beads and *spread* them evenly around the center of your table. Then *collect* them in a pile in the center of the table.

— Take a handful of the beads and *scatter* them over the table. Return all the beads to the box.

— Take a glass of water and *sprinkle* two or three handfuls on a plant in the room.

Subject:
walk, stagger, march (barcollare, dondolare, erigersi).

Commands: —

— *Walk* naturally to the end of the room farthest from your table.

— *March* back to your seat as though you were keeping time to music.

— *Stagger* across the room as though you were very dizzy.

Subject:

take, seize, catch (acchiappare, acciuffare, afferrare).

Commands: —

— Walk to the cabinet and *take* a box of counters in your hands.

— Run to the sofa, *seize* the sofa-pillow, and run around the room with it, holding it in your arms.

— Roll your handkerchief into a ball, toss it into the air and try to *catch* it before it falls to the floor.

### LESSONS WITH EXPERIMENTS

The function of the verb can be still more interestingly emphasized by suggesting actions designed to increase the child's knowledge in the direction of elementary science. Here the teacher, instead of executing simple movements, performs experiments, which on the same day or on succeeding days the child can imitate guided by the directions in the commands.

Subject:

stir, mix, beat, flavor (mescolare, emulsionare, stemperare).

Commands: —

— Take a bowl half full of water and drop into it a half cup of flour; *stir* with a spoon until the mixture is thick.

— Place a table-spoonful of vinegar and a table-spoonful of olive-oil in a clean bowl; *beat* them together until an emulsion is formed.

— Place a tea-spoonful of chocolate and a tea-spoonful of sugar in a cup and *mix* them thoroughly. What color was the chocolate? What color was the sugar? What color is the mixture?

— Take a little milk in a cup and taste of it; add a drop of vanilla extract. Then taste of the milk again. Do you taste the vanilla? In the same way *flavor* a glass of water with the vanilla. *Flavor* another glass of water with vinegar.

Subject:

dissolve, saturate, be in suspension (sciogliere, fare la sospensions, saturare).

Commands: —

— Place a spoonful of sugar in a glass of warm water and *dissolve* the sugar by stirring with a spoon. Is the water still clear?

— *Saturate* the water with sugar by continuing to add sugar and stirring till you can see the sugar at the bottom of the glass. Allow the water to rest a moment. Is the water still clear?

— Mix a spoonful of starch in the water. The water becomes white, since the starch does not *dissolve* but remains *in suspension* in the water.

Subject:

strain, filter (decantare, filtrare).

Commands: —

— Take the glass containing the water saturated with sugar and the one with the starch in suspension, and allow the starch and sugar to settle for some time, until the water is clear. Taste the water in each glass, and then *strain* each glass of water separately.

— *Filter* the water saturated with sugar and the water with the suspended starch. Then taste of each.

By the time all these commands have been executed, the child will have developed a keen desire to go on, becoming so interested in the meaning of verbs as not to require further commands to stimulate his study of these words. The most frequent question now is " How many verbs are there in the language? " " Are there more in other languages? " etc. To satisfy this new curiosity of the children we have dictionaries of synonyms and antonyms, and word-charts. But meantime they have been building their own dictionaries. One by one they begin to own copy books (rubrics) with illuminated letters of the alphabet. Under the proper letter the child copies his words as fast as he learns them. We are still experimenting on the question of the exact amount of information that may successfully be offered to elementary school children of various ages and stages of development, with the word material required for the notions of natural history, physics and chemistry they may be expected to acquire. We can say, at this moment, simply that each experiment involves the use of a certain number of new words (nouns, adjectives and verbs), which are copied into the word-books (rubrics) as fast as they occur.

# VII

## PREPOSITIONS

### ANALYSES

Here also the first exercise is to compose sentences analyzed with the colored cards. This grammar box has five compartments, each with a small title card of the color corresponding to the different parts of speech, red for the verb, black for the noun, brown for the adjective, tan for the article and *violet* for the *preposition*. In the compartment at the rear of the box are six cards with printed sentences. The colored cards do not correspond exactly to the number of words used in the sentences because the words of one sentence which are repeated in the next are not duplicated in the cards. In this case it is the change in preposition only which alters the meaning of the sentence. Here are the series of sentences, some of which the teacher may have used already in previous lessons (commands).

### SERIES A

#### (Prepositions of space relations)

— Take the box *with* the colored beads. (con, senza, insieme con).
Take the box *without* the colored beads.
Take the box *together with* the colored beads.

— Place the prism *under* the cylinder. (sotto a, sopra a).
Place the prism *upon* the cylinder.

— Lay the pen *in front of* the ink-well.  (avanti a, dietro a, a lato di).

Lay the pen *behind* the ink-well.

Lay the pen *beside* the ink-well.

— Put the green bead *into* the box.  (in, dentro).

Put the green bead *inside* the box.

— Arrange a few beads *between* the red counters.  (in mezzo a, tra).

Arrange a few beads *among* the red counters.

— Set one chair *opposite* another chair.  (dirimpetto a, accanto a).

Set one chair *next to* another chair.

## SERIES B
### (Space relations continued)

— Lay the counter *inside* the box.  (dentro, fuori, di).

Lay the counter *outside* the box.

— Place a chair *on this side of* the door.  (di là da, di qua da, oltre).

Place a chair *on that side of* the door.

Place a chair *beyond* the door.

— Stand *in front of* the blackboard.  (di fronte a, di fianco a).

Stand *to one side of* the blackboard.

Stand *to the other side of* the blackboard.

— Arrange the chairs *along* the wall.  (lungo, contro).

Arrange the chairs *against* the wall.

— Place the blue cone *near* the pink cube.  (vincino a, accosto a).

Place the blue cone *against* the pink cube.

## SERIES C
### (Possession, material, use, purpose)

[NOTE: — Such relationships are expressed in English preferably by adjectives: *cloth of cotton = cotton cloth;* or by the

Grammar Boxes, showing respectively four and five parts of speech. (Note: The cards forming the sentence, "Place the blue cone against the pink cube," should have been arranged in one continuous line, not in two lines.)

Grammar Boxes, containing respectively six and seven parts of speech. (Note: In the sentence on the right, the cards should be in one line, not two.)

possessive inflection with -*s*: *the drawing of George* =*George's drawing*. In Italian they are expressed by the prepositions *di, per, da,* etc.: *stoffa di cotone* "cotton cloth," *piattino di vetro* "glass saucer." For Signora Montessori's simple exercise we suggest for English the following definitions (TR.)].

— Cotton cloth is cloth *of* cotton.
Woollen cloth is cloth *of* wool.
Silk cloth is cloth *of* silk.

— The iron triangle is a triangle *of* iron.
The wooden triangle is a triangle *of* wood.

— The glass saucer is a saucer *of* glass.
The china saucer is a saucer *of* china.

— A shoe-brush is a brush *for* shoes.
A clothes-brush is a brush *for* clothes.

— George's hat is the hat *of* George; George's hat belongs *to* George.
Mary's hat is the hat *of* Mary; Mary's hat belongs *to* Mary.

— A drinking-cup is a cup *for* drinking.
A copy-book is a book *for* copying.

### SERIES D

#### (Direction and source of motion)

— Turn *from* the right *to* the left.   (da...a, a...da)
Turn *from* the left *to* the right.

— Draw a line *from* the bottom of the paper *to* the top.
Draw a line *from* the top of the paper *to* the bottom.

— Go *from* your seat *to* the cabinet.
Go *from* the cabinet *to* your seat.

— Change the pen *from* your right hand *to* your left hand.
Change the pen *from* your left hand *to* your right hand.

## Permutations

The child has built the first sentences on each of the slips with his cards, and he has reproduced the others by changing simply the preposition cards. In this way he has seen how the position of objects relative to each other is determined wholly and only by the use of the preposition. The preposition, therefore, determines the *relation of words,* the relation of a *noun* to some other word, here to another *noun* or to a *verb.* In the phrase,

Set one chair opposite another chair,

if we take away the preposition, leaving,

Set one chair another chair,

the relation that formerly existed between the words *chair* and *another chair* is lost. The teacher must not forget the rules for the position of the preposition. The preposition must always precede its object and no other word can come between it and the word or words it controls.

Here are some examples of sentences in the above exercises from which the preposition has been taken away by the teacher:

Go from your seat the cabinet.
Place a chair the door.
Lay the counter the box.
Place the prism the cylinder.
The china saucer is made china.

To give the child an idea of the normal position of prepositions a series of permutations may be made leaving the preposition and its object in their normal positions. In this case some meaning is still left to the sentence:

Stretch a string from the door to the window.
From the door to the window stretch a string.
Stretch from the door a string to the window.
From the door to the window a string stretch.
From the door stretch to the window a string.

But the child will recognize that the right sentence is the simplest and the clearest:

Stretch a string from the door to the window.

On the other hand if we separate the preposition from its object or invert their normal position, the meaning is entirely lost:

Stretch a string the door from the window to.
Stretch a string from the door window to the.
String from the stretch door to the a window.

And likewise with these other sentences:

Run from the wash-stand to the table.
Run wash-stand table (*definition of motion lacking*).
Run wash-stand from the table to the.
From the run wash-stand to the table.
Wash-stand from the to the run table.

### Lessons and Commands on Prepositions

The teacher may also take groups of children and give them short lessons on the preposition to explain the meaning, selecting if possible two or three synonyms or antonyms each time. The lessons should always be practical and full of action. The child should come to understand in this case the relationship established by this or that preposition between the object (noun) and the action (verb) to be performed. As soon as this has been made clear by the teacher the commands are distributed to the children who put them into execution. Here is the material that we use:

Subject:
Of (di).

Command: —

— Go and get a boxful *of* counters. Go and get a glass *of* water. Bring me a piece *of* cloth.

Subject:
near (to), next (to), beside, far away from (vicino, accosto, lontano).

Command: —

— One of you boys stand in the middle of the room. Now you others go and stand *near* him. One of you stand *next* to him on the right, another *beside* him on the left. Now all go *far away from* him.

Subject:
in, into, inside, out of (in, dentro, fuori).

Command: —

— Rise from your chairs and go *into* the next room. Stay *in* that room a moment and then come back *into* this one. Go back on tip-toe and lock yourselves *inside* the next room. Come *out of* the next room *into* this one.

Subject:
On this side of, on that side of, beyond (di là da, di qua da, oltre).

Command: —

— Leave your places and form a circle *on that side of* the door; form a circle then *on this side of* the door. All of you go and stand somewhere *beyond* the door.

Subject:
except, save (tranne, eccetto).

Command: —

— All the children, *except* George and Mary, walk on tip-toe around the room.

— All the children, *save* George and Mary, walk on tip-toe around the room.

Subject:

side by side with, opposite, in front of, along (di fianco, di fronte, avanti).

Command: —

   — Form a line *side by side with* each other.

   — Form a line *along* the wall *opposite* the door.

   — Form two lines *in front of* the piano.

Subject:

before, behind (dirimpetto, dietro).

Command: —

   — Two of you come and stand *before* me.

   — The rest of you go and stand *behind* me.

Subject:

on, about, along (su, secondo, lungo).

Command: —

   — Each of you place one counter *on* the table. Now arrange the same counters *along* the far edge of the table. Now scatter the same counters *about* the center of the table.

Subject:

between, among (fra, in mezzo a).

Command: —

   — One of you go and stand *between* the door and the piano.

   — Place ten white counters on the table. Now go and scatter two or three red counters *among* the white ones.

Subject:

from, to, as far as (da, a, fino a).

Command: —

   — Rise and walk *from* your places *to* the piano; wait a moment and then continue *as far as* the door of the next room.

Subject:

around, about (attorno, intorno).

Command: —

   — Walk in couples, arm in arm, *around* the room twice; when you reach the piano on the second round, form a circle *about* the piano.

Subject:
   toward, against (verso, contro).

Command : —
   — Take your chairs and move them three steps *toward* the wall in front of you.   Next, arrange your chairs in a row with their backs *against* the wall behind you.

Subject:
   across, through (attraverso, per).

Command : —
   — Roll your handkerchiefs into balls and throw them *across* the room.
   — Pick them up as they lie and try to throw them *through* the door into the hall.

Subject:
   With, without (con, senza).

Command : —
   — Walk around the room *with* your chairs in your hands.
   — Walk around the room *without* your chairs.

Subject:
   to, in order to, so as to (per).

Command : —
   — Wash your hands *in order* not *to* soil the cloth.   Then close your eyes and feel this cloth *so as to* recognize it.

# VIII

## ADVERBS

### ANALYSES

Again the exercise consists of sentences analyzed by means of colored cards and commands. The grammar box contains six compartments having, like the others, the names of the different parts of speech on title cards of proper color. The card for the adverb is pink. In the rear compartment are six slips for each exercise, and in the sections the usual number of corresponding colored cards for the necessary words.

### GROUP A

#### (Adverbs of Manner)

— Walk *slowly* to the window.
  Walk *rapidly* to the window.

— Rise *silently* from your seat.
  Rise *noisily* from your seat.

— Speak *softly* into the ear of your nearest comrade.
  Speak *loudly* into the ear of your nearest comrade.

— Take five steps toward the door; turn *abruptly* to the left.
  Take five steps toward the door; turn *gradually* to the left.

— Take your nearest comrade *lightly* by the arm.
  Take your nearest comrade *roughly* by the arm.

— Look *smilingly* into the mirror.
  Look *scowlingly* into the mirror.

85

## GROUP B

### (Adverbs of place and time)

— Place your pencil *there*.
Place your pencil *here*.

— Lay your book *somewhere* on the table.
Lay your book *elsewhere* on the table.

— Walk to the window *constantly* clapping your hands.
Walk to the window *occasionally* clapping your hands.

— Drink the water in the glass *now*.
Drink the water in the glass *by and by*.

— Carry the pink tower *upstairs*.
Carry the pink tower *downstairs*.

— Write a word on the blackboard *immediately*.
Write a word on the blackboard *soon*.

## GROUP C

### (Adverbs of quantity, comparison)

— Walk along the hall swinging your arms *somewhat*.
Walk along the hall swinging your arms *a great deal*.

— Bend your head a *little*.
Bend your head *much*.

— Walk *slowly* to the window.
Walk *less slowly* to the window.
Walk *more slowly* to the window.

— Place on the table your *most* beautiful drawing.
— Place on the table your beautiful drawing.

— Make a broad mark on the blackboard.
Make a *very* broad mark on the blackboard.

## GROUP D

### (Adverbs of comparison, correlative adverbs)

— Look for a piece of cloth softer *than* velvet.
— Look for a piece of cloth *as* soft *as* velvet.

— Find among your colors a shade *as* black *as* the blackboard.

— Find a piece of cloth *not so* shiny *as* satin.

— Find among the plane insets a rectangle *as* broad *as* half the square.

— Bring a rod longer *than* your copy-book.

— Bring a rod *as* long *as* your copy-book.

— Bring a rod *not so* long *as* your copy-book.

— Find a piece of cloth *less* rough *than* the canvas.

## PERMUTATIONS

The sentences to be analyzed are reproduced as usual by building the first sentence on each slip; and then, by changing the adverb, the child gets the second or third sentence. One of the first permutations is to remove the adverb from those sentences where it performs the function of an *adjective to the verb,* thereby causing one action to be changed into another. For example take the two sentences:

Walk slowly to the window.
Walk rapidly to the window.

Taking away the adverb we have:

Walk to the window.

The child can perform the action which, now, is a simple one. The adverb, however, changes, *modifies,* the action. If the teacher in play puts the two adverbs together in the same sentence the child has the problem of interpreting two contrary movements. That is, he is to go to the window *slowly* and *rapidly* at the same time. Taking away the adverb cards the sentence left is *Go to the window.* This action the child can perform. But how shall he perform it, in what way? With the help of adverbs! Similarly in the following sentences:

Bend your head *a little.*
Bend your head *much.*

Written without the adverb they indicate one action. What slight changes in the position of the head can be brought about by these adverbs!  It is the *adverb* which really shows fine differentiations in movement!

In other sentences also where the adverb is, so to speak, an *adjective* to an *adjective* and therefore really affects the object (noun), similar permutations may be made.

Make a broad mark on the blackboard.
Make a *very* broad mark on the blackboard.

Here by the use of an adverb two different *objects* (nouns) are distinguished which, though they have the same quality (breadth) differ in degree (broad, very broad).   Take, for instance, two objects belonging to the same series:

Place on your table the prism which is most thick.
Place on your table the prism which is least thick.

If the adverbs are taken away the factor determining the degree of quality (thickness) disappears and we have sentences which are far less precise in their meaning:

Place on your table the prism which is thick.

As the teacher proceeds to make permutations in the different sentences she should remember (for Italian) that the normal position of the adverb is after the verb (in the compound tenses it comes between the auxiliary and the participle).

(Note: In English the position of the adverb is much freer than in Italian; it often stands at the end of the sentence and even between subject and verb,— something quite foreign to normal Italian usage. We retain the text entire.)

In the sentences analyzed by the child it is sufficient to recall that the adverb modifies the verb and follows the verb it modifies. Take the sentence:

Bend your head a little as you write.

If the adverb is placed after the second verb the meaning changes:

Bend your head as you write a little.

The same is true in the following:

Walk along the hall swinging your arms somewhat.
Walk somewhat along the hall swinging your arms.

General shifting of position would give results as follows:

Bend a little your head as you write.
A little bend your head as you write, etc., etc.
Somewhat walk along the hall swinging your arms.
Walk along somewhat the hall swinging your arms, etc., etc.

The child is quick to recognize by ear the accurate, the normal position of the adverb.

On the other hand, adverbs of quantity and comparison precede the adjective:

Make a very broad mark on the blackboard.
Place on your table the prism that is least thick.

Permutation gives the following results:

Make a broad very mark on the blackboard.
Place on your table the prism which thick least is, etc., etc.

Adverbs of time and place often ring like trumpet calls to attention at the beginning of the sentence:

Drink the water in the glass now.

Now drink the water in the glass.

(Note: In English the adverb of time, placed at the end of the sentence, gains quite as much emphasis. So for adverbs of place.)

### Lessons and Commands on Adverbs

Subject:

straight, ziz-zag (diritto, a zig-zag).

Command: —

— Run *straight* into the other room; return to your place walking *zig-zag*.

Subject:

lightly, heavily, sedately (leggermente, gravemente, pesantemente).

Command: —

— Walk *lightly* into the other room; return to your place walking *sedately* as though you were a very important person; walk across the room and back again resting *heavily* on each step as though it were hurting you to walk.

Subject:

suddenly, gradually (ad un tratto, gradatamente).

Command: —

— Form in line and walk forward beginning *suddenly* to stamp with your left foot. Return to your places letting the stamping *gradually* cease.

Subject:

meanwhile, frequently, occasionally (sempre, spesso, raramente).

Command: —

— Form in line and march slowly into the next room, stopping *frequently*. Return to your places stopping *occasionally*.

— Walk into the next room and back again, *meanwhile* keeping your eyes closed.

Subject:

back, forward, to and fro (avanti, indietro, su e giù).

Command: —

— Form in line and walk *forward* to the other side of the room; then come *back* to your places.

— Walk *to and fro* across the room with your heads lowered and your hands behind your back.

Subject:

forwards, backwards.

Command: —

— Stand in the middle of the room; then walk *backwards* to the window, being careful to walk in a straight line. Return to your places walking *forwards*.

Subject:

slowly, abruptly (lentamente, bruscamente).

Command: —

— Rise *slowly* from your seats.

— Rise *abruptly* from your seats.

Subject:

politely, cordially (gentilmente, garbatamente).

Command: —

— Offer your chair *politely* to your nearest neighbor.

— Shake hands *cordially* with your nearest neighbor.

Subject:

alternately, in succession, simultaneously (successivamente, alternativamente, simultaneamente).

Command: —

— Raise your two hands *alternately* above your heads.

— Raise your two hands *simultaneously* above your heads.

— One of you children walk around the room bowing to each pupil *in succession*.

Subject:

Well, badly, fairly, best, worst (bene, male, meglio, peggio, così così, benino, maluccio, benissimo, malissimo).

Command: —

— One of you call the children to the end of the room, carefully observing how they walk; judge their carriage without speaking and distribute the following cards where they belong: *well, badly, fairly, best, worst.*

Subject:

away, back (via).

Command: —

— One of you stand in the center of the room; the others gather round him. Suddenly all of you run *away* from him. Then come *back* to him again.

Subject:

here, there, somewhere, elsewhere (qui, qua, costì, costà, lì, là, altrove).

Command: —

— Form in line and the first four children come to me *here;* the rest go and stand *there* by the window. Now go and stand *somewhere* in the other room. Remain where you are a moment, then go and stand *elsewhere.* Finally all come back *here* to me.

Subject:

thus, likewise (così).

Command: —

— One of you walk around the room holding his arms in a certain position. The rest of you do *likewise.*

— All of you hold your hands *thus,* as I am doing.

Subject:

up, down, upward, downward.

Command: —

— Roll your handkerchiefs into balls and throw them *up* to the ceiling.

— Pick them up and throw them *down* again to the floor.

— Look *upward* to the ceiling. Now look *downward* to the floor.

Subject: ·
    crosswise, lengthwise.

Command: —
    — Lay two rods *crosswise* on the table.  Then lay them *lengthwise* on the table.

Subject:
    sharply, sullenly, gently, kindly.

Command: —
    — *Sharply* order your nearest neighbor to rise from his seat.
    — Ask him *gently* to sit down again.
    — Sit *sullenly* in your chair with your eyes lowered.
    — Smile *kindly* at your nearest neighbor.

### A Burst of Activity:

#### The Future of the Written Language in Popular Education

In our own private experiments when we reached the adverb there occurred among the children a veritable explosion into a a new kind of activity.  They insisted on making up commands themselves.  They invented them and then read them aloud to their companions or had their companions interpret the slips which they had written.  All were most enthusiastic in performing these commands and they were rigorously scrupulous in acting them out down to the minutest detail.  The executions came to be a literal, intensely real dramatization: if a word was inexact or incorrect, the interpretation of the command threw the error into noisy relief, and the child who had written it saw before him an action quite different from what he had in mind.  Then he realized that he had expressed his thought wrongly or inadequately and immediately set to work to correct his mistake.  The revelation seemed to redouble his energy.  He would hunt among his numerous words for the one necessary to translate his idea into a living scene before his eyes.  Suppose a child had written the following sentence involving the use of the adverb *sempre* " always " :

Walk about the room (sempre) *always* on tip-toe.

meaning that the child should *all the while* go on tiptoe; if the child began to walk on tip-toe and continued to do so for a long time, trying to express *sempre* (always — forever) he would find himself facing a serious problem.  Hence the spontaneous query: " What must I do to express myself correctly ? "

A little girl once wrote " Walk around the tables," meaning that the children should form a line and walk in and out around each table.  Instead she saw her companions form a line and walk round the entire group of tables.  Red in the face and out of breath she kept calling: " Stop, stop.  That isn't the way," just as if this difference between the thought she actually had in mind and the way it was being executed were hurting her intolerably.

This is only a passing suggestion of something which, I think, will merit much further development later on, after more thorough experiment.  It will suffice, however, to bring to the teacher a notion of a most fertile field for the development of the written language in its most rigorous purity.  It is evident that the experiment shows the possibility not only of having spontaneous compositions without grammatical errors (just as the mechanical writing was spontaneous and without errors), but of developing a love for clearness and purity of speech which will be a potent factor in improving the literary appreciation of the masses, and popular culture generally.

When the children are seized with this passion for accurate expression of their thoughts in writing, when, spontaneously, clearness becomes the goal of their efforts, they follow the hunt for words with the keenest enthusiasm. They feel that there are never too many words to build with exactness the delicate edifice of thought. Problems of language come to them as a revelation. " How many words are there? " they ask. " How many nouns, how many verbs, how many adjectives? Is there any way for us to learn them all? " They are no longer content with their little copy-books of words. They ask for a wealth of word material which they now enjoy with all the delight of attractive and orderly interpretation. They never get tired of it.

These developments in our work suggested to us the idea of giving the children a large vocabulary comprising a sufficient number of nouns, verbs, and adjectives and containing *all* the words of the other parts of speech. The difference in bulk between the real content of language (substance and modification, that is, nouns with their adjectives, and verbs with their adverbs) and the other words which serve to establish relations and consolidate this content, is something very impressive to children of eight. It is for them that we tried to prepare our word charts and the dictionaries of synonyms for nouns, verbs, and adjectives. Here, meanwhile, are some of the commands which the children wrote themselves — things which they improvised all of a sudden, by an explosion of energy, as it were, developed as the result of inner maturity. Compare the aridity and uniformity of the commands we invented ourselves with the variety and richness of ideas appearing in the children's commands! We very evidently show the weariness the preparation of the material caused us.  They, on the contrary, reveal an ardent, vivacious spirit, a life full of exuberance.

### COMMANDS IMPROVISED BY THE CHILDREN

— Build the pink tower *very badly*.

— Make *accurately* a pose for each of the pictures in the room.

— Pretend you were two old men: speak *softly* as if you were very sad; and one of you say this: " Too bad poor Pancrazio is dead! "  And the other say:  " Shall we have to wear our black clothes to-morrow? "  Then walk along *silently*.

— Walk along limping *heavily;* then *suddenly* fall *prostrate* on your faces as though you were exhausted.  Return tripping *lightly* to your places, without falling and without limping.

— Walk *slowly* with lowered heads as though you were very sad; return then *joyfully* and walking *lightly*.

— Take a flower and run *eagerly* and give it to the lady.

— Go half way round the room limping; the rest of the way *on all fours*.

— Silence *immediately; silently* act out poses for the pictures in the room.

— Go from your seats to the door *on all fours; then* rise and limp *lightly* half way round the room; do the other half back to the door *on all fours; there* rise and run *lightly back* to your seats.

— Walk *silently* into the next room; walk three times around the big table and *then* return to your places.

— Go into the next room running *quite fast;* come back *gradually* reducing speed until you reach your places.

— Go to the cabinet *immediately;* take a letter-chart, and walk twice around the room with the chart on your head, trying *never* to let it fall; go back to your places *in the same way*.

— Walk around the large hall, walking *wearily;* sit down, as though you were tired, and fall asleep; wake up *shortly after* and go back to your places.

— Form in line and march forward till you reach a clear

space; *there* form a circle; *next* a rhombus; *then* a square; *finally* a trapezium. Go into the big hall conversing *softly; suddenly* fall to the floor *lightly* and go to sleep; then wake up and look around, saying, " Where are we?" Then go back to your seats.

# IX

## PRONOUNS

Material: — The box has seven compartments marked
with the colored title slips; tan for the article, black for
the noun, brown for the adjective, red for the verb, violet for the preposition, pink for the adverb, and *green* for
the *pronoun.* In the rear space are the slips for the sentences to be analyzed. There are, as usual, fewer cards
than words. The exercise is to substitute the pronouns
for nouns.

### GROUP A

### (Personal Pronouns)

— George's sister was weeping. George soothed his sister with
a kiss.

George's sister was weeping. *He* soothed *her* with a kiss.

— The book fell to the floor. Emma replaced the book on
the table.

The book fell to the floor. *She* replaced *it* on the table.

— The children gave their mother a surprise. The children
wrote a letter to their mother.

. The children gave their mother a surprise. *They* wrote
*her* a letter.

— The teacher said: The drawing is beautiful! Will *you*
give the drawing to the teacher?

The teacher said: *It* is beautiful! Will *you* give *it* to *me?*

98

— Charles has gone into the other room. Can you find
  Charles?
  Charles has gone into the other room. Can you find *him?*

(Demonstratives (questo, cotesto, quello) " this, that,
these, those, this one, that one)

(As already noted for the adjective English lacks the
demonstrative of the second person: that *near you.*)

— Show a child the prisms of the brown stair; *this* prism is
  thicker than *that* prism; *that* prism is thinner than *these*
  prisms.
  Show a child the prisms of the brown stair; *this* is thicker
  than *that; that* is thinner than *these.*

— Let us look at the children: *this* child is taller than *that*
  child; *that* child is shorter than *this* child.
  Let us look at the children: *this one* is taller than *that one;*
  *that one* is shorter than *this one.*

— Here is a cone on top of a cylinder: try to put the cylinder
  on top of the cone.
  Here is a cone on top of a cylinder: try to put *this* on top
  of *that.*

— Let us show the cubes of the pink tower to a little girl:
  *this* cube is the largest; *those* cubes are the smallest of
  the series.
  Let us show the cubes of the pink tower to a little girl:
  *this one* is the largest; *those* are the smallest of the series.

(Relatives and Interrogatives: (che, il quale, cui, chi?
quale?) who, whom, whose, which, that, who? whose?
whom? what? which? where, when?)

Note: The situation with the relatives is different in English:
*who* refers to persons; *which* to things; *that* to either persons or
things; whereas *che* and *il quale* are interchangeable referring to both

persons and things, *il quale* having special rhetorical advantages over *che*, in addition to showing gender and number. *Cui* is used after prepositions; and, for the possessive Italian has *il cui, la cui,* etc., "whose."

— Ask the children:   Which child wants to see my drawing?
Ask the children:   *Who* wants to see my drawing?

— Ask Charles for the pencil; Charles put the pencil into the drawer.
Ask Charles for the pencil *which* Charles put into the drawer.
Ask Charles for the pencil *that* he put into the drawer.

— Thank Charles.   Charles gave you the pencil.
Thank Charles *who* gave you the pencil.

— Look at the children.   You hear the children in the next room.
Look at the children *whom* you hear in the next room.

— Yesterday you put the flowers into a vase: change the water in the vase.
Change the water in the vase into *which* you put the flowers yesterday.
Change the water in the vase *where* you put the flowers yesterday.
Change the water in the vase *that* you put the flowers into yesterday.

— Choose among the pieces of cloth the cloth most like your dress.
Choose among the pieces of cloth *the one which* is most like your dress.
Choose among the pieces of cloth *the one that* is most like your dress.

— Here is the little girl.   We found her pocketbook.
Here is the little girl *whose* pocketbook we found.

— Here is the boy.   We saw him yesterday.
Here is the boy *whom* we saw yesterday.

— Select an inset from the insets used for drawing.

Select an inset from *those which* are used for drawing.

Select an inset from *those that* are used for drawing.

### GROUP D

(Possessives: mine, yours, his, hers, ours, yours, theirs)

— This book is my book
This book is *mine*

— That house is our house
That house is *ours*

— This book is your book
This book is *yours*

— This money is your money
This money is *yours*

— Those pencils are his pencils
Those pencils are *his*

— Those seats are their seats
Those seats are *theirs*

— Those pencils are her pencils
Those pencils are *hers*

— This place is its place
This place is its

### PERMUTATIONS

The function of the pronoun as a substitute for a noun has been made clear in the analysis of the above sentences. After the children themselves have composed the first sentence with the colored cards they form the second sentence by taking away the noun card and substituting the corresponding pronoun. In the work done by the teacher to give the child an idea of the normal position of the pronoun, let her remember that in Italian personal pronouns precede the verb except in interrogation (where the subject may follow) and in cases where the subject is specially emphasized and where the pronouns appear as a suffix (infinitive, participle and imperative).

He soothed her with a kiss.
He her soothed with a kiss, etc., etc.

[It will become apparent that in English the personal pronoun takes the position of the noun, whereas for Italian the pronoun shifts to a position in front of the verb.

Considerable variety develops in English when the noun is replaced by a relative pronoun. However, the different problems arising in connection with pronouns generally are so complex that we return to this subject, especially to the question of subject and object forms, in dealing with sentence-analysis later.]

LESSONS AND COMMANDS ON THE PRONOUN

Subject:

Subjective Personal Pronouns: I, you, he, she, we, you, they (io, tu, egli, essa, noi, voi, loro, etc.).

Explain these pronouns as briefly and practically as possible from the point of view of speaker and listener, etc., one child commanding the others while they *execute* the command along with him. Example: The teacher, named for instance Anna Fedeli, explains in this way: " I don't say *Anna Fedeli;* I say *I.*" " To Carlino here I don't say Carlino; I say, *you.*" " Of Gigino, over there, I don't say Gigino; I say *he,*" etc., etc.

Command: —

The command is given by a child; but he himself executes the first personal form along with the other children:

| | |
|---|---|
| —*I* walk around the table | —*I* raise my arms |
| —*You* walk around the table | —*You* raise your arms |
| —*She* walks around the table | —*She* raises her arms |
| —*He* walks around the table | —*He* raises his arms |
| —*We* walk around the table | —*We* raise our arms |
| —*You* walk around the table | —*You* raise your arms |
| —*They* walk around the table | —*They* raise their arms |
| | |
| —*I* lift the chair | —*I* take the ink-stand |
| —*You* lift the chair | —*You* take the ink-stand |
| —*He* lifts the chair, etc., etc. | —*He* takes the ink-stand, etc., etc. |
| | |
| —*I* wave my handkerchief | |
| —*You* wave your handkerchief, etc., etc. | |

From these exercises the notion gradually develops that:

the *first person* is the one who *speaks;*
the *second person* is the one who *listens;*
the *third person* is the one spoken of.

Other commands may be dramatized by small groups as follows:

— The first person must put a question the second must answer, and the third from a distance must try to hear both of them.

— Let the first one write, the second one watch, and the third one say " That is not right."

The following commands may be read aloud by the child:

— *I* ask you a question very softly. *You* answer *me;* and *he,* over there, must try to hear both of us.

— *I* shall write; *you* must act as if you were trying to read what I am writing; and then *he,* over there, will call out: " That is not right."

Subject:
Direct Objective Personal Pronouns: me, you, him, her, us, you, them (mi, ti, si, lo, la, ci, vi, si, li, le).
Reflexives and reciprocals: myself, yourself, etc., each other.

Command: —
(Here too one child commands executing the first personal forms, while the others act out the second and third):
— I touch the oil-cloth on the table; I touch *myself;* I touch *you;* you touch *yourself;* I touch *him;* you touch *her;* let us touch *each other;* you touch *me.*
— Charles, take the whisk-broom and brush the table; Charles, brush *me;* Charles, brush *him;* Charles, brush *her;* Charles, brush *yourself.*
— Mary and I bow to the teacher; now we bow to *you;* now we bow to *him;* now we bow to *her;* now we bow to *each other.*

— I lead George by the hand to the window; I lead *you* by the hand to the window; I lead *him* by the hand to the window; he leads *us* by the hand to the window; we lead *her* by the hand to the window.

Subject:

Indirect object personal pronouns: me, te, se, mi, ti, si, le, gli, lui, lei, noi, voi, ci, vi, loro (the disjunctive pronouns, used after prepositions, etc., do not differ in English from the simple direct object forms).

(The commands are still executed as above):

Commands: —

— I am going to distribute these pencils: one to *you,* one to *him,* one to *her;* one to *myself.*

— Louis, give *me* a command; give *him* a command; give *her* a command; give *yourself* a command.

— Attention! Charles, give *her* a blue bead! Mary, give *him* a red bead!

— Alfred, give a white bead to *me;* give *me* also a yellow bead!

Subject:

Demonstratives for persons (questi, costui, colui; the second person, " that one near you," is lacking in English, which also fails to distinguish between persons and things and between genders).

When the distinctions in space represented by these pronouns have been taught as above the children read and execute as follows:

Commands: —

Distribute the pronouns to different children in the class; *questi,* " this one (near me)," *costei* (feminine); *costui,* " that one (near you)," *costei* (fem.); *colui,* " that one (over there)," *colei* (fem.); when the children are in their proper places, give to each child a different command.

— Call to you a boy and a girl, and then command: *that one* (*costui*) go and get a case; *that one* (*costei*) go and get a counter; *those* (*costoro*) keep far away and preserve complete silence.

— Point to two children, one standing near you and one far away; then command: *that one* (*colui*) go and fetch an arm-chair for *that one* (fem. *costei*) and a chair for *this one* (*questo*); then have him return to his place. Then have all the children execute the commands which *those* (*costoro*) will now give.

In case the class is made up either entirely of girls or entirely of boys, the children find considerable amusement in trying to imitate the manners of whichever opposite sex is missing.

Subject:

Demonstratives of things (questo, cotesto, quello, ciò, ne; here also English has no pronoun of the second person (*that near you*), nor does it possess the general indefinite *ciò* (referring to a general idea: *that* (ciò) *is true*).

When the meaning of these words, in terms of space location, has been taught, the children execute as follows:

Commands: —

— You children divide into three groups; then go and occupy three different places; change places as follows: you leave *that* (*cotesto*) and occupy *that* over there; the others leave *that* (*quello*) and occupy *this* (*questo*).

Subject:

Possessives: mine, yours (thine), his, hers, its, ours, yours, theirs.

Commands: —

— Point out various objects, saying: This is my slate; that one is *yours*, that is *hers*, and this one is *his*.

— Point at the different seats, saying: Here are our places, that is *mine* and this is *yours*. Those over there are *theirs*.

— Pass around little baskets, saying: This is my basket. Whose is that? Is that *yours*? Is this *hers*? Are these *ours*? Is this one *his*?

We dealt with the relatives only incidentally in the analyses (Group C above); we do not treat them here, postponing the study of them in detail to the chapter on sentence-analysis.

## PARADYMS

In teaching the declension of the pronouns we use the method employed by us in teaching all inflections: bundles of cards, of which one group is tied separately and serves as a guide. The child arranges the cards on the table, working first on the guiding group and putting the pronouns in order of persons: first, second, third.

### GROUP A
### (Personal Pronouns)

|  |  | Masculine | | Feminine | |
|---|---|---|---|---|---|
| I | we | io | noi | io | noi |
| you, thou | you | tu | voi | tu | voi |
| he | they | egli | loro | ella | loro |
| she | they | esso | essi | essa | esse |
| it | they | lo | li | la | le |
| me | us | lui | | lei | |
| you, thee | you | gli | | le | |
| him | them | | | | |
| her | them | | | | |
| it | them | | | | |

### GROUP B
### (Demonstratives of Person)

|  |  | Masculine | Feminine |
|---|---|---|---|
| this | these | questi | costei |
| that | those | costui | costei |
| this one | these | colui | colei |
| that one | those | costoro | costoro |
|  |  | coloro | coloro |

## (Demonstratives of Things)

|  |  | *Masculine* |  | *Feminine* |  |
|---|---|---|---|---|---|
| this | these | questo | questi | questa | queste |
| that | those | cotesto | cotesti | cotesta | coteste |
| this one | these | quel(lo) | quegli, quei | quella | quelle |
| that one | those | ciò |  | ciò |  |
|  |  | ne |  | ne |  |

## (Relatives)

*Persons*

|  | *Persons and Things* | |
|---|---|---|
|  | *Masculine* | *Feminine* |
| who | il quale  i quali | la quale  le quali |
| whose | che | che |
| whom | chi | chi |
| that | cui | cui |

*Things*

which                   chi (compound ="he who")
that

what (compound = that which)

## (Possessives)

| mine | its |
|---|---|
| yours (thine) | ours |
| his | yours |
| hers | theirs |

## (Interrogatives)

| *Persons* | *Persons* |
|---|---|
| who? | chi? |
| whose? |  |
| whom? | quale? |
| which? |  |

| *Things* | *Things* |
|---|---|
| | che? |
| what? | cosa? |
| | che cosa? |
| which? | quale? |

### AGREEMENT OF PRONOUN AND VERB

The cards given to the child for this work are green for the personal pronoun subjects, and red for the verb forms of the three simple tenses, present, past, and future. There are, for Italian, three groups corresponding to the three conjugations: *amare, temere, sentire.* The child's work is to place the pronouns in the proper order of person (first, second, third, singular and plural) and to put after each pronoun the corresponding verb form. Each child corrects his work by his own sense of the language; however, the teacher looks it over to verify it. The resulting exercises when correctly performed are as follows:

#### GROUP A

| io **amo** ("I love" etc.) | Io amavo ("I was loving") | io amerò ("I shall love") |
|---|---|---|
| tu ami | tu amavi | tu amerai |
| egli ama | egli amava | egli amerà |
| noi amiamo | noi amavamo | noi ameremo |
| voi amate | voi amavate | voi amerete |
| essi amano | essi amavano | essi ameranno |

#### GROUP B

| io temo ("I fear") | io temevo ("I was fearing") | io temerò ("I shall fear") |
|---|---|---|
| tu **temi** | tu temevi | tu temerai |
| egli teme | egli temeva | egli temerà |
| noi temiamo | noi temévamo | noi temeremo |
| voi temete | voi temevate | voi temerete |
| essi temono | essi temevano | essi temeranno |

## GROUP C

| | | |
|---|---|---|
| io sento ("I hear") | io sentivo ("I was hearing") | io sentirò ("I shall hear") |
| tu senti | tu sentivi | tu sentirai |
| egli sente | egli sentiva | egli sentirà |
| noi sentiamo | noi sentivamo | noi sentiremo |
| voi sentite | voi sentivate | voi sentirete |
| essi sentono | essi sentivano | essi sentiranno |

## FOR ENGLISH

### GROUP A

### (Simple Tenses)

| | | |
|---|---|---|
| I love | I loved | I shall love |
| you love | you loved | you will love |
| he loves | he loved | he will love |
| we love | we loved | we shall love |
| you love | you loved | you will love |
| they love | they loved | they will love |

### GROUP B

### (Progressive Forms)

| | | |
|---|---|---|
| I am loving | I was loving | I shall be loving |
| you are loving | you were loving | you will be loving |
| he is loving | he was loving | he will be loving |
| we are loving | we were loving | we shall be loving |
| you are loving | you were loving | you will be loving |
| they are loving | they were loving | they will be loving |

### GROUP C

### (Interrogative Forms)

| | | |
|---|---|---|
| do I love? | did I love? | will I love? |
| do you love? | did you love? | shall you love? |
| does he love? | did he love? | will he love? |
| do we love? | did we love? | will we love? |
| do you love? | did you love? | shall you love? |
| do they love? | did they love? | will they love? |

### GROUP D

### (Intensive and Negative Forms)

| | | |
|---|---|---|
| I do (not) love, etc. | I did (not) love etc. | I shall (not) love etc. |

The child can shuffle his cards in various ways, mixing the verb forms of the three different Italian verbs, or the four tense forms of the English verb; passing then to a reconstruction of the different tenses according to the pronouns, the order of which has by this time become familiar to him.

The next step is to conjugate properly.

### Conjugations of Verbs

#### MATERIAL

In our material we offer (for Italian) the conjugation of the two auxiliary verbs (*essere* " to be," *avere* " to have ") and the model verbs of the first, second and third conjugations. The colors used for the five verbs are all different, yellow for *essere* " to be," black for *avere* " to have," pink for *amare* " to love," green for *temere* " to fear," light blue for *sentire* " to hear." Each card has both pronoun and verb form. This is not only to simplify and expedite the exercise but also to make sure of auto-exercise, since the pronoun guides the order of the forms in each tense. These verb forms of a given verb preceded by the pronouns are, accordingly, made into a little package. Here, however, the groups are not so simple as in other cases. For the verb, the cards are kept in a sort of red envelope tied with a ribbon. The infinitive of the verb is written on the outside of the envelope, which, though very simple, is most attractive. When the whole verb is wrapped in its package and tied with the ribbon, it forms a small red prism of the following dimensions: cmm. 35 × 4 × 5.5. On untying the ribbon and opening the envelope the child finds inside ten little " volumes " with red covers. These volumes represent the *moods* of the verb and they have the following titles inscribed on the first page:

> Indicative Mood
> Conditional Mood (for Italian)
> Subjunctive Mood
> Imperative Mood
> Verbals

To facilitate replacing these materials in an orderly way and to be sure that this order is recognized, the child finds in the corner of each envelope a Roman numeral (I, II, III, IV, V); and besides that, an Arabic numeral indicating the number of tenses in the given mood. On opening the little volume and taking off the cover we find many other tiny volumes with red covers. These are the tenses. In the middle of each cover is written the name and, to one side, the number indicating the relative position of the tenses in the following manner: the *simple* tense is marked with the letter *S* and the *compound* tense with the letter *C*. The titles, then, of the eight booklets contained in the little volume for a given mood are:

> Present Tense   1s
> Past Tense   2s
> Future Tense   3s
> Perfect Tense   1c
> Pluperfect Tense   2c
> Future Perfect Tense   3c

(For Italian the tenses are:   Present, 1s, Imperfect 2s, Remote Past 3s, Future 4s, Perfect 1c, Pluperfect 2c, Past Anterior 3c, Future Perfect 4c.)

Finally, on opening each of these little booklets (which, by the way, are 3.5 × 4 cmm. and only a bare millimeter thick) we have the cards with the verb forms preceded by the corresponding pronoun.

This rather resembles the famous egg in which a number of smaller and smaller eggs were enclosed. For this beautiful package forming as a whole the entire conjugation of the verb contains the booklets of the different moods, which in their turn contain the smaller booklets of the tenses. The orderly enumeration of the moods and tenses, together with the pronouns which serve to show the order of the verb forms, allows the child to conjugate the entire verb by himself and to study the classification of the different forms that make it up. In fact the children need no help in this exercise. Once they have this attractive, complicated, and mysterious little red package, they evolve on their little tables in an orderly way the entire conjugation of the verb. Having learned the verb forms little by little they shuffle the cards of the different tenses in various ways and then try to put them in their regular order. At length they are able to shuffle all the cards in the entire verb as the children in the " Children's House " did with the sixty-four colors; and to reconstruct correctly the whole conjugation by tense and by mood. They themselves finally ask to write the verb and they prepare of their own accord new booklets writing out the new verbs as they meet them.

For this purpose we have included in our materials many booklets likewise covered in red and filled with *blank* cards of a variety of colors. The children themselves fill out these cards in conjugating their new verbs.

The exercises both of working out the conjugation of the verb and of writing out new verbs may be performed at home.

# X

## CONJUNCTIONS

Material: This box has eight compartments for the title cards, which are tan (article), black (noun), brown (adjective), red (verb), violet (preposition), pink (adverb, green (pronoun), and *yellow* (*conjunction*). It also has the usual place for the sentences that are to be analyzed. These again are given in groups.

### GROUP A

### Coordinate Conjunctions

#### (Copulative, Disjunctive, Illative, Adversative)

— Put away the pen *and* the ink-stand.
Put away the pen *or* the ink-stand.
Put away *neither* the pen *nor* the ink-stand, *but* the paper.

— The table, therefore, is bare *and* in order.
*For* all your things are in their places.

— Do not leave the objects you use here and there about the room, *but* put them all back in their places.

— Speak to your nearest school-mate not aloud *but* in a whisper.

— Move your table forward a little, *but* only a little *and* without making any noise.

GROUP B

## Subordinate Conjunctions

### (Time, condition, cause, purpose)

— You can push down a key of the piano without making any sound *if* you push it down slowly.

— You could write with your left hand *if* you " touched " the letters with that hand.

— You will get silence from the children *as soon as* you write " silence " on the blackboard.

— That child is happy: he always sings *while* he works.

— Always shut the door *when* you go from one room to another.

— Everybody must be orderly *in order that* the " Children's House " may look neat.

GROUP C

## Subordinate conjunctions, *continued*

### (Cause, concession, alternative)

— The " Children's House " is attractive *because* it is pretty and *because* it is so easy to keep busy all the time.

— I shall give it to you *since* you have asked me for it very politely.

— We shall go to walk in the park rather *than* in the crowded streets.

— I shall give you that toy *although* I should have preferred to let you have a beautiful book.

— You may promise to go and visit him to-morrow *provided* you keep your promise.

Grammar Boxes, showing respectively eight and nine parts of speech.

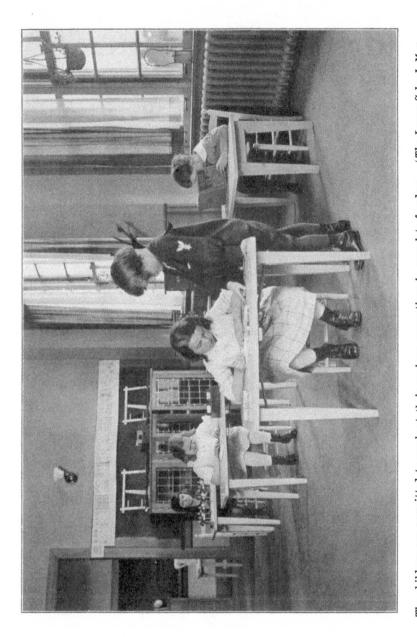

The children are permitted to work at their various occupations in complete freedom. (*The Lenox School, Montessori Elementary Class, New York.*)

## PERMUTATIONS

The removal of the conjunction destroys the relationship between the words, and this brings out its function in the sentence:

Put away the pen and the ink-stand.
Put away the pen the ink-stand.

Put away the pen or the ink-stand.
Put away the pen the ink-stand.

You could write with your left hand if you touched the letters with that hand.
You could write with your left hand you touched the letters with that hand.

The conjunction must be placed between the words it connects: otherwise the meaning is changed or destroyed:

Put away the pen and the ink-stand.
Put and away the pen the ink-stand.

The " Children's House " is attractive because it is pretty.
The " Children's House " is attractive it is pretty.

### LESSONS AND COMMANDS ON THE CONJUNCTIONS

Subject:
Coordinate conjunctions: and, or, neither, nor (e, o, nè).

Commands: —

— Come to " silence " where you are *and* move only at my call.

— Come to " silence " where you are *or else* move silently among the chairs.

— Walk on tip-toe about the room, being careful *neither* to meet *nor* to follow one another.

Subject:
Declarative: that (che).

Command: —

— Tell two of your schoolmates *that* you know a conjunction.

Subject:

Adversatives: but, however, instead (ma, invece).

Command: —

— Form two lines; now one line face about turning from left to right; the other line, *instead*, turn in the opposite direction.

— Form in one long line and advance; when you reach the end of the room, do not stop, *but* turn to the left.

Subject:

Condition: if (se).

Command: —

— You will be able to hear this drop of water fall, *if* you remain for a moment in absolute silence.

Subject:

Time: while, when, as soon as (mentre, quando, appena).

Command: —

— A few of you walk about among the tables; then stop in the center of the room, *while* the others gather round you and try to cover your eyes with their hands.

— One of you start to leave the room. *When* you are about to cross the threshold, the others will block the way compelling you to stop.

— All of you ready! *As soon as* I say "Go!" run to the other end of the room.

Subject:

Purpose: so that, in order that (affinchè, perchè).

Command: —

— One of you stand in the middle of the room; the others try to pass near him quickly *so that* he cannot touch you.

— I am going to whisper a command: listen in perfect silence *in order that* you may hear what I command.

Subject:

Alternative: rather than (piuttostochè, anzichè).

Command: —

— Those children who would *rather* work *than* go out of doors rise from their places.

Subject:

Cause: because, since (perchè, poichè).

Command: —

— Before beginning to work let us become entirely quiet, *because* then we can think about what we are going to do.

Subject:

Exception: except, save (fuorchè, salvochè).

Command: —

— Get the counters and place one on every table in the room *except* on this one. Gather up all the counters *save* the red ones. Return all the counters to their box.

## COMPARISON OF ADJECTIVES
### SERIES A

— Of these two long rods, this one is the *longer.*
Of these three rods, which is the *longest?*

— This rod is *longer* than that.
That rod is the *longest* of the three.
Which is the *longest* of the series?

— This cloth is *smoother* than that.
This cloth is *smoothest* of all.

— Of these two shades of red which is the *darker?*
Of all these shades of red which is the *darkest?*

— Of these two prisms which is the *thicker?*
This prism is *thicker* than that.
Of these three prisms, which is *thickest?*

— Which of these two children is the *taller?*
Which is the *tallest* child in the room?

— Which of these two pictures is the *more* beautiful?
This picture is *more* beautiful than that.

— Which of these three pictures is *most* beautiful?
Which is the *most* beautiful picture in the room?

— Which of these two games is the *more* amusing?
This game is *more* amusing than that.
This game is *most* amusing of all.

— This drawing is good.
That drawing is *better.*
That drawing is *best.*

— There are some beads on this table.
There are *more* beads on that table.
There are *most* beads on that table.

— There is a little water in this glass.
There is *less* water in that glass.
There is *least* water in that glass.

— Of these two children John is the *elder.*
Of these three children Mary is the *eldest.*
Mary is *older* than John.
John is *older* than Laura.

A set of exercises may be arranged to bring out the
paradymns of comparison by means of suffixes (*-er, est*)
and of adverbs (*more, most*).   Here the series of cards
for the positive adjectival forms are, as usual, brown, the
phonograms for *-er* and *-est* in lighter and darker shades
of brown respectively.   The cards for *more* and *most* as
adverbs are colored pink.   When properly arranged, the
cards appear as follows:

| long | tall | thick | smooth |
|------|------|-------|--------|
| long *er* | tall *er* | thick *er* | smooth *er* |
| long *est* | tall *est* | thick *est* | smooth *est* |

| short | dark | light | rough |
|-------|------|-------|-------|
| short *er* | dark *er* | light *er* | rough *er* |
| short *est* | dark *est* | light *est* | rough *est* |

|  |  |  |
|---|---|---|
| beautiful | amusing | interesting |
| *more* beautiful | *more* amusing | *more* interesting |
| *most* beautiful | *most* amusing | *most* interesting |

A second exercise contains cards for each of the forms for these same words. There are three colors: brown, light brown and dark brown (superlative). There are in addition similar cards for the adjectives of irregular comparisons, and three title cards: *Positive, Comparative, Superlative.* The exercise results as follows:

| *Positive* | *Comparative* | *Superlative* |
|-----------|--------------|--------------|
| long | longer | longest |
| tall | taller | tallest |
| thick | thicker | thickest |
| smooth | smoother | smoothest |
| short | shorter | shortest |
| dark | darker | darkest |
| light | lighter | lightest |
| rough | rougher | roughest |
| beautiful | more beautiful | most beautiful |
| amusing | more amusing | most amusing |
| interesting | more interesting | most interesting |
| old | elder | eldest |
| many | more | most |
| good | better | best |
| bad | worse | worst |
| little | less | least |

# XI

## INTERJECTIONS

Since this is the last part of speech to be studied the children are now able to recognize *all* the different parts of speech and it is no longer necessary to make sentences containing only parts of speech which the children know. Therefore in our Italian lessons we choose henceforth sentences from the classic authors (mostly from Manzoni). Since the interjection is really a thought expressed in an abbreviated form it lends itself readily to dramatic interpretation. With the same sentence the children accordingly can now perform the two-fold exercise of general analysis and "interpretative reading." They now recite sentences which they have picked out and studied instead of the commands. At this time also they are given a chart containing the complete classification of interjections. The children read them, interpreting each as they go along by voice and gesture. This is the first table of classification to be presented. Later on all the parts of speech will be given on charts with their definitions and classification.

### ANALYSES

Material: The grammar box is complete. It now has nine separate compartments for the colored cards, article (tan), noun (black), adjective (brown), verb (red), preposition (violet), adverb (pink), pronoun (green), conjunction (yellow), and *interjection* (*blue*). In the compartment for the sentence slips are groups of cards which correspond exactly to the number of the words contained in the sentences.

### GROUP A

(Per amor del cielo! oibò! addio! ehm! misericordia! ah!)

*Please!* Don't make so much noise!
*Shame on you!* exclaimed Henry, much shocked at those words.
*Good-by!* We shall see you to-morrow.
*Look out!* If you drop that vase, you will break it.
*Mercy on us!* What is the matter with the poor man?
*Aha!* now I understand!

### GROUP B

(Eh via! bravo! bene! ehi! poh! per carità! oh!)

*Come, come!* Do you think I am going to believe all that non-sense?
*Goodness!* I hope the child is not going to fall.
*Thanks!* It was kind of you to help me put my objects away.
*Cockadoodledoo!* sang the rooster in the yard!
*Ding-dong, ding-dong!* The engines were passing by. There was a fire!
*Cheer up!* There is no harm done!

### GROUP C

(Ohè! ih! toh! poveretto! ahi! ohi! eh! animo! uh! ton!)

*Farewell!* The ship gradually drew away from the shore! The houses faded from view one by one. The hills formed a low line on the horizon. *Farewell!* It would be months, years perhaps, before George would see the old familiar town again. *Farewell!*
*Help! Help!* came a voice through the fog! A man was drowning.
*Hush!* Do you hear that bird singing in the distance?
*Alas!* It was too late! When the doctor came, the poor man was dead!

*Hurrah! Hurrah!* The soldiers were now almost at the top of
the hill. *Hurrah! hurrah!* The red-white-and-blue was
waving at last where the enemy had held out so long!
*Bang!* In the still night the sound of a gun roused the sleeping inhabitants.

CHART OF CLASSIFIED INTERJECTIONS

(For interpretative reading)

ITALIAN INTERJECTIONS:

*Pain:* ahi! ohi! oihmè! ahimè! ah! oh! poveretto!
*Prayer:* deh! mercè! aiuto! per carità! per amor di Dio!
*Surprise, wonder:* Oh! ih! nientedimeno! poh! toh! eh! corbez-
zoli! bazzecole! caspita! cospetto! uh! oooh! misericordia!
diavolo! bubbole!
*Threat:* ehm! guai!
*Disgust, horror:* puh! puah! brr!
*Anger:* oibò! vergogna!
*Doubt:* uhm!
*Weariness:* auf! auff!
*Calls, silence:* ehi! ohè! olà! alto là! pss! st! psst!
*Demonstratives:* ecco! riecco! eccomi! eccoci!
*Encouragement:* orsù! via! suvvia! animo! coraggio! arri là!
hop hop!
*Greeting:* salve! vale! addio! arrivederci! ave! ciao!
*Applause:* bene! bravo! viva! evviva! gloria! osanna! alleluja!
*Onomatapoetic:* crac! patatrac! piff paff! din don! ton ton!
zum zum! bum bum!
*Animal sounds:* gnau! chicchirichì! coccodè! cra cra cra!
uè uè uè! glu glu glu! pi pi pi! cri cri! fron fron! bu bu!
*Curses:* accidenti! accidempoli! perbacco! canchero! malanag-
gia!

ENGLISH INTERJECTIONS:

*Pain:* oh! alas! ah! ouch! my!
*Joy:* oh! ah! oh my! good! splendid!
*Surprise:* ha! aha! oh! really! you don't say! indeed! well, well!
upon my word!
*Contempt:* fudge! pshaw! fie! nonsense! bother!

*Hesitation:* hum!
*Resolution:* by Jove!
*Silence:* hush! hist! listen! shh!
*To animals:* whoa! gee! haw! geddap! kitty-kitty! puss-puss!
*Onomatapoetic:* ding-dong! bang! whiz! bing! crack! snap!
    etc., etc.

(In general the use of interjections, especially of capricious character, is much more characteristic of the best Italian writing and speech than it is of English.)

# XII

## SENTENCE ANALYSIS

### I

#### SIMPLE SENTENCES

The material for logical analysis consists of little rolls of fairly stiff paper, on which are printed simple, compound and complex sentences, in carefully prepared series.

There is also a chart, divided into two columns of rectangular spaces, with the name of one sentence element printed in each space. The sentence read on the roll can be torn off part by part, and each of these parts is placed in one of the rectangles, according to the name printed on it. This is another application of the compartment box method used to analyze first the alphabet, then the sounds which go to make up the word, finally the words as parts of speech. Here, the compartments are reduced to a simple design.

The charts for logical analysis are on colored paper and are artistically drawn and decorated. We have charts of four different kinds as regards ornament and color, for such details exert a considerable influence upon the work of the children. On the following page is a sample of the charts with its " sections."

The two spaces at the top, subject and predicate, are somewhat larger and are more conspicuously decorated than the other rectangles below. The words *subject* and *verb* are printed entirely in large capitals. The other

CHART A

| VERB<br><br>(The verbal or nominal predicate.) | Who is it that?<br>What is it that?<br><br>SUBJECT |
|---|---|
| Who? What?<br><br>(Direct object.) | To whom? To what?<br><br>(Indirect object.) |
| By Whom? By What?<br><br>(Agent.) | Of whom? Of what?<br><br>(Possessive, material.) |
| When?<br><br>(Time.) | Where?<br><br>(Place.) |
| Whence?<br><br>(Source.) | How?<br><br>(Manner.) |
| Why?<br><br>(Cause.) | What for?<br><br>(Purpose.) |
| By means of whom?<br>By means of what?<br><br>(Instrument.) | With whom?<br>With what?<br><br>(Accompaniment.) |
| (Attributive (phrases).) | (Vocative.) |

spaces, however, are much more simply decorated and the words are in small letters. This helps to distinguish the principal from the secondary elements in the sentences. The names of the parts of speech, and the questions which bring out the meaning of these names, are in different colors: for instance, the names may be black and the questions red, or the names may be in red and the questions in green. And the letters of the questions are larger than the letters of the names, except in the two upper spaces, where the words *subject* and *verb* are in the largest type.

The child begins to see what a sentence is: that is, he begins to *concentrate* on this particular question. How many times he has read sentences, pronounced sentences, composed sentences! But now he is examining them in detail, *studying* them. The simple sentence is a short proposition, with completed meaning, which expresses an action or a situation, organizing its different parts around a *verb*.

The first exercise for the child must be to find the verb, a task not very difficult after the preceding exercises on the parts of speech have been performed. When he has found the verb, it becomes essential for him to find the subject. The subject may be found by asking the question: *Who is it that — ?* For example:

The child reads.

The word *reads* is the verb. The section of the roll where the word *reads* appears is torn off and placed in the space marked *Verb*. Then ask: " *Who is it that* reads?" The answer is, " *The child* reads." The section containing the word *the child* is torn off and placed in the space marked *Subject*.

Another sentence: on the roll the child finds written:

*The glass is broken.*

The teacher can briefly explain that the verb taken by itself, has no special meaning. *Is* means nothing! " *Is?* Is *what?* " Some attribute must be added: " Is *broken!* " Here we get a *nominal predicate.* When the verb contains some definite meaning in terms of action, for instance *reads,* we get a *verbal predicate.* The section of the roll containing *is broken* is torn off, accordingly, and placed in the space of the verb. But *what* is broken? *The glass!* The section containing the words *the glass* is placed in the space of the subject. All of this can be copied off by the child by hand, as follows:

Simple sentence: The child reads.
The child: Subject.
Reads: Predicate (verbal).

### Series I

#### (Simple Sentences)

The first roll contains the following simple sentences without modifiers of any kind:

— The child reads.
— The glass is broken.
— Charles is tall.
— The trees are blossoming.
— The blackboard is clean.
— Who has come?
— The pencil is broken.
— The sky is blue.
— I am reading.
— I am studying.
— The children are playing.
— Time flies.
— The teacher sings.

(Simple Sentences, containing a few modifiers)

The roll contains the following sentences, written one after another:

— The mother loves her child dearly.
— Johnny brought his teacher a rose.
— You may keep the book for some days, Louis.
— Mary, give the poor man a penny.
— Where have you been, Mary?
— I will do it, mother.
— Little Harry, only three years old, has cleaned the whole blackboard.
— Who drew the pretty picture?
— Last night I showed the letter to father.
— In the yard a red white and blue flag is waving.
— Did you go to the theater last night?
— The rain was beating against the window panes.
— The dog is barking at the cat.
— The poor deaf-mutes talk with their hands.

Example of application: The section containing the first sentence,

The mother loves her child dearly

is first torn off from the roll. Then the section containing the word *loves* is placed in the space marked *verb*. *Who* loves? — *the mother.* The section containing the words *the mother* is placed in the space marked *subject.* The mother loved *whom? Her child.* The section containing *her child* is torn off and placed in the space marked *direct object.* By thus reading the names printed in the spaces of the chart the child learns to classify the various kinds of modifiers. *How* does the mother love her child? *In what manner? Dearly.* The section containing the word *dearly* is placed in the space marked *Manner* and the sentence is completed.

Now the child can copy off these analyses immediately or make others, as he thinks best. The copy may be as follows:

> The mother loves her child dearly.
> The mother: Subject.
> Loves: Predicate (verbal).
> Her child: Direct object.
> Dearly: Adverb, manner.

In classifying the vocatives and attributives, a little help from the teacher may be required. Example:

> You may keep the book for some days, Louis.

The word *Louis* can be dramatized somewhat into a kind of invocation, as — *O Louis, you may keep the book* and so on. Vocatives can almost always be identified by trying the exclamatory *O* before them.

In the sentence,

> Little Harry, only three years old, has cleaned the whole blackboard.

*only three years old* is an attributive of Harry. It should be torn off and placed in the space marked *Attributive*.

### SERIES III

(Simple sentences with two or more modifiers of the same kind)

The roll contains the following sentences in sections which may be read and torn off one after the other as the child unrolls the strip:

> — The child sleeps and dreams.
> — Everybody likes fruit and flowers.

— He took paper, pen and ink to write to his friends.
— Charles opened and closed the book.          ,
— The doctor and the father left the sick child's room.
— The women recommended calmness, patience and prudence.
— In the beginning God created heaven and earth.
— He will always have money and friends.
— In the street we could see crowds of men and a few women.

## Series IV

(Elliptical sentences with subject understood)

[This situation does not however arise in English, which, save in the imperative, always requires at least a pronominal subject for the verb.]

Here, the child interprets the sentence, completing it and finding the element that is lacking.

— La ringrazio (*I* thank you).
— Verrete? (Will *you* come?)
— Sono stanco (*I* am tired).
— Non mi sento bene oggi (*I* don't feel well to-day).
— Com'è andata? (How did *it* turn out?)
— Dico la verità (*I* will tell you all about it).
— Siamo contentissimi (*We* are delighted).
— Vi saluto (*I* bid you good-by).
— Vado a casa (*I* am going home).
— Lampeggia (*It* is lightening).
— M'impose silenzio (*He* told me to say nothing).
— Ascolto (*I* am listening).

## Series V

(Elliptical sentences where the predicate is understood)

— Silence!
— Why all this noise?
— After me, the deluge!
— The sooner the better!
— Good luck to you, sir!

— What nasty weather!

— What an attractive school!

— O for a calm, a thankful heart!

— A horse, a horse, my kingdom for a horse!

— Away with him!

— Fire! Fire!

— Here, here, quick!

— Honor to the brave!

### SERIES VI

(Elliptical sentences where the direct object is understood:
*incomplete predication*)

— They drove away.

— He spends like a millionaire.

— He drinks like a fish.

— The farmer's boy had just milked.

— Do you understand?

— The cavalry spurred across the field at full speed.

— Did you see?

— The child did not hear.

### SERIES VII

(Sentences with numerous modifiers and of increased
difficulty)

— The poor boy came home that night, all tired out, covered
with mud from head to foot, with his coat torn and with
a black and blue lump on his forehead.

— Ethel hurried home as fast as possible.

— We heard the clatter of horse's hoofs on the pavement.

— And so through the night went his cry of alarm

To every Middlesex village and farm.

— The beautiful child with the black hair is here on the
lawn.

— And yet through the gloom and the night
  The fate of a nation was riding that night.

— The woman walked along in front of me with the child in
  her arms.

— The girl's voice sounded distinctly above all the others.

— To-morrow I shall come to town on foot.

— He spent the summer every year with his parents in their
  old home on the mountain side.

— That evening the old house was more lonely than ever.

— They are very busy this morning.

— I never did such a thing in my life!

— Every now and then a group of people hurriedly crossed
  the street.

— The doctor whispered something into the Mayor's ear.

— Just then some one knocked at the door.

— Here I am back again at my work.

— Mary had a little lamb
  With fleece as white as snow.

### The Order of Elements in the Sentence: Permutations

Rules:

The English (the Italian) language tends to follow the direct order in prose, inversion being very rare.

In poetry, inversion is very common.

The direct order consists in placing: first, the subject, then the predicate, then the objects, direct and indirect; then the modifiers follow according to the importance they derive from the meaning of the sentence.

These ideas are after all so simple and clear that the child rarely has any difficulty in understanding them. Nevertheless, it is much easier to give the child a vivid impression of them by the permutation of parts than by explanation. This permutation is made very convenient by the sentences being printed in sections which may be moved about and combined at will. Just as the sequence of the various parts of speech was made clear by transposing the parts, here the same result can be accomplished by transposing the sections of the printed slip. Example:

We          heard          the clatter          of the horse's hoofs
(subject)   (predicate)    (direct object)      (attribute)
on the pavement.
(place: adverb)

The following combinations are possible results of permutation:

We — heard — the clatter — of the horse's hoofs — on the pavement.

We — the clatter — heard — on the pavement — of the horse's hoofs.

We — of the horse's hoofs — on the pavement — the clatter — heard.

Of the horse's hoofs — on the pavement — heard — the clatter — we, etc., etc.

## Series VIII

### (The inverted order)

The effect of direct and inverted order can be shown in every sentence. But it is better to try examples of inversion from poetic language. In this series, all the sentences show inversion of one type or another:

— Meanwhile, impatient to mount and ride,
Booted and spurred, with a heavy stride
On the opposite shore walked Paul Revere.

— Upon the roof we sat that night!
The noise of bells went sweeping by;
Awesome bells they were to me.

— Still sits the school-house by the road.

— Before them under the garden-wall
Forward and back
Went drearily singing the chore-girl small.

— And day by day more holy grew
Each spot of the sacred ground.

— There thronged the citizens with terror dumb.

Exercises on the putting together of sentence elements can lead to practise in the identification and use of grammatical forms as parts of speech, which the study of single words would not at first permit; as for instance, forms of the verbs used as nouns (infinitive and gerund as subject and object), the difference between personal pronouns used as direct or indirect objects, and so on.

## SERIES IX

### (The forms of the verb)

The roll contains the two forms of the verb, active and passive, in sections. The analysis is conducted on the chart for the simple sentence:

| ACTIVE VOICE (Action performed by subject) | PASSIVE VOICE (Action performed by agent) | REFLEXIVE (*Middle Voice*) (Subject is direct object) |
|---|---|---|
| Mary dresses the little girl. | The little girl is dressed by Mary. | The little girl dresses herself. |
| The teacher praised Charles for the drawing. | Charles was praised by the teacher for the drawing. | Charles praised himself for the drawing. |
| The little girl excused George for his roughness. | George was excused for his roughness by the little girl. | George excuses himself for his roughness. |
| The janitor accused the boy. | The boy was accused by the janitor. | The boy accused himself. |
| The old man liked Albert very much. | Albert was very much liked by the old man. | Albert liked himself very much. |
| The nurse tucked the child into the warm bed. | The child was tucked into the warm bed by the nurse. | The child tucked himself into the warm bed. |

| ACTIVE VOICE (Action performed by subject) | PASSIVE VOICE (Action performed by agent) | REFLEXIVE (*Middle Voice*) (Subject is direct object) |
|---|---|---|
| The girl rocked her little friend to sleep in the rocking-chair. | The little friend was rocked to sleep in the rocking-chair by the little girl. | Her little friend rocked herself to sleep in the rocking-chair. |
| The teacher saw Henry in the large mirror. | Henry was seen in the large mirror by the teacher. | Henry saw himself in the large mirror. |
| The angry boy hurt Louis. | Louis was hurt by the angry boy. | Louis hurt himself. |

## SERIES X

### (Use of the personal pronoun)

The sentences previously given for analysis in teaching the personal pronouns can be used over again at this point for analysis on the sentence-chart.

— The children wrote a letter to their mother
 The children wrote her a letter
 They wrote it to her

— They gave their mother a surprise
 They gave her a surprise

— I told father all about it
 I told him all about it

— Charles soothed his sister with a kiss
 He soothed her with a kiss

— Will you give your drawing to the teacher?
 Will you give her your drawing?
 Will you give it to her?

— Don't think badly of your schoolmates
 Don't think badly of them

— Show those dirty hands to the teacher
 Show her those dirty hands
 Show them to her

— Tell the story to the children in the other room
 Tell it to the children in the other room
 Tell it to them there

The exercise in permutation brings out the relative positions of the direct and indirect objects; as also the conditions under which the preposition *to* is required before the indirect object.

II

### Compound and Complex Sentences

Here we are dealing with a number of propositions (clauses) which combine into one complete meaning. The clauses fit together in the sentences just as did the various elements in the simple sentence. The material for the analysis is therefore analogous to that used in the analysis of the simple sentence: strips of paper in rolls on which are written the sentences to be analyzed, and a chart with spaces where the detached pieces may be placed, according to the designation of these spaces.

The principal space on the chart is reserved for the main clause, around which the other clauses are arranged, as coordinate or subordinate.

Since the work of logical analysis of the complex sentence is sufficiently interesting to attract the attention of the child to various forms of study, the material contains in addition to the rolls and the chart, a number of test-cards where the analysis is completed and logically demonstrated. These cards serve as tests of the accuracy of the work done by the children, and as actual charts for analytical study. Of course, when the child is doing his exercise with the strips of paper and the chart, he does not have these test-cards before him. He should, however, always have free access to them. His interest in the game is to succeed by himself in placing the different propositions where they belong.

CHART B

| PRINCIPAL CLAUSE | |
|---|---|
| INCIDENTAL CLAUSES (Parenthetical clauses) | |
| SUBORDINATE ATTRIBUTIVE CLAUSE (Adjective or Relative clauses) | |
| who is it that . . . ?<br><br>subordinate *subject* clause<br>(subject clause) | whom . . . ? what . . . ?<br><br>subordinate *object* clause<br>(object clause) |
| when . . . ?<br><br>subordinate clause of *time*<br>(temporal clause) | where . . . ?<br><br>subordinate clause of *place*<br>(locative clause) |
| for what purpose . . . ?<br><br>subordinate clause of *purpose*<br>(purpose clause) | why . . . ? for what cause?<br><br>subordinate clause of *cause*<br>(causal clause) |
| how . . . ? than what?<br><br>subordinate clause of *manner* or *comparison*<br>(modal clauses) | on what condition . . . ?<br><br>subordinate clause of *condition*<br>(conditional clause) |
| in spite of what . . . ?<br><br>subordinate clause of *concession*<br>(concessive clause) | with what result . . . ?<br><br>subordinate clause of *result*<br>(result clause) |

## Series I

### (Compound Sentences)

The clauses are independent of each other. Each contains a complete meaning, and each therefore could stand alone. It is a question of simple sentences *coordinated* with each other.

— I hunted carefully everywhere and at last I found it.
— She started in fear, lifted her face and shaded it from the strong sun.
— The bees hummed in the warm sunshine and the cat sat purring at her side.
— She dropped her sewing and went to the door.
— The girl covered her eyes with her hands and wept.
— They looked into each other's faces: each of them had a question to ask and neither dared to speak.
— I am a lowly peasant and you are a gallant knight.
— They all looked at the speaker, and crowded round him and waited for his next word to attack him.
— Then he began to weep and he tore his hair in anguish.
— Louis clapped his hands for joy and began to dance around the room.
— He looked into the mirror, straightened his tie, smoothed his hair and went out to greet his two friends.
— She went to the window and looked out over the stormy sea.

The child divides these sentences into clauses, analyzing each separately. Then, placing one under the other, he is impressed by the fact that each has a complete meaning and can stand by itself; save that in English the subject of the first clause is often carried over to the second:

I hunted carefully everywhere.
And at last I found it.

I am a lowly peasant.
And you are a gallant knight.

Louis clapped his hands for joy.
 began to dance around the room.

He looked into the mirror.
 straightened his tie.
 smoothed his hair.
*and* went out to meet his two friends.

The bees hummed in the warm sunshine.
And the cat sat purring at her side.

Then he began to weep.
And he tore his hair in anguish.

The girl covered her face with her hands.
 *and* wept.

They looked at the speaker.
 crowded around him.
 *and* waited for his next word to attack him.

## SERIES II

### (The Complex Sentence)

Here only the main clause has a complete meaning. The other clauses make sense only when they are united with the main clause.   On this roll, the subordinate clauses are attributes of one of the elements of the main clause (relative clauses).

— The gold ring which you found yesterday on the stairs belongs to mother.
— The man who brought me to school this morning was my uncle.
— He was educated by his sister who taught him many beautiful things.
— The colors which Aunt Anna gave me Christmas are very good.
— A little girl who was at a party sat looking with longing eyes at a plate of sandwiches.
— The knife with which you sharpened my pencil was very dull.

— Bees don't care about the snow!
I can tell you why it's so:
Once I caught a little bee
Who was much too warm for me.—(F. D. SHERMAN)
— We have at home the prettiest cat you ever saw.
— Here are the pennies my mother gave me.
— The children I play with did not come to school to-day.
— The house we live in is beautiful and airy.
— Stars are the little daisies white
That dot the meadow of the night.—(SHERMAN)

## TEST CARDS

| PRINCIPAL CLAUSE (The words modified by the relative clause are in *italics*). | ATTRIBUTIVE SUBORDINATE CLAUSE (Relative or Adjective Clauses) (The clause has no meaning until united with some noun in the main clause). |
|---|---|
| The gold *ring* belongs to mother | which you found on the stairs yesterday |
| The *man* was my uncle | who brought me to school this morning |
| He was educated by his *sister* | who taught him many beautiful things |
| The *colors* are very good | which Aunt Anna gave me Christmas |
| A little *girl* sat looking with longing eyes at a plate of sandwiches | who was at a party |
| Once I caught a little *bee* | who was much too warm for me |
| Stars are the little *daisies* white | that dot the meadow of the night |

### RELATIVE OMITTED

| | *What word is omitted?* |
|---|---|
| Here are the *pennies* | — my mother gave me |
| The *children* did not come to school to-day | with — I play |
| The *house* is beautiful and airy | in — we live |

SERIES III

In the preceding roll, the subordinate clauses completed the meaning and constituted an attribute of *one word* of the principal clause. Here, however, the subordinate clauses refer to the whole content of the main clause and complete *the whole thought* of the main clause. They have, therefore, a logical dependence on the main clause. The child will be guided in finding the place of the different subordinate clauses and in classifying them according to the designations of the spaces by the questions which appear in the analytical chart. It is presupposed that he can readily identify the main clause itself.

The following sentences come one after the other on the rolled strip of paper:

— Do not forget that your objects are not in their places.
— Will you play with me when you have finished your work?
— When the sun is low our shadows are longer.
— I hope that you will write me a long letter as soon as you arrive in Europe.
— The little girl stood on tiptoe so that she could see the queen as the procession went by.
— Brer Rabbit thought it was the worst time he had had in all his life.
— All is well that ends well, says the proverb.
— The people mourned when the good President died.
— It is not right that the big boys should have all the candy.
— As she sat there reading, a beautiful red bird flew in through the window.
— They could not play in the yard because the ground was too wet.
— Remember that you must thank the lady who gave you the book.

## TEST CARD

| PRINCIPAL AND INCIDENTAL CLAUSES | QUESTION | SUBORDINATE AND ATTRIBUTIVE CLAUSES |
|---|---|---|
| Do not forget | what? | that your objects are not in their places. |
| Will you play with me | when? | when you have finished your work? |
| Our shadows are longer | when? | when the sun is low. |
| I hope | what? | that you will write me a long letter |
|  | when? | as soon as you arrive in Europe. |
| The little girl stood on tiptoe | why? | so that she could see the queen |
|  | when? | as the procession went by. |
| Brer Rabbit thought | what? | (that) it was the worst *time* he had had in all his life (*attributive, relative pronoun omitted*). |
| All is well says the proverb (*incidental clause*) |  | that ends well (*attributive*). |
| The people mourned | when? | the good President died. |
| It is not right | what? | that the big boys should have all the candy. |
| A beautiful red bird flew in through the window | when? | as she sat there reading. |
| They could not play in the yard | why? | because the ground was too wet. |
| Remember | what? | that you must thank the *lady* who gave you the book (*attributive*). |

## SERIES IV

Here we have sentences both compound and complex, containing both coordinate and subordinate clauses.

— As he said this, he rose from his chair and left the room.
— The two friends shook hands and said they would always be faithful to each other.

— When the wolf came out, Brer Rabbit threw the stone on him and laughed.

— When the lady knocked on the door, a smiling old man appeared and asked what he might do for her.

— The children walked along in the forest and became very hungry because they had had nothing to eat since morning.

— The king's face grew very red and he angrily ordered that the deceitful general be put to death.

— Since the wind was blowing hard, the captain told the children to keep off the deck and a sailor carried them to their state-rooms.

— The dogs began to bark and the people all ran out into the streets as the uproar of the combat increased.

— Where that tree now stands, there was once a beautiful house and a fine road led up to it.

— He had left the village and mounted the steep,
And under the alders that skirt its edge,
Now soft on the sand, now loud on the ledge,
Is heard the tramp of his steed as he rides.

## Test Card

| Principal Clause | Coordinate Clause | Question | Subordinate and Attributive Clauses |
|---|---|---|---|
| He rose from his chair | and left the room | when? | as he said this |
| The two friends shook hands | and said | what? | that they would always be faithful to each other |
| Brer Rabbit threw the stone on him | and laughed | when? | when the wolf came out |
| A smiling old man appeared | and asked | what? | what he might do for her |
|  |  | when? | when the lady knocked on the door |
| The children walked along in the forest | and became very hungry | why? | because they had had nothing to eat since morning |
| The king's face grew very red | and he angrily ordered | what? | that the deceitful general be put to death |
| The captain told the children to keep off the deck | and a sailor carried them to their state-rooms | why? | because the wind was blowing hard |
| The dogs began to bark | and the people all ran into the streets | when? | as the uproar of the combat increased |
| There was once a beautiful house | and a fine road led up to it | where? | where that tree now stands |

| PRINCIPAL CLAUSE | COORDINATE CLAUSE | QUES-TION | SUBORDINATE AND ATTRIBUTIVE CLAUSES |
|---|---|---|---|
| He had left the village | and mounted the steep | | |
| | under the *alders* now soft on the sand, now loud on the ledge, is heard the tramp of his steed | | that skirt its edge (attributive). |
| | | when? | as he rides |

## SERIES V

### (Correlative Sentences)

The clauses are here dependent upon each other:

— The flowers were so beautiful that we picked them all.
— That day he was so lazy that he did not get his work done.
— She sings much better than she plays.
— The more one studies, the more one learns.
— Either you return your objects to their places or some one else must do it.
— Not only was the man very cross, but he actually punished the little boy.

## TEST CARD

| PRINCIPAL CLAUSE | QUESTION | SUBORDINATE CLAUSE |
|---|---|---|
| The flowers were so beautiful | with what result? | that we picked them all. |
| That day he was so lazy | with what result? | that he did not get his work done. |
| She sings much better | than what? | than she plays. |
| The more one studies | with what result? | the more one learns. |
| Either you return your objects to their places | with what result? | or some one else must do it. |
| Not only was the man very cross | with what result? | but he actually punished the little boy. |

## SERIES VI

### (The Order of Clauses in Sentences: Sentence Forms in Prose and Verse)

Our material makes it very easy for the children to understand the mutual dependence of the subordinate

clauses. We take the commonest cases within easy reach
of the children. There are clauses of the first degree of
subordination, dependent directly on the principal clause.
There are others of the second degree of subordination
which depend on a subordinate clause (clause subordinate
to a subordinate). We have the same situation in coor-
dinates. We have the first degree of coordination when
the clause is parallel with the principal clause, and the
second degree when the clause is parallel with a subordinate clause.

Since the slips have as many sections as there are
clauses, the clauses may be arranged on the table in the
order of their subordination, keeping, for example, the
principal clause to the left, and arranging the subordinate
clauses downward and downward to the right. Take, for
instance, the sentence:

— The old man liked to tell stories; and he would laugh
    heartily when the women were frightened at the terrible
    things that he had to relate.

As the different clauses are torn off they are placed on a
chart marked into sections by vertically placed arrows: the
principal clause to the right of the first arrow; the first
subordinate clause to the right of the second; the subordinate to the subordinate to the right of the third, and so on.
The above sentence results as follows:

| Principal and Coordinate | 1st subordinate | subordinate to subordinate |
|---|---|---|
| The old man liked to tell stories | | |
| and he would laugh heartily | | |
| | when the women were frightened at the terrible things | |
| | | that he had to tell. |

CHART C

| Principal and coordinate (incidental) | 1st subordinate and its coordinates | subordinate to subordinate |
|---|---|---|
| ↑ I shall feel better | | |
| | ↑ if you will let me sit next to the window | |
| | | ↑ where there is more air. |

Here is another example:

— I often sit and wish that I
Could be a kite up in the sky,
And ride upon the breeze, and go
Whatever way it chanced to blow.

| Principal and Coordinates | 1st subordinate and coordinate | subordinate to subordinate |
|---|---|---|
| ↑ I often sit and wish | | |
| | ↑ that I could be a kite up in the sky and ride upon the breeze and go whatever way | |
| | | ↑ it chanced to blow. |

Here, finally, is another:

— I was a bad boy, I admit, but no one ever paid any attention to me, unless I was to be blamed for something wrong that I had done, or was accused of doing.

↑ I was a bad boy
I admit   (incidental)
but no one ever paid
any attention to me

↑ unless I was to be
   blamed
   for something  wrong

↑ that I had done,
   or  was  accused  of
   doing.
   (coordinate of second
      subordinate)

In using this material, the child tears off the clause-slips using the analytical sentence-chart (Chart B).   This gives him the classification of the clauses. The strips are then to be placed on the dependence chart (Chart C) according to the indications of the arrows. This brings out the mutual relation of the clauses.

## Permutations

The preceding exercises have created in the child a notion of sentence construction and of the position of the clauses which make it up. Our material permits, of course, as an exercise supplementary to the analyses, dislocations and translocations of parts just as was true with the simple sentence. To derive the full benefit of this possibility, the teacher should have in mind the general rules for location of clauses:

Adjective clauses (relative, attributive) always follow, and most often directly, the noun they modify.

Subject subordinate clauses may stand either before or after the principal clause. If the subject clause follows, it is usually anticipated before the verb by the pronoun *it* (just as a following noun subject is anticipated by *there*).

(In Italian, if the object clause precedes the main clause, it is usually repeated before the noun by a conjunctive object personal pronoun.)

The position of the other clauses depends on considerations of emphasis.

The direct order for complex sentences is in general similar to that for simple sentences:

> subject clause
> principal clause
> object clause
> adverbial clauses.

Coordination is possible with subordinate as well as with principal clauses.

The special exercises on the complex sentence conclude with some practise in turning simple inversions as found in poetry into direct sentence order.

### SERIES VII

The detachable strips are used here also.   The exercise should be conducted with reference to the sentence charts.

#### 1

— Just where the ·tide of battle turns,
Erect and lonely stood old John Burns . . .
And buttoned over his manly breast
Was a bright blue coat with a rolling collar.

Old John Burns stood, erect and lonely just where the tide of battle turns. . . .
A bright blue coat, with a rolling collar, was buttoned over his manly breast.

#### 2

— It was terrible: on the right
Raged for hours the deadly fight,
Thundered the battery's double bass,
Difficult music for men to face;
While on the left, where now the graves
Undulate like the living waves
That all that day unceasing swept
Up to the pits the rebels kept,
Round shot ploughed the upland glades.
BRET HARTE.— *John Burns of Gettysburg.*

It was terrible: the deadly fight raged for hours on the right; the battery's double bass thundered,— difficult music for men to face; while round shot ploughed the upland glades on the left, where now the graves undulate like the living waves that swept unceasing all that day up to the pits the rebels kept.

#### 3

— Merrily rang the bridle reins, and scarf and plume streamed gay,
As fast beside her father's gate the riders held their way . . .

The bridle reins rang merrily and scarf and plume streamed gay, as the riders, held their way fast by her father's gate.

"Now break your shield asunder and shatter your sign
and boss,
Unmeet for peasant-wedded
warms, your knightly
knee across.
WHITTIER.— *King Volmer.*

Now break your shield asunder
and shatter across your knightly
knee your sign and boss unmeet
for peasant-wedded arms.

### 4

The breaking waves dashed high
On a stern and rock-bound coast;
And the woods against a stormy
sky
Their giant branches tossed.
And the heavy night hung dark
The hills and waters o'er,
When a band of Pilgrims moored
their bark
On the wild New England shore.

The breaking waves dashed
high on a stern and rock-bound
coast; and the woods tossed their
giant branches against a stormy
sky.
The heavy night hung dark
*over* (*o'er*) the hills and waters,
when a band of Pilgrims moored
their bark on the wild New England shore.

Not as the conqueror comes
They the true hearted came,
Not with the roll of the stirring
drums
And the trumpet that sings of
fame.
MRS. HEMANS.

They, the true hearted, came
not as the conqueror comes, not
with the roll of the stirring
drums and the trumpet that
sings of fame.

### 5

My golden spurs now bring to me
And bring to me my richest mail,
For tomorrow I go over land and
sea
In search of the Holy Grail.
Shall never a bed for me be
spread,
Nor shall a pillow be under my
head,
Till I begin my vow to keep;
Here on the rushes will I sleep,
And perchance there may come a
vision true
Ere day create the world anew.
LOWELL.

Bring to me now my golden
spurs and bring to me my richest
mail; for I go in search of the
Holy Grail tomorrow over land
and sea; a bed shall never be
spread for me, nor shall a pillow
be under my head till I begin to
keep my vow; I will sleep here
on the rushes, and perchance a
true vision will come *before* (ere)
day creates the world anew.

### 6

Glad tidings of great joy I bring
To you and all mankind:
To you, in David's town this day
Is born of David's line
The Saviour, who is Christ the
    Lord,
And this shall be the sign:
The heavenly Babe you there
    shall find
To human view displayed,
All meanly wrapt in swaddling
   bands
And in a manger laid.
    TATE.— *While Shepherds
    Watched.*

I bring to you and all mankind glad tidings of great joy. The Saviour, who is Christ the Lord, is born to you this day in David's town, of David's line; and this shall be the sign: you shall find the heavenly Babe there displayed to human view, all meanly wrapt in swaddling clothes and laid in a manger.

### 7

The harp that once through
    Tara's halls
The soul of music shed,
Now hangs on Tara's walls
As if that soul were fled.
So sleeps the pride of former
    days,
So glory's thrill is o'er,
And hearts that once beat high
    for praise
Now feel that pulse no more.

No more to chiefs and ladies
    bright
The harp of Tara swells;
The chord alone that breaks at
    night
Its tale of ruin tells.
Thus Freedom now so seldom
    wakes,
The only throb she gives,
Is when some heart indignant
    breaks
To show that still she lives.
    THOMAS MOORE.

The harp, that once shed the soul of music through Tara's halls, now hangs on Tara's walls, as though that soul were fled. So the pride of former days sleeps, so glory's thrill is over, and hearts that once beat high for praise now feel that pulse no more. The harp of Tara swells no more to chiefs and bright ladies: the chord alone, that breaks at night, tells its tale of ruin. Thus Freedom now wakes so seldom (that) the only throb she gives is when some indignant heart breaks to show that she still lives.

8

| Childhood is the bough where slumbered | Childhood is the bough where many numbered birds and blossoms slumbered: Age encumbered that bough with snow. |

Birds and blossoms many numbered;

Age that bough with snows encumbered.

LONGFELLOW.

## TEST CARDS

1

| Just where the tide of battle turns | subordinate of place (locative) |
| Erect and lonely stood old John Burns | principal |
| And, buttoned over his manly breast, | (verbal attributive phrase) |
| Was a bright blue coat with a rolling collar | coordinate of principal. |

2

| It was terrible | principal |
| on the right raged for hours the deadly fight | coordinate of principal |
| thundered the battery's double bass | coordinate of principal |
| Difficult music for men to face | (verbal attributive phrase in apposition). |
| While on the left (round shot ploughed, etc.) | subordinate of time (temporal) begun |
| where now the graves | (*While* may be considered as adversative coordinate) |
| Undulate like the living waves | subordinate to subordinate (locative) 2d degree |
| That all that day unceasing swept | attributive subordinate (relative adjectival clause modifying *waves*) of 3d degree |
| up to the pits | |
| the rebels kept | attributive subordinate (relative pronoun omitted) of 4th degree |
| Round shot ploughed the upland glades | subordinate of time (concluded). |

### 3

| | |
|---|---|
| Merrily rang the bridle reins | principal |
| and scarf and plume streamed gay | coordinate |
| As fast beside her father's gate the riders held their way | subordinate of time |
| Now break your shield asunder | principal |
| and shatter your sign and boss Unmeet for peasant-wedded arms your knightly knee across | coordinate |

### 4

| | |
|---|---|
| The breaking waves dashed high On a stern and rock-bound coast | principal |
| And the woods against a stormy sky Their giant branches tossed. | coordinate |
| And the heavy night hung dark The hills and waters o'er | principal (coordinated in paragraph) |
| When a band of pilgrims moored their bark On a wild New England shore | subordinate temporal |
| Not | principal begun |
| as the conqueror comes | subordinate of manner (modal) |
| They the true hearted came | principal concluded |
| Not with the roll of the stirring drums and the trumpet | coordinate (elipsis of verb *they came* continued from principal) |
| that sings of fame | attributive (relative) subordinate to coordinate. |

### 5

| | |
|---|---|
| My golden spurs now bring to me | principal |
| And bring to me my richest mail | coordinate |

For tomorrow I go over land and
  sea
In search of the Holy Grail — subordinate of cause (causal);
may be considered *coordinate*
of *reason*

Shall never a bed for me be
  spread — principal

Nor shall a pillow be under my
  head — coordinate

Till I begin my vow to keep — subordinate of time (temporal)

Here on the rushes will I sleep — principal

And perchance there may come a
  vision true — coordinate

Ere day create the world anew — subordinate temporal.

### 6

Great tidings of great joy I
  bring
To you and all mankind — principal

To you in David's town this day
Is born of David's line
The Saviour — principal

      who is Christ the Lord — attributive (relative) subordinate

And this shall be the sign — coordinate

The heavenly Babe you there
  shall find
To human view displayed
All meanly wrapt in swaddling
  bands
And in a manger laid. — simple sentence with three coordinate verbal phrases.

### 7

The harp — principal begun
      that once through
            Tara's hall
The soul of music shed — attributive subordinate (relative)

| | |
|---|---|
| Now hangs on Tara's walls | principal concluded |
| As if that soul were fled | subordinate of manner (modal) |
| So sleeps the pride of former days | principal |
| So glory's thrill is o'er | coordinate |
| And hearts | coordinate begun |
|     that once beat high for praise | attributive relative subordinate |
| Now feel that pulse no more | coordinate concluded. |
| No more to chiefs and ladies bright<br>The harp of Tara swells | principal |
| The chord alone | coordinate begun |
|     that breaks at night | attributive relative subordinate |
| Its tale of ruin tells | coordinate concluded. |
| Thus freedom now so seldom wakes | principal |
| The only throb | subordinate result begun (conjunction *that* omitted) |
|     she gives | subordinate to subordinate (2d degree; relative omitted) |
| Is when some heart indignant breaks<br>To show | subordinate result concluded |
|     that still she lives | subordinate object (noun) clause of 2d degree. |

8

| | |
|---|---|
| Childhood is the bough | principal |
|     where slumbered<br>Birds and blossoms many-numbered | subordinate locative (of place) |
| Age that bough with snows encumbered | coordinate. |

(Note: the best English poetry makes far less use of inversion than does Italian. Such exercises as the above could be profitably applied to the analysis of the different kinds of phrases (adjective, adverbial, etc.). It should be noted that Dr. Montessori in her own exercises treats verbal phrases (participles and infinitives) as subordinate clauses.— Tr.)

### Coordinating and Subordinating Conjunctions

This study of the complex sentence leads the child to a more precise comprehension of the values of certain parts of speech as, notably, the conjunction. We have found, in fact, that little difficulty is experienced in realizing the distinction between the terms *coordinating* and *subordinating* as applied to conjunctions which *unite* clauses but in different ways. The following charts serve to cover the vast majority of cases that the child is likely to meet. We may add that at this point it may be found useful to have the child analyze the complex sentences which appeared in the commands and readings already familiar to him (see below under *Reading*).

#### COORDINATING CONJUNCTIONS

*Copulatives:* and, also, too, besides, moreover, further, furthermore, nor.

*Disjunctives:* or else, otherwise, rather.

*Adversatives:* but, nevertheless, however, notwithstanding, yet, still, while, only, instead.

*Declaratives:* namely, in other words, that is.

*Asseverative:* in fact, assuredly, really.

*Illative:* hence, therefore, then, accordingly, so.

#### PRINCIPAL AND COORDINATE CLAUSES MAY BEGIN WITH ONE OF THESE CONJUNCTIONS

## CHART D
## THE CONJUNCTIONS IN THE SUBORDINATE CLAUSE

| PRINCIPAL CLAUSE | |
|---|---|
| Incidental (parenthetical) clause | |
| Adjective (relative, attributive) clause<br>who, which, that, whose, whom | |
| Subordinate subject clause<br>that | Subordinate object clause<br>that |
| Subordinate clause of<br>time<br>(temporal)<br>when, while, as soon as,<br>before, after, till, until | Subordinate clause of<br>place<br>(locative)<br>where, whence, wherever,<br>whither |
| Subordinate clause of<br>purpose<br>(final, purpose clause)<br>that, in order that, so that | Subordinate clause of<br>cause<br>(casual clause)<br>as, because, for, since, in<br>as much as |
| Subordinate clause of<br>manner and comparison<br>(modal clause)<br>as (manner), than (com-<br>parison) | Subordinate clause of<br>condition<br>(conditional clause)<br>if, unless, provided, pro-<br>vided that |
| Subordinate clause of<br>concession<br>(concessive clause)<br>though, although, even if,<br>however, notwithstand-<br>ing that | Subordinate clause of<br>result and correlatives<br>that, so that (result)<br>so . . . as,   so . . . that<br>(correlative, degree) |

## Sequence of Tenses

A special series of exercises on the relations of the subordinate to the principal clause brings out the changes in tense made necessary in the subordinate clause as the tense of the principal clause varies.

## Series VIII

### Sequence of Tenses

#### Group A

##### (Causal Clauses)

— I am writing to you because I have some important news.
    "   wrote   "  "    "   " had    "       "       "

— I shall not go because I must attend to my work.
    " did    "  "    "   " had to   "    " "    "

— I am glad that you have done so well.
    " was  "    "    " had    "   ."    "

— I will give it to you since you insist   on having it.
    " gave      " " "   "     " insisted "     "     "

— He does not answer because your letter is   insulting.
    " did     "      "       "      "   " was     "

#### Group B

##### (Miscellaneous Clauses)

— I shall   be proud of you if you become a fine scholar.
    " should "    "     "   "   "   " became " "     "

— I believe   that only the rich can   be happy.
    " believed "    "    "     " could "     "

— I am waiting here till my father returns   from town.
    "    waited    "   " "     " returned    "     "

— They expect   that something will   happen before long.
    " expected "      "     would "     "     "     "

— He is doing that for you, in order that you may   go to school.
    ” did   ”  ”  ”  ”  ”  ”  ” might ” ”   ”

— He will let you know where he has been.
    ”  let   ”   ”    ”   ” had  ”

### GROUP C

#### (Object Clauses)

— They are   telling me what they have been doing.
    ” were   ”    ”    ”    ” had   ”    ”

— I promise  you that I will   do everything punctually.
  ” promised   ”    ”  ” would ”     ”       ”

— I think   he will   not be back before Wednesday.
  ” thought ” would ” ” ”     ”      ”

— Do  you know that your friend has gone away?
  Did ”   ”    ”     ”    ” had ”   ”

— I assure  you that I will   take good care of it.
  ” assured   ”    ”  ” would  ”    ”   ”   ” ”

— I repeat   that you ought to be     ashamed of yourself.
  ” repeated   ”    ”     ”   ” have been    ”    ”    ”

### GROUP D

#### (Conditional Sentences)

— I would     read this book too, if I could.
  ”   ”    have read ”   ”   ” ” ” had been able.

— If I see him, I shall   tell him what you say.
  ” ” saw ”  ” should ”   ”    ”   ” said.

— I will   finish this work, if you can   wait.
  ” would   ”    ”    ”   ”   ” could   ”

— I shall   come sooner if I can.
  ” should   ”     ”   ” ” could.

— He would     give  it to you if you     asked him for it.
   ”   ”    have given ” ” ” ”  ”   had asked  ”   ”   ”

— He would     give   it to you if you should ask him for it.

— I shall     go    there if I      have time.
   " should     "     "   " "      had   "
   " shall      "     "   " " should have   "
   " should have gone   "   " "    had had    "

# XIII

## PUNCTUATION

The permutations of clauses permitted by our materials give empirical evidence of the pauses and accordingly of the functions of the orthographical signs of suspense in the sentence. These signs are included also in our alphabets. All the exercises hitherto given require more or less spontaneous attention to punctuation. We offer, however, in addition, several series of sentences for analysis in illustration of the principal rules for the use of punctuation points. Almost all of our Italian sentences are taken from Manzoni, a writer especially noteworthy for his care in punctuation. (The majority of the sentences below are taken from the *Book of Knowledge,* by special permission of the publishers.)

### SERIES I

The comma may separate coordinate elements.

— The mother took a glowing pride in the beauty of her children's faces, the grace and strength of their bodies, their reckless daring and unflinching courage.
— The little star fell plump into the middle of a big puddle, and there it lay sad and shaken and quaking with fright.
— It was dumb and half blind, it had a soiled face, and could give no more light.
— A mouse was just then peeping from its hole to see whether it was going to rain, and whether it would be safe to cross the fields.
— The mouse started running again, and ran until it was tired out and had to sit down.

160

— The little star poured a flood of bright light over the poor woman, and made her bright and cheerful and strong again, and then the little girl became very happy.

## SERIES II

A comma isolates vocatives and incidental clauses.

—" Cæsar, let your men go forward," said the guide.
— Why do you want to find your father, Mora?
—" No," said he, " I shall be very well presently."
—" Boys," said our host, " I know whose hand it is."
— That, excuse me for saying so, is not the way to speak to a friend.
—" Come with us, you handsome young huntsman," he cried.

## SERIES III

A comma separates clauses, especially for clearness, when the elements of one clause might seem to apply equally well to another clause, and when one clause is interpolated between the essential elements of another.

— Mohammed taught that men should pray at stated times, wherever they are.
— George, who was only five years old, could not go with his father to fight.
— The tribemen, after quarreling a long time, decided to march away.
— He went that evening, as he had planned, to the doctor's house.
— The poor Indian had been kept moving, ever since he was born, to regions farther and farther north.
— The child crept to the bed, and, taking his little fan, stood over his father all night fanning him.

## SERIES IV

A comma indicates a pause caused by the ellipsis of some word or idea (in such cases longer suspense can be indicated by a colon or a semi-colon).

— Very well, what of it?
— Good-by, all you nice people!
— Just what I wanted: a plate of wild strawberries with real
    cream!
— Please, mother, just a little more, a very little more!
— Silence, obedience, and everybody at work!
— Enough said; I know exactly what the matter is!

## SERIES V

A semi-colon marks a considerable halt between clauses.
In some special cases, a colon is used. The dash. Quotations.

— The knight mounted a superb steed; the old huntsman did
    the same.
— Some carriages opened at the back, with the driver sitting
    perched high above the door; others had the driver's seat
    at the side, and in all sorts of queer positions.
— The first trams were drawn, usually, by horses; though many
    people can remember when London street-cars were drawn
    by mules — two big ones or three little ones for each car.
— The letter began: "I hope you will let me know if this let-
    ter does not reach you."
— Patrick Henry said: "Give me liberty, or give me death!"
— The boy's mind was full of love and romance but not of sad-
    ness for —

        Singing he was and fluting all the day:
        He was as fresh as in the month of May.

— The king will ask you three questions: "How old are you?"
    "How long have you been in his service?" "Are you
    satisfied with your food and lodgings?"
— How happy they were: all kinds of toys to play with; all
    sorts of good things to eat; and a kind old father to satisfy
    their every want!
— Slowly one of the dialects of English — the language of Lon-
    don — came to be regarded as standard English.
— Washington is called "the Father of his Country."

— When he got home, he said to his wife: "See, I have brought you a present."

— He shouted gleefully: "I am a lion — a terrible lion."

## SERIES VI

### (Other Punctuation Points)

The period, question mark, exclamation point and other signs of punctuation:

In this series should be given dialogues, interesting stories, passages which express emotional states of mind vividly portrayed. Such selections, as is true also of our shorter passages, ought to be taken from the best writers, distinguished by the naturalness and vivacity of their style and the use of an accurate orthographical technique. At this point we make use of the selections used for our "interpretations," since the question of punctuation coincides with the problems of text interpretation itself.

# XIV

## WORD CLASSIFICATION

### The Kinds of Words

In doing the work outlined thus far, the children have acquired considerable resources in vocabulary. They have seen all the articles, prepositions, pronouns, conjunctions, interjections, many of the adverbs; and they know many nouns, adjectives, and verbs, which will be increased in number as their culture is widened. They know something also of the use of the parts of speech and their functions in the expression of thought. This is the natural place for a classification in retrospect of those words which the children have in writing before them on the cards and slips of different colors. Separate tables should be used for these exercises in word grouping.

This new step is preparatory to a *theoretical study* of language to be developed in later courses in the second period of their education.

### WORDS CLASSIFIED ACCORDING TO FORMATION

Root  
Derived [1]  $\Big\}$ words  
Compound [2]

[1] Under this heading we include all derivations by suffix: some suffixes change one part of speech into another: *love* (verb), *lovable* (adj.), etc.; others, such as *diminutives, peggioratives, augmentatives*, etc., change the quality of a word's meaning. In adjectives we have suffixes of degree (comparison: *-er, -est*).

[2] Under this heading we include all words formed by the union of two words or by prefixes.

CLASSIFICATION OF WORDS ACCORDING TO INFLECTION

There are two kinds of words, thus considered: variable and invariable:

INVARIABLES: { preposition / conjunction / interjection { They may be simple or compound, made up, that is, of one word or more.

VARIABLES:

in gender and number } nouns { may be of masculine, feminine, neuter or common gender. form their plurals by adding -s or by changing the root vowel (umlaut)

in gender, number, person and case } pronouns { have special words for each form: e.g. he, him, who, whom, I, me, etc.

in degree { adjectives adverbs { -er for comparative -est for superlative

in person, number, tense and mood } verbs { show third person singular by adding -s, and old second person singular by adding -st show moods by adding -ing, -ed or by vowel change for participles; or by special forms (I be, he be, etc.) for subjunctive. show tense by suffix -ed, -t; or by vowel change (I go, I went). show irregular forms.

for phonetic reasons } definite article indefinite { the has two pronunciations according to the following word. a becomes an before a vowel.

CLASSIFICATION OF WORDS ACCORDING TO THEIR USE

(Parts of Speech)

| | | |
|---|---|---|
| Article | Verb | Pronoun |
| Noun | Adverb | Conjunction |
| Adjective | Preposition | Interjection |

NOTE: In actual usage the parts of speech perform not only their own functions, but also the functions of other parts of speech, for instance, the adjective, verb, adverb, conjunction, etc., may be used as nouns.   The participles, etc., may be used as adjectives, or as clauses, etc.

### THE NOUN

| | |
|---|---|
| Proper .................... | Common |
| Concrete ................. | Abstract |
| Collective ............... | Individual |

### THE ARTICLE

Definite — the
Indefinite — a, an

### THE ADJECTIVE

Descriptive:   Properties, qualities of things and living beings.

Quantitative:

Definite (numeral)
- *cardinal:* one, two three, four, etc.
- *ordinal:* first, second, third, fourth, last, etc.
- *multiple:* single, double, triple, quadruple, etc.
- *fractional:* half, third, etc.

Indefinite
- many, all, some, much, enough, no, more, most, other, little, few, whatever, each, every, certain, several, somewhat, etc.

Demonstrative (position in space) : this, that, these, those, such, same.
Possessive: my, thy, his, her, its, our, your, their.
Interrogative: what? which?

### VERB

The verb indicates:
existence: *to be.*
state or condition: *nominal predicate* (copular) : e. g., She *is* beautiful.
action: *verbal predicate:* e. g., I *run.*

Transitive (action upon an object different from subject)
- lay, throw, toss, hurl, roll, raise, lower, attach, touch, tie, cover, uncover, undo, invert, rub, spread, collect, scatter, sprinkle, stir, beat, mix, dissolve, flavor, arrange, clean, dust, sweep, button, lace, hook, brush, wash, wipe, embrace, etc., etc.

Intransitive (action remains in subject)
- grow, die, smile, laugh, stare, walk, stagger, march, sing, whistle, speak, hum, dance, shout, dine, bark, think, burst, blossom, remain, stand, rise, go, run, breathe, sigh, hesitate, weep, sleep, etc., etc.

Note: Certain verbs may be by nature both transitive and intransitive (incomplete predication).

Impersonals (the subject is *it* without reference to a specific object): { rain, snow, hail, dawn, lighten, thunder, etc.

## ADVERBS

of Manner: { slowly, rapidly, silently, noisily, abruptly, loudly, strongly, weakly, moderately, well, ill, better, worse, otherwise, differently, thus, so, lightly, heavily, etc., etc.

of Place: { here, there, elsewhere, up, down, forward, backward, upstairs, downstairs, etc., etc.

of Time: { always, ever, never, again, still, yesterday, tomorrow, today, now, occasionally, before, afterwards, soon, etc., etc.

of Quantity: { much, little, enough, nothing, more, less, least, most, about, only, too, very, etc.

of Comparison: more, less, than, etc.

of Affirmation: { yes, certainly, precisely, indeed, surely, assuredly, truly, even, etc.

of Negation: no, never, not, at all, etc.
of Doubt: perhaps, perchance, almost, probably, etc.

## PREPOSITION

Simple: { of, to, by, from, in, with, on, among, above, through, under, around, beside, behind, save, except, near, next, like, during, off, etc.

Compound (preposition phrases): in place of, out of, away from, as to, on board, with regard to, etc.

## PRONOUN

Personal { subject: { I, thou, he, she, it, we, you, they

object: { me, thee, him, her, it, us, you, them

Demonstrative { definite: { this, this one, that, that one, these, those

indefinite: { one, ones, some, somebody, everyone, each, each one, no one, nobody, none, nothing, etc.

**Relative**

of person:
- subject: who, that
- possessive: whose
- object: whom, that

of thing: which, that

indefinite: whoever, which ever

compound (antecedent understood): **what** (that which), whereof, wherewith, etc.

**Interrogative:**

of person
- who
- whose
- whom
- which

of thing
- what
- which

**Possessive:** mine, yours (thine), his, hers, ours, yours, theirs.

## CONJUNCTION

**Disjunctive:** or, or else, otherwise, rather.

**Copulative:** and, also, too, besides, moreover, further, furthermore, nor, etc.

**Adversative:** but, nevertheless, notwithstanding, yet, still, while, however, only, on the contrary, instead, etc.

**Declarative:** namely, in other words, that is, etc.

**Relative:** that.

**Illative:** hence, therefore, wherefore, then, accordingly, so, with the result that, etc.

**Temporal** while, when, as soon as, after, before, until, till, hardly, etc.

**Concessive:** though, although, even if.

**Purpose (Final):** that, in order that, to the end that, etc.

**Conditional:** if, unless, provided, provided that, etc.

**Causal:** as, because, for, since, seeing that, etc.

**Result:** that, so that, etc.

**Locative:** where, whence, whither, whereto, wherefrom, etc.

**Degree and Comparison:** as, than.

## INTERJECTION

See list already given on pp. 122–123.

# PART II

# READING

# I

## EXPRESSION AND INTERPRETATION

### MECHANICAL PROCESSES

Reading begins in the " Children's House " as soon as the children *reread* the word they have already composed with the movable alphabet. This early effort is not indeed the true reading of the word, since interpretation is lacking. The children, it has been seen, know the word because they have actually put it together. They have not gained an understanding of it from the simple recognition of the graphic symbols. What they have done is, nevertheless, an important contribution to real reading. As one considers all of the details of this period of development, it is apparent that its mechanism is closely allied with that of the spoken language.

When the child's attention has been intensively applied to the recognition of the written word, it can easily be fixed on the analysis of the sounds which make up the word. At a certain age the child's interest was aroused by " touching " the letter. He can now be interested in hearing the sounds of the word when pronounced by others and in pronouncing it himself. We have shown that the work on the written language in the exercises with the alphabet was *necessary* for developing and perfecting the spoken language. It is by so doing that we make it possible to correct defects in speech and to pass naturally over the period when such defects are formed.

We now aim at finding an *exercise* in the actual mechanism of pronunciation which can be started at the moment of its natural development in such a way that its growth to perfection will follow as a matter of course. It is a question of bringing the children rapidly to pronounce without hesitation. In so pronouncing well, in performing extensive exercises in hearing words and in the interpretation of them from graphic signs, the child brings together in a unit of effect the basic processes of reading and writing.

A good pronunciation of the word read is of great importance. We may say that in the elementary schools of our day this is the principal purpose of reading. Nevertheless, it is very difficult to obtain a good pronunciation when defects have been allowed to develop and become habitual in the child's previous work. In fact, the elimination of these defects, which have been the result of a fundamental error in education, comes to absorb all of the energies of the reading class in ordinary primary schools. So far along as the fifth grade we see teachers struggling to make the children read, that they may acquire a good " pronunciation," and in our reading books there are graduated exercises constructed on the basis of " Difficulties in Pronunciation." It is apparent that all of this stress on the *physiological mechanics* of pronunciation is foreign to *true reading*. It is, rather, an impediment to the development of true reading. Such reading exercises constitute, as it were, a foreign body, which operates like a disease to prevent the development of the high intellectual activity which interprets the mysterious language of written symbols and arouses the child's enthusiasm with the fascinating revelations they can give. The eagerness of the child to learn is curbed and cheated when he is compelled to stop his mind from working because his tongue refuses to act properly and must be laboriously trained to work right. This training, if begun at the proper time, when the child's whole psychic and nervous organism yearns for the perfection of the mechanism of speech, would have been a fascinating task; and once started along the right path, the pupil would have continued to follow it with alacrity and confidence. When the time comes for the intelligence to try its wings, its wings should be ready. What would happen to a painter, if at the moment of inspiration, he had to sit down and manufacture his brushes!

## Analysis

Our first publication on the methods used in the " Children's House " made clear two distinct operations involved in reading: the interpretation of the meaning and the pronunciation aloud of the " word." The stress we laid on that analysis as a guide to the development of reading was the result of actual experience. Those who followed this work during its initial stages saw how the children, when they read for the first time, interpreting the meaning of the words before them, did so without speaking,— reading, that is, mentally. Interpretation, in fact, is a question of mental concentration. Reading is an affair of the *intelligence.* The pronunciation aloud is quite a different thing, not only distinguished from the first process, but secondary to it. Talking aloud is a question of speech, involving first hearing and then the mechanical reproduction of sounds in articulate language. Its function is to bring into immediate communication

two or more people, who thus, exchange the thoughts
which they have already perfected in the secret places of
their minds.

But reading stands in a direct relation with writing.
Here there are no sounds to be heard or pronounced.  The
individual, all by himself, can put himself into communication not only with human beings actually alive on the
earth, but also with those who lived centuries and centuries ago down to the dawn of history.  Such communication is made possible not by sound but by the written
symbol.  The mind takes in these symbols in silence.
Books are mute, as far as sound is concerned.

It follows that reading aloud is a combination of two
distinct operations, of two "languages."  It is something
far more complex than speaking and reading taken separately by themselves.  In reading aloud the child speaks
not to express his own thoughts, but thoughts revealed by
the written symbol.  The "word" in this case no longer
has that natural stimulus from within which creation
gives it.  In fact, it is something forced and monotonous,
something like the language of the deaf-mute.  Words
which are the product of the interpretation of individual
alphabetical symbols come with effort, and the meaning
which comes from the interpretation of the entire sentence, as the eye reads word by word, and translates into
sound, is apprehended and reduced to expression with
great difficulty.  To give a fairly intelligible expression
to the meaning, the eyes have been obliged rapidly to
traverse the sentence as a whole, while the tongue has been
laboriously and monotonously pronouncing one word after
another.  Just imagine adding to such a complex problem for the child of the primary schools the additional task
of correcting his pronunciation!  It is no wonder that

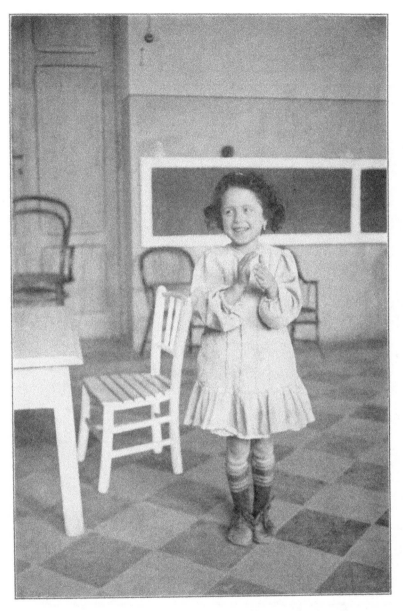

Interpreted reading: " Smile and clap your hands." The child reads silently
an order written on a slip of paper; then proves that she understands
by acting the direction given. (*A Montessori School in Italy.*)

Interpreted reading: "Take off your hat and make a low bow."    (*A Montessori School in Italy.*)

reading is one of the rocks on which the rudderless ship
of elementary education inevitably runs aground.

The experiments we have succeeded in conducting on
the subject of reading are perhaps among the most complete we have made. We found the key to the problem
when we discovered that the child passed from the mental
reading of the words written on the cards directly to interpretation in action. This interpretation, ready and
facile, as all the acts of children are, reveals to us what the
child has understood and accordingly what he is capable
of understanding. We have thus been able to obtain an
experimental graduation of passages for reading, which
on being gathered together, show the nature of the difficulties which successively present themselves to the child.
The children have made for themselves specimen clauses
and sentences which an expert grammarian could not have
devised better for facilitating the study of language. As
we went on with this work, we became more and more con-
vinced that the study of grammar may be made a help in

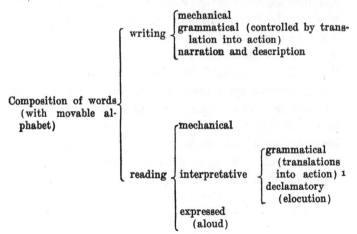

Composition of words
(with movable al-
phabet)

writing
- mechanical
- grammatical (controlled by translation into action)
- narration and description

reading
- mechanical
- interpretative
  - grammatical (translations into action) [1]
  - declamatory (elocution)
- expressed (aloud)

[1] The first readings consist of a special grammar and a dictionary.

the up-building of the child's language and that it makes
its influence felt in reading and in the written composition. The table (p. 175) may be useful in showing the
successive steps actually traversed by the child in the
phenomena of reading.

The fundamental point to realize is that *interpretation*
alone constitutes true reading. Reading aloud, on the
other hand, is a combination of reading and articulate
expression, in other words, a combination involving the
two great mechanisms of the spoken language and the
written language. Reading aloud permits an audience to
take part in the reading communicated to it by means of
articulate speech. Even here, the mental effort required
to listen to the voice of a man passionately interested in
the narration of things which he himself has experienced
is not the same as that demanded in listening to a reading of the same things by a person who has not experienced
them, and who, to narrate them, must perform the rapid
and intense effort of interpretation. In this reading, so
to speak, by " transmission," the most serious difficulties
are encountered. We all know by experience how difficult it is to endure a reading, and how rare an endowment
the " gift of reading " is. However, the person who is
thus gifted can get a hearing almost as well as the person
who speaks. The teaching of reading, then, in this sense,
is not merely the teaching of the interpretation of the
meaning,— all that would be necessary, if the sole function of reading were to gain new ideas for the reader.
Reading, thus conceived, represents really the addition
of *an art of expression* to simple reading, and since this
expressive art is purely dramatic, the *teaching of reading*
involves the development of *dramatic art*. Only through

dramatic art can the transmission of reading to a group of people be made possible.

It is clear that the oftener the exercise of identifying oneself with what is read is repeated and perfected, the greater the possibility of expression becomes. It follows that in the perfection of this art we should be less concerned with *timbre,* with tone of voice and gestures, all extrinsic aspects of this art, than with intense vivid *interpretation* which brings the child to an identification of himself with what he reads. And this interpretation will realize its objects if it is practised as a habit and as *a form of reading.*

The proof of correct interpretation was the child's ability to reproduce in action what was described in the words he read. Similarly, the proof of the interpretation in reading aloud is the repetition of the things heard by means of the spoken language. That is, the children, in order to prove to us that they have understood something read aloud, should be able to repeat in narrative form what they have heard.

The practical results of our efforts in this direction were very interesting to watch. Some children can say noth-thing. Others offer to tell the whole story. Their story is not clear or perhaps it is defective in some respect. Immediately other children are ready to correct the ones telling the story: " No, no, that's not what happened, that's not what happened," or, " Wait, you have forgotten something," and so on. In fact, to understand and to be able to narrate what has been understood is not the same thing. In telling a story there is a successive unfolding of very complex mental activities which are based on and added to the primal activity of " having understood." It is a question again of the three different stages noted by us in the first lessons given to children:

*First stage,* the causing of the perception:   (*That is red, that is blue*);

*Second stage,* the perfection of recognition:   (*What is red or blue?*);

*Third stage,* the provocation of expression:   (*What about this or that?*).

Thus, the child who succeeds in expressing, even in an imperfect way, what he has understood of the passage he has read, is in a more advanced state of development than other children who are unable to tell the story.   However, these children who are not able to relate what they have heard said may very well be in the preceding stage in which they are capable of " recognition."   These latter are the relentless critics, the constant " hecklers " of those who are trying to relate —" No, no,— that's not so," " You have forgotten this, or that."   Let one of us teachers try to tell the story in the most perfect and complete manner, and these tiny impetuous hecklers listen to us in ecstasy, showing their approval in every form of approbation of which they are capable.   By studying such manifestations in the children, we can get sufficient psychological data for determining what reading is adapted to children of different ages, the best ways of reading aloud, and the line of development followed by each child in that hidden mental world of his which is cut off from our gaze. But to derive these benefits from reading, it is perfectly clear that the children must be left absolutely *free* in the expression of what goes on in their minds.

According to the method used in ordinary schools a child is called upon to read aloud, and the teacher herself continually interrupts, either to correct the pronunciation, or to assist by explanations and suggestions in the interpretation of the meaning. This is all useless for experimental purposes. We have no certain means of determining whether the pupil has understood either what he has read or the explanations of the teacher. Furthermore the corrections of pronunciation have centered the child's attention on this detail which is entirely without relation to the meaning of the text he is interpreting. Another situation not infrequently arises. A child is selected at random to tell in his own words what has been read. Often the selection is not made at random, but some pupil is called on because he has shown himself the most inattentive, the least interested in what is being done — the recitation thus becoming correctional in character! While the child is telling his story, there is a constant suppression of interruptions: "Hush, I did not call on you," "Wait till you are called on," "It is not polite to interrupt some one who is talking," etc. It is clear that the teacher will never learn anything about her pupils in this way.

This explains why, from the psychological point of view, our present-day schools have not been able to contribute anything new to a reformed scientific pedagogy of reading.

### EXPERIMENTAL SECTION: READING ALOUD

Although we lay all possible stress on interpretative reading, we nevertheless put into the hands of the child a little reading book which he can go over by himself first in a low voice, and then, when he has grasped the meaning, aloud, provided he can express himself clearly and easily.

The simplicity of these texts occasions surprise when

one observes how completely and enthusiastically absorbed in them the children become.   They find them so delightful that the books get literally worn out with the reading and rereading to which they are subjected.   Sometimes a book is read from beginning to end.   Again the child opens it by chance and reads the page he happens on. Some children like to read the whole book over and over. Others prefer to read some particular page a great many times.   One frequently sees these tiny things suddenly rise with great decision and read aloud one of the pages which has been so seriously examined.

The little book was composed very carefully on the basis of rigid experimentation.   As the book is opened only one page of print appears, the tergo of the right hand page being always blank.   Nor does the text always cover the entire page.   The spaces above and below the print are decorated with designs.

The twenty pages of this beginners book are as follows:

Page  1.  My school is the " Children's House."

Page  2.  In the " Children's House " there are ever so many little chairs and tables for us.

Page  3.  There are also some pretty cabinets.  Each child has his own drawer.

Page  4.  There are green plants and beautiful bouquets of flowers everywhere about the rooms in our school.

Page  5.  I often stop to look at the pictures which are hanging on the walls.

Page  6.  We are busy all the time.  We wash our faces and hands.  We keep everything where it belongs.  We dust the furniture.  We study and try to learn all we can.

Page  7.  Can you guess how we learned to dress ourselves? We kept our fingers busy working on the canvas frames, lacing and unlacing, fastening and un-

fastening the hooks and eyes, buttoning and un-
buttoning, tying and untying knots.

Page 8. There are ten blocks for this tower, all of different
sizes. First I spread them around on this carpet.
It is great fun to put them together again, taking
one after the other and choosing the largest each
time.

Page 9. I use the tower too in a balancing game. Just try
to carry the tower around the room without letting
it fall to pieces! Sometimes I succeed and then
again I sometimes fail.

Page 10. I like the long rods, too! I must put the rods near
each other according to their length. I must be
careful to place the blue sections near the blue ones
and the red ones near the red. Thus, I build
some pretty stairs with red and blue steps.

Page 11. But to get a real stair case I use the brown prisms.
These prisms are of different sizes. I put one beside the other according to size, and I get some
fine stairs with ten steps.

Page 12. I have also some solid insets of wood into which I fit
little cylinders of different dimensions. They differ in length and breadth. The game is to put
these cylinders in their places after looking at them
and touching them carefully.

Page 13. We often make mistakes in working with the insets.
When we put a cylinder where it doesn't belong,
we find that at the end of the game we have one
cylinder left over and it won't fit in anywhere.
Then the exercise becomes very exciting. We look
at the inset carefully; we find the mistake and begin all over again. The most skilful pupils work
on the insets with their eyes closed.

Page 14. These colors are called: red, black, green, yellow, blue,
brown, pink and violet.

Page 15. I amuse myself by picking out and putting together
pieces of the same color from the collection spread
out over my table. I get thus a long strip of different colors.

Page 16. We learn to arrange sixty-four different colors by gradations. We get eight beautiful blends of colors, each formed by eight tints of different tones. When we become skilful we can make a pretty rug with blending strips.

Page 17. We also have two little chests full of pieces of cloth. The cloths are of all kinds from the roughest and hardest to the smoothest and softest: canvas, cotton, linen, wool, flannel, velvet, etc. If we keep our hands clean, we can learn to recognize all sorts of things with the tips of our fingers!

Page 18. A child is blindfolded. He mixes the pieces of cloth with his little hands. He feels about among the pieces of cloth. At last he smiles and holds up his hands with two pieces of cloth, both alike. Though he could not see, the child has found out, just by using his fingers, that the two pieces were of the same cloth.

Page 19. These are my plane insets. Here are the blue tablets. I must fit them into the frames, which have just enough room for them. I run two fingers, the forefinger and the middle-finger, around the edge of the tablet, and then around the edge of the frames. Next I fit the tablet into its proper place. After a little practise I can put the six tablets in their places even with my eyes blindfolded.

Page 20. With the plane insets I have learned to recognize many figures: the square, the circle, the rectangle, the ellipse, the triangle, the oval, the pentagon, the hexagon, the heptagon, the octogon, the enneagon, the decagon. I learned all these hard names very easily because the insets are so amusing!

### INTERPRETATIONS

Reading with the object of interpretation is conducted as in the first experiments of the " Children's House," with cards. From the graduated series we have prepared the child selects a card. He reads it mentally and then executes the action indicated on the card. Our later experiments became very interesting when they were based upon a more rigorous method. When we gave a card describing two actions to a child of five years, he would execute only one of the actions. Take the following for example:

— She leaned over the back of a chair.
— She covered her face with her hands and wept.

The child would act out either the first sentence (*She leaned over the back of the chair*) or the second (*She covered her face with her hands and wept*). In spite of the fact that this child seemed extraordinarily eager to get the cards into his hands and to interpret them, those containing two sentences always aroused in him less enthusiasm than those containing a single sentence or indicating a single action (for instance, *The boy ran away as fast as he could*). In this latter case the enthusiasm of the little ones, their care in interpreting the action vividly, their eagerness to repeat it, their flushed faces and shining eyes, told us that at last we had the reading adapted to their psychology.

Our *first series* of readings accordingly is entirely " tested " or *experimental*. It is made up of simple sentences something like those analyzed in the lessons on grammar (Verb to Pronoun).

## Series I

— She gazed slowly around the room.
— He looked at them out of the corners of his eyes.
— The boy ran away as fast as he could.
— She threw herself on her knees before him.
— The man paced slowly up and down the room.
— The little girl stood with lowered head.

— The teacher nodded her approval.
— The little child sat with folded arms.
— He started rapidly toward the door.
— He began to walk to and fro about the room.
— His mother tenderly stroked his head.
— She motioned to him to keep away.
— He whispered in her ear.
— She placed her hand on his shoulder.
— They knocked at the door.
— The little girl frowned.

The children carry out the indicated action after they have read mentally, but they put what amounts to artistic expression into their interpretations, which are never executed listlessly. For them it becomes a real " interpretation." They often " study " the action, trying it over and over again, as though rehearsing for a play. Their aptitude for this is something remarkable. Furthermore the words have, for the most part, already been studied in the grammatical exercises, so that the meaning of each word is becoming more and more clear. This helps in the interpretation. For example, the sentence *The little girl stood with lowered head* does not mean simply " she lowered her head." If the child has understood he will stand for some time with lowered head in an attitude more or less expressive according to the vividness of his feeling of the situation. In the sentence *She threw herself on her knees before him* there will not be a simple act of kneeling, but something more dramatic. The child will assume the kneeling posture with some indication of emotion. The children take no end of interest in each other's interpretations.

In a *second series* of readings we have two coordinated clauses, the children executing two consecutive actions instead of one.

## Series II

— He opened the door and came in.

— He left the room and locked the door behind him.

— He went on tiptoe to the door and carefully opened it.

— She covered her face with her hands and began to sob violently.

— She gave a cry of joy and ran to the door.

— She burst into a laugh and clapped her hands.

— He took off his cap and made a low bow.

— She shook her head sadly and smiled.

— He threw the window wide open and looked into the garden.

— He hurried to the table and rang the bell.

— With a sigh of relief he stretched himself out on the sofa, and lay there looking at the ceiling with his mouth open.

— He shut his eyes and fell asleep.

In the *third series,* there are sentences with one or more coordinate clauses.

## Series III

— She opened the door, smoothed her hair slowly and came in.

— He went to the window, opened it a little and peered into the street.

— He closed the window, went back to his desk and then began to walk hurriedly up and down the room.

— The doctor bent over the sick man, felt his pulse with one hand and placed the other on his forehead.

— He took a key out of his pocket, opened the door and came in.

— She uttered a cry of joy, ran to her mother and sank on her knees before her.

— He put his left elbow on his knee, rested his forehead in his left hand and began to stroke his beard with his right.

— She leaned over the back of the chair, covered her face with her hands and wept.

— He went to the table, found the picture and joyfully took it in his hands.

— She took her handkerchief out of her pocket, unfolded it and wiped the tears from her eyes.

— The child was sleepy. He rested his head on his arms on the table and went to sleep.

— He looked toward the door fixedly, with an expression of terror on his face and waited for the man to come in.

## SERIES IV

### (Complex sentences with one subordinate clause)

— While he was making the drawing, he kept examining the flower very carefully.

— She covered her eyes with her hands, as if she were trying to collect her thoughts.

— She closed her eyes so that she could feel more intensely the softness of the piece of velvet.

— She looked tenderly after the little boy, till he disappeared through the door.

— When he had succeeded in turning the knob without making any noise, he stealthily opened the door and peered into the room.

— George held the book before his face so that no one could see him laughing.

— She walked slowly across the room and with bowed head, as though she were in great sorrow.

— The old man stroked the little boy's head as though he were much amused.

— After she had motioned to the child to be silent, the lady smilingly approached and took him by the hand.

— They stopped suddenly and listened, as though wondering what it could be.

— When Mary opened the door, George went to meet her with a cheery smile of welcome.

## SERIES V

### (Sentences somewhat more involved; descriptions more complex; an exact interpretation sometimes requires the pronunciation of words aloud)

— The child rose from her seat, and with her face buried in her handkerchief, walked slowly, sadly, toward the window.

— He lay back in his chair, his head sunk between his shoulders, while his arms were pressed tightly across his breast, as though he were cold.

— He dropped wearily into a chair and sat there looking at the floor, his right elbow on his knee and his chin resting on his hand.

— He stood at the open window, with figure erect, and his hands resting on the window-sill, while in deep breaths he took into his lungs the delicious fresh air that was coming into the room.

— The boy lowered his head, and rubbed his forehead with his hands as though he were trying to collect his thoughts.

— There she knelt, her face turned heavenward, her hands crossed in her lap, while her body drooped gently as though she were very, very tired.

— When he reached the door of his house, he hastily unlocked the door, opened it, went in, and carefully locked the door again behind him; and in his eagerness to confide his secret to some one he could trust, he went down the hall calling "Mother, Mother!"

— His eyes filled with tears as he went to the wall where the picture of his father hung, and there with his head resting on his arm against the wall, he sobbed bitterly.

— Rizpah spread the cloth on the ground at the foot of the tree, seated herself upon it, and with her arms resting limp upon her knees, her eyes set in unutterable woe, watched the birds and thought about her lost children.

— The man was lying, sprawling, on the couch, but he jumped up and ran to the door and angrily motioned to his servant to come to him.

— The old lady sat shivering near the stove, holding out her hands to get the warmth and nervously opening and closing them so that the tips of her fingers kept rubbing her palms.

— "I see," thought the boy as he stood with folded arms looking fixedly at the floor.

— He took the handkerchief, examined it a moment and said: "It doesn't belong to me!"

— He stooped over and picked up a pencil that was lying on the floor: "Pshaw," said he, "it is broken!"

— Pecopin, feeling that all was over, threw himself face down-
    ward on the ground, and moaned: " I shall never see her
    again! "
— On waking, Rip Van Winkle rubbed his eyes and looked
    around for his gun; as he rose to walk he found himself
    stiff in the joints and wanting in his usual agility.
— The clergyman folded his hands before his breast and, bend-
    ing his head above them, prayed fervently.
— The girl knelt beside the fallen soldier, while with her right
    hand she waved her handkerchief to and fro in the air.
— As the door opened, Florence ran to meet him, crying, " Oh,
    dear, dear papa! " and she held out her arms to him; but,
    as he paid no attention to her, she put her handkerchief to
    her face and burst into tears.
— Beatrice came through the door holding her skirt with one
    beautiful arm, while with the other she held a candlestick
    above her head, so that the light shone upon her face.
— She advanced holding forward her head as if she would have
    him kiss her as he used to when she was a child; but then
    remembering herself, she made him a deep curtsy, sweep-
    ing down to the ground almost, looking up meanwhile with
    the sweetest smile.
— She closed the door very carefully behind her, and then leant
    back against it, her hands folded before her, looking at the
    boy who was kneeling beside his trunk to pack it.
— He took the paper and stepped to the window; then holding
    the sheet so that the light fell full upon it, he examined it
    carefully, folded it as though musing on its contents and
    put it into his vest pocket.
— My Lord was lifting the glass to his lips, when Esmond en-
    tered; but at the sight of the familiar face, the movement
    of his arm ceased when the glass was on a level with his
    chin; he held it there a moment in astonishment, then,
    suddenly setting it on the table he rushed toward Esmond
    with outstretched arms, and would almost have embraced
    him: " I thought you were in France," he exclaimed.
— The Prince was lying on the bed, but at the sound of the
    footsteps, he rose on his elbow in alarm, while he reached

Interpreted reading: "Whisper to him." (*The Lenox School, Montessori Elementary Class, New York.*)

In a similar manner, the children act out or interpret poses and expressions in pictures. (*A Montessori School in Italy.*)

under the pillow for his pistols: "Who goes there?" he
shouted sternly.
— The child playfully drew his cap down over his eyes as though
he were a very fierce bandit, and rushed into the room
holding out his arm and pointing his fore-finger like a
pistol.
— As the ladies rode up, the old gentleman raised his hat and
stood with bowed head till they had passed.
— The young man picked up the glove from the floor, pressed it
fervently to his lips and clasped it tenderly against his
bosom, as though it were a priceless treasure.

## SERIES VI

### (More difficult interpretations with occasional speaking)

— Dunsey threw himself into a chair by the window, drew another chair before him, threw one leg over it, and began to
beat on the window sill with the points of his fingers.
— Godfrey stood with his back to the fire, moving his fingers
uneasily among the contents of his side-pockets and looking
at the floor.
— Aaron replied by rubbing his head against his mother's skirt,
passing the backs of his hands over his eyes and peeping
through his fingers at Master Marner.
— Mr. Macey screwed up his mouth, leaned his head further on
one side and twirled his thumbs rapidly, with his two
hands resting on his lap and touching at the finger-tips.
— Silas sat with his elbows on his knees, his forehead pressed
rigidly into his two palms, his eyes closed, deep sighs that
were almost groans shaking his slender frame.
— The little tot squatted on the coat and spread out her hands
to the fire; but the little eyes refused to stay open, and
finally the golden head sank down upon the floor fast asleep.
— Presently the child slipped from his knee and began to walk
about; but suddenly she fell into a sitting posture and
began to pull at her little boots, as though she were trying
to get at her toes.
— "At last," he said, stretching back in the arm chair, crossing

his legs and joining his hands behind his head: "I can now have a minute to myself!"

— "Ssshh," said the boy, frowning, and waving his right arm with hand outspread towards his companion.

## Series VII

### (Interpretations requiring more than one person)

— As Rip Van Winkle approached the town, the people all stared at him with marks of surprise and invariably stroked their chins, so that Rip was induced involuntarily to do likewise: his beard was a foot long.

— A self-important old gentleman pushed through the crowd, shoving the people to the right and left with his elbows as he passed; and planting himself before Van Winkle, with one hand on his side, the other resting on his cane, he demanded with an austere tone: "What are you doing here?"

— As Rip Van Winkle told his story, the bystanders began to look at each other, nod, and wink significantly and tap their fingers against their foreheads.

— An old woman came tottering forward, put her hand to her brow and peering under it into his face for a moment, exclaimed: "Sure enough, it is Rip Van Winkle!"

— As the Emperor stepped into the court-yard, the ladies were all so busy crowding about the young prince, holding his hands and counting the kisses, that they did not see the old gentleman: "What's all this, what's all this?" he shouted in rage; and they all scampered off in every direction.

— Trotty sat down in his chair and beat his knees and laughed; he sat down in his chair and beat his knees and cried; he got out of his chair and hugged Med; he got out of his chair and hugged Richard; he got out of his chair and hugged them both at once. He was constantly getting up and sitting down, never stopping in his chair a single minute, being beside himself with joy.

— "Here, little girl, can you tell us the way to town?" "That's not the way. The town is over in this direction!" But as the little girl was turning to point out the road, one of the men seized her by the waist and lifted her from the ground. Lucia looked back over her shoulder terrified and gave a shriek. (Manzoni.)

(The children were delighted with this little action and rehearsed it over and over again.)

— With a start, Evangeline looked wildly about her: "Where is Gabriel?" she asked dazedly. "Where is Gabriel? Where is Gabriel?" "He is on that ship that is just sailing out of the harbor!" some one answered. For a few moments Evangeline stood shading her eyes with her palm, gazing after the vessel, fast disappearing into the horizon. At last she spoke half aloud: "I will follow you and find you wherever they may take you, Gabriel," she said, as though taking a vow. Then she turned to the soldier and said: "Lead on to the boat, I am coming, I am coming."

— "Give me the bow," said Tell. Tell chose two arrows; one he fitted to the bow-string, the other he thrust into his girdle. Then for a moment he stood, a little bowed of shoulder, with his eyes downward: he was praying. You might have heard a leaf fall, so still was the place. Then Tell raised his head; his eyes were steady, his hands had become still; his face was like iron; he brought the cross bow to his shoulder and laid his eye to the feather of the shaft: "Twang," the apple fell. A cheer arose from the crowd. Tell laid his hand upon the arrow in his girdle. "If the first had hurt my child," he said, "this one by now would have been through your heart, O Gessler!"

The children by no means restrict themselves to acting out these little scenes and poses. In a second stage they read aloud all these slips which they have interpreted, and in view of the preparation they have had, their reading shows considerable power of expression. They tend to read the slips over and over again, many times, and not infrequently commit them to memory. To take advantage of this new activity we got together a number of poems, making up a little book of children's verse. The pupils read them both mentally and aloud, ultimately committing them to memory and reciting them. Here are some specimens of our Italian collection:

### IL BACIO

Dormiva nella cuna un bel bam-
bino,
E la mamma lo stava a rimirare;
Voleva dargli il bacio del mattino,
Ma il bacio lo poteva risvegliare;
Svegliarlo non voleva, e con la
mano
Gli buttò cento baci da lontano.

### THE KISS

"A pretty child was sleeping in its cradle; its mother was looking at it. She wanted to give it the morning kiss; but the kiss might awaken it. To avoid this, she threw it a thousand kisses with her hand."

### UN SOGNO

Vidi una fata un giorno
Che avea le trecce d'oro
E un abito di perle
Più ricco d'un tesoro.

"Vieni con me," mi disse,
"Che ti farò regina."
"Non vengo, bella fata;
Io sto con la mammina."

### A DREAM

I saw a fairy one day, with golden hair and a dress of pearls, richer than a treasure.

"Come with me," the fairy said, "and I'll make you a queen." "I cannot, pretty fairy," I replied, "I must stay with mother."

### LA NEVE

Lenta la neve fiocca, fiocca,
fiocca,
Senti, una culla dondola pian
piano.
Un bimbo piange, il piccol dito
in bocca,
Canta la vecchia, il mento in su
la mano.

### THE SNOW

The flakes of snow are falling, falling, falling. Listen, a cradle is gently, gently rocking; a baby cries, his finger in his mouth; the old nurse sings, her chin in her hand.

### LA GALLINA

Io vi domando se si può trovare
Un più bravo animal della gal-
lina.
Se non avesse il vizio di raspare

### THE HEN

I leave it to you: is there a nicer animal than the hen? If only she wouldn't scratch, I would like to have one with me

Ne vorrei sempre aver una vicina.
Tutti i giorni a quell'ora: "Coccodè"!
Corri a guardar nel covo e l'ovo c'è!

all the time. Every day, at a certain hour: "Cut-cut-cut-cut-cadakut!"
Run and look in the nest, and an egg is there!

### LA POVERA BAMBINA
Disse: "Mia madre è morta!
Io son digiuna
E la stagion è cruda;
In terra a me non pensa anima alcuna:
Sono orfanella e ignuda."

### THE POOR ORPHAN CHILD
She said: "My mother is dead; I have nothing to eat; the weather is cold. There is no one left to think of me. I am a ragged orphan girl."

### IL PESCE
Un dì fuor della vasca del giardino
Guizzò imprudentemente un pesciolino.
Gigi lo vide, e tutto disperato
Gridò alla mamma: un pesce s'è annegato!

### THE FISH
One day a little fish jumped imprudently out of the garden pool. Gigi saw it and all excitedly cried out: "Mamma, mamma, a fish has drowned himself."

### QUEL CHE POSSIEDE UN BAMBINO
Due piedi lesti lesti
per correre e saltare.
Due mani sempre in moto
per prendere e per fare.
La bocca piccolina
per tutto domandare.
Due orecchie sempre all'erta
intente ad ascoltare.
Due occhioni spalancati
per tutto investigare.
E un cuoricino buono
per molto, molto amare.

### A CHILD'S POSSESSIONS
Two little lively feet to run and jump with.
Two busy hands to take and do things.
One little mouth to ask questions with.
Two ears always awake to hear everything with.
Two bright eyes always open to see everything with.
One little heart to love with.

### IL BUON ODORE
"Ma, bimbo mio, perchè
Sciupar questo bel fiore?"
"Cercavo il buon odore,
Non so capir dov'è."
LINA SCHWARZ.

### THE FLOWER'S FRAGRANCE
"Why spoil that pretty flower, my child?"
"I was looking for the sweet smell and I haven't been able to find it."

### NINNA-NANNA DI NATALE

Ninna-nanna, gelato è il foco-
lare;
fanciul, non ti svegliare.
Per coprirti dal freddo, o mio
bambino,
Cucio in un vecchio scialle un
vestitino.

Ma il lucignolo trema e l'occhio
è stanco,
bimbo dal viso bianco.
Chi sa se per domani avrò finito
Questo che aspetti povero vestito!

ADA NEGRI.

### CHRISTMAS LULLABY

Lullaby, the fire is out, my
child, do not awaken. To keep
you warm, my little child, I
must make you a little dress
from this old shawl.

But the lamp is dim and my
eyes are tired, O child of the
white face. Who knows if even
by tomorrow I can have this
poor dress for you.

A corresponding book of English verse might include
something like the following:

### THE WHOLE DUTY OF A
### CHILD

A child should always say what's
true,
And speak when he is spoken to,
And behave mannerly at table —
At least so far as he is able.

STEVENSON.

### THE RAIN

The rain is raining all around,
It falls on field and tree,
It rains on the umbrella here
And on the ships at sea.

STEVENSON.

### THE COW

Thank you, pretty cow, that
made
Pleasant milk to soak my bread,
Every day and every night
Warm and fresh and sweet and
white.

ANN TAYLOR.

### THE RAIN

The rain is raining all around,
Kittens to shelter fly,
But human folk wear over-shoes
To keep their hind-paws dry.

O. HERFORD.

### FISHES

How very pleasant it must be
For little fishes in the sea!
They never learn to swim at all:
It came to them when they were
small.
"Swim out like this," their
mother cried,
"Straight through the water,
foam and tide."
They waved their fins and
writhed their scales,
And steered their little rudder
tails.
Already they know what to do —
I wish that I could do it too!

ALICE FARWELL BROWN.

THE LITTLE COCK SPARROW

A little cock-sparrow sat on a
  green tree,
And he chirruped, he chirruped,
  so merry was he;
A naughty boy came with his
  wee bow and arrow,
Determined to shoot this little
  cock-sparrow.

"This little cock-sparrow shall
  make me a stew,
And his giblets shall make me a
  little pie too."
"Oh, no!" said the sparrow, "I
  won't make a stew";
So he flapped his wings and
  away he flew.
               BOOK OF KNOWLEDGE.


THE TREE

What do we do when we plant
  the tree?
We plant the houses for you and
  me;
We plant the rafters, the shin-
  gle, the floors,
We plant the studding, the laths,
  the doors,
The beams and siding — all parts
  that be!
We plant the house when we
  plant the tree.
               HENRY ABBEY.

THE LAMB

Little lamb, who made thee?
Dost thou know who made thee,
Gave thee life and bade thee feed
By the stream and o'er the mead;
Gave thee clothing of delight,
Softest clothing woolly bright;
Gave thee such a tender voice,
Making all the vales rejoice?
Little lamb who made thee?
Dost thou know who made thee?
               W. BLAKE.


Let dogs delight to bark and bite,
For God hath made them so;
Let bears and lions growl and
  fight,
For 'tis their nature too.
But, children, you should never
  let
Such angry passions rise:
Your little hands were never
  made
To tear each others' eyes.
               WATTS.

The sunshine flickers through
  the lace
Of leaves above my head,
And kisses me upon the face
Like Mother before bed.

The wind comes stealing o'er the
  grass
To whisper pretty things;
And though I cannot see him
  pass
I feel his careful wings.
               STEVENSON.


After this preparation the children are able to "understand" what they read. All their difficulties in grasping the sentences and their most complicated constructions
have been overcome. They have an insight into the grammatical form of language; and the construction of a sen-

tence, as well as the meaning of the words in it, interests them. There has been created within them a fund of suppressed energy which will very soon break forth into intense activity. In fact, in our school, after these exercises the passion for reading began to show itself. The children wanted " reading, reading, more reading." We got together hastily a few books but never enough to satisfy the eagerness of the children. We found a surprising lack of reading for little children in Italian. The American system of opening special rooms in public libraries for the use of little readers seems to me an excellent thing.

But to take full advantage of this awakened enthusiasm for reading and to cultivate at the same time the art of reading aloud we must not neglect another element in reading: audition.

## AUDITION

When the child has advanced to some extent in the exercises of interpretation, the teacher may begin reading aloud. This should be done as artistically as possible. We recommend for the training of teachers not only a considerable artistic education in general but special attention to the art of reading. One of the differences between the traditional teacher of the past and the teachers we should like to create is that the former used to speak of an " art of teaching," which consisted of various devices to make the child learn, in spite of itself, what the teacher wanted to teach. Our teachers, rather, should be *cultivators* of the fine arts. For in our method art is considered a *means to life*. It is beauty in all its forms which helps the inner man to grow. We have repeatedly emphasized that both in the environment at school and in the materials used, everything should be carefully considered in its artistic bearings, to provide ample room for development for all the phenomena of attention and persistence in work which are the secret keys of self-education. The Montessori teacher should be a cultivator of music, drawing and elocution, responsive to the harmony of things; she must, that is, have sufficient " good taste " to be able to lay out the school plant and keep it in condition; and sufficient delicacy of manner — the product of a sensitive nature — to be alive to all the manifestations of the child spirit.

In the matter of reading aloud the teacher has an important task to accomplish. We found the drawing hour best adapted for this work. It was our experience that it is easier to gain a hearing when the children are busy with something which does not require great concentration and which is not sustained by any particular inspiration. During the drawing lesson, in the placid silence which comes from work, and while the children are intent on their designs, the teacher may begin her reading aloud. It sometimes happens that the substance of what she reads will be sufficient to engage the interest of the whole school. But this is not always an easy task. It is more often the musical quality of the teacher's execution which will attract the little ones with a sense for art and bring them to that motionless attention which is the evidence of eager enjoyment. Possibly a really perfect reader might be able so to hold the whole group of children with some absorbing selection.

The readings we used were numerous and of great variety: fairy tales, short stories, anecdotes, novels, historical episodes. Specifically there were the tales of Andersen, some of the short stories of Capuana, the *Cuore* of De

Amicis, episodes of the life of Jesus, *Uncle Tom's Cabin,* *The Betrothed* (*I promessi sposi* of Manzoni), *Fabiola,* stories from the Italian wars for independence (Nineteenth Century), Itard's *Education of the Young Savage of Aveyron.*

## The Most Popular Books

In general the child will listen to anything that is really interesting. But certainly some surprise will be occasioned by our discovery that the children liked above everything else the readings on Italian history and the *Education of the Savage of Aveyron.* The phenomenon is sufficiently curious to merit further consideration. The history we used was not one commonly thought adapted to young readers. Quite the contrary: it was Pasquale de Luca's *I Liberatori* (*Makers of Freedom,* Bergamo, 1909), written to arouse a feeling of patriotism among the Italian emigrants of Argentina. The special feature of this publication is its contemporary documents reprinted in *fac-simile.* There are, for instance, telegrams, notices in cipher published on the walls of the towns on the eve of uprisings, commemorative medals, a receipt given by an executioner for whipping publicly an Italian patriot, etc. Patriotic songs are given with the music (these the children learned by heart, following the piano) ; there are also copious illustrations.

This documented history was so absorbing that the children became entirely possessed by the situations. They started animated discussions on various subjects, arguing and deciding. They were particularly outraged at an edict of the king of Naples which was intended to mislead the public. They raged at unjust persecutions, applauded heroic deeds, and ended by insisting on acting

out some of the scenes.   They formed little companies of
three or four and " acted " the episodes with a most impressive dramatic sense.    One little girl was moved to bring to
school a collection of all the Italian patriotic songs.    It
fascinated many of the children, who learned several by
heart and sang them in chorus.   In a word, the Italian
Risorgimento came to live in those little hearts with a freshness it has long since lost in the souls of their elders.
Many of the children wrote down their impressions of their
own accord, often giving surprisingly original judgments.
Finally they began to " take notes."   They asked the
teacher to give an outline of the principal events, which
they took down in their copy-books.   This whole experience corrected many of my own ideas on the teaching of
history.   I had thought of preparing moving-picture films
and giving historical representations.   But that, naturally,
being beyond my resources, I had been compelled to give
up the plan.   The reading of De Luca's book was a revelation.   To teach history to children it is sufficient to give
a *living documented truth*.   We need, not more cinemato-
graphs, but different school books.   Children are much
more sensible to the true and beautiful than we.   They
must be shown complete pictures of reality, which vividly
suggest fact and situation.   De Luca, moved by affection
for his distant brothers, tried to write a book flaming both
with truth and with love, which would awaken them and
bring them back to live among us as Italians.   Our task
is the same.   We must be filled with a similarly intense
human zeal: we must call back to us the distant souls of
the children.   They too are brothers living far away in
a distant country.   We must arouse them, bring them
back to us as partners in our own life.

After our readings from Itard's *Savage,* the parents

of the children kept coming to us with inquiries:
"What have you been reading to our children? We
should like to hear it ourselves." The little ones had told
of hearing an extraordinary story about a child who had
lived with the animals, beginning little by little to understand, to feel, to live like us. All the psychological details
of his study, his attempts at education, seemed to have
touched the children deeply. It occurred to us to take the
older of such children to a "Children's House" and show
them our educational method. They took the greatest interest in it, and some of them are now collaborators in the
foundation of other "Children's Houses." Such children
are able to follow the development of the child mind with
extraordinary sympathy. However, if we reflect that the
best teachers for children are children themselves, and that
little tots like the company of another child much better
than that of an adult, we need not be surprised at the down-
fall of another prejudice.

We have conceived of children according to a fantastic
idea of our own, making of them a sort of human species
distinct from that to which adults belong. As a matter
of fact, they are our children, more purely human than
we ourselves. The beautiful and the true have for them
an intense fascination, into which they plunge as into
something actually necessary for their existence.

The results here witnessed led us to many a reflection.
We succeeded in teaching history and even pedagogy by
means of "reading." And, in truth, does not reading
embrace everything? Travel stories teach geography;
insect stories lead the child into natural science; and so
on. The teacher, in short, can use reading to introduce
her pupils to the most varied subjects; and the moment
they have been thus started, they can go on to any limit

Interpreted reading: "She was sleepy; she leaned her arms on the table, her head on her arms, and went to sleep." Notice the slip of paper which the child has just read. (*The Lenox School, Montessori Elementary Class, New York.*)

Exercises in interpreted reading and in arithmetic. (*The Rivington Street Montessori School, New York.*)

guided by the single passion for reading. Our task is to offer the child the instruments of education, to keep pure within him the springs of his intellectual growth, of his life of feeling. The rest follows as a matter of course. As the ancients said: "*Necessary* education is the three 'r's': reading, writing and arithmetic," for these are things which the child cannot discover by himself. We can only add that "method" must be scientifically determined only at the points where it becomes necessary to assist the "formation of man," that he may develop his activities by strengthening them and not by repressing them, that he may receive essential help without losing any of the pure freshness of his interior activities. But this does not mean that "a rigorous method must guide the child at all times and in every step that he takes." When he has become strong and is in possession of his tools for discovery, he will be able to uncover many of life's secrets by himself. We tied the child to the materials in his sensory exercises, but we left him free to explore his environment. This must be the method for all his later steps in advance: he must be given the instrument and the strength to use it, and then left free to find things out for himself.

The fondness of children for reading and their preference for the "true" is something already demonstrated by experiments conducted elsewhere. I may refer here to the investigations on readings for children conducted by the "Education" section of the Federation for School Libraries of the province of Emilia (Italy). The questionnaire was as follows:

Do you remember what books you have read and which you
  liked best?
How did you get them?
Do you know the title of some book you would like to read?

202 MONTESSORI ELEMENTARY MATERIAL

> Do you prefer fairy-tales, or rather stories of true or probable facts? Why?
>
> Do you prefer sad or humorous stories?
>
> Do you like poetry?
>
> Do you like stories of travel and adventure?
>
> Do you subscribe to any weekly or monthly newspaper? If so, to which?
>
> If your mother were to offer you a choice between a subscription to a weekly or a monthly and an illustrated book, which would you take? And why?

The answers, very carefully sifted, showed that the vast majority of children preferred readings which dealt with fact. Here are some of the reasons alleged by the children in support of their preference for "truth": "Facts teach me something; fairy-tales are too improbable; true stories don't upset my thinking; true stories teach me history; true stories always convey some good idea; fairy-stories give me many desires impossible to satisfy; many good ideas come from actual experiences; fantastic tales make me think too much about supernatural things"; etc., etc. In favor of the fairy-tales we find: "They amuse me in hours free from work; I like to be in the midst of fairies and enchantments"; etc. Those who preferred sad or serious stories justified themselves as follows: "I feel that I am a better person, and realize better the wrong I do; I feel that my disposition becomes more kindly; they arouse in me feelings of kindness and pity." Many supported their preference for humorous tales on the ground that "when I read them, I am able to forget my own little troubles." In general, a great majority denied any educational value to joy and humor. In this conviction — or rather this feeling — so widely diffused among children, have we not evidence that something must be wrong in the kind of education we have been giving them?

# PART III
# ARITHMETIC

# I

## ARITHMETICAL OPERATIONS

### Numbers: 1 — 10

The children already had performed the four arithmetical operations in their simplest forms, in the "Children's Houses," the didactic material for these having consisted of the rods of the long stair which gave empirical representation of the numbers 1, 2, 3, 4, 5, 6, 7, 8, 9, 10. By means of its divisions into sections of alternating colors, red and blue, each rod represented the quantity of unity for which it stood; and so the entrance into the complex and arduous field of numbers was thus rendered easy, interesting, and attractive by the conception that collective number can be represented by a *single* object containing signs by which the relative quantity of unity can be recognized, instead of by *a number of different* units, represented by the figure in question. For instance, the fact that five may be represented by a single object with five distinct and equal parts instead of by five distinct objects which the mind must reduce to a concept of number, saves mental effort and clarifies the idea.

It was through the application of this principle by means of the rods that the children succeeded so easily in accomplishing the first arithmetical operations: $7 + 3 = 10$; $2 + 8 = 10$; $10 - 4 = 6$; etc.

The long stair material is excellent for this purpose. But it is too limited in quantity and is too large to be handled easily and used to good advantage in meeting the demands of a room full of children who already have been initiated into arithmetic.   Therefore, keeping to the same fundamental concepts, we have prepared smaller, more abundant material, and one more readily accessible to a large number of children working at the same time.

This material consists of beads strung on wires: i.e., bead bars representing respectively 1, 2, 3, 4, 5, 6, 7, 8, 9, 10.   The beads are of different colors.   The 10-bead bar is orange; 9, dark blue; 8, lavender; 7, white; 6, gray; 5, light blue; 4, yellow; 3, pink; 2, green; and there are separate beads for unity.[1]   The beads are opalescent; and the white metal wire on which they are strung is bent at each end, holding the beads rigid and preventing them from slipping.

There are five sets of these attractive objects in each box; and so each child has at his disposal the equivalent of five sets of the long stairs used for his numerical combinations in the earliest exercise.   The fact that the rods are small and so easily handled permits of their being used at the small tables.

This very simple and easily prepared material has been extraordinarily successful with children of five and a half years.   They have worked with marked concentration, doing as many as sixty successive operations and filling whole copybooks within a few days' time.   Special quadrille paper is used for the purpose; and the sheets are ruled in different colors: some in black, some in red, some

[1] At the present time, because of the difficulty of getting beads of certain colors, owing to war conditions, the following colors have been approved by Dr. Montessori to replace those originally used:   10-bead bar, gold; 9, dark blue; 8, white; 7, light green; 6, light blue; 5, yellow; 4, pink; 3, green; 2, yellow-green; 1, gold.   These same colors are retained for the bead squares and the bead cubes.   They will be supplied by The House of Childhood, 16 Horatio Street, New York.

in green, some in blue, some in pink, and some in orange. The variety of colors helps to hold the child's attention: after filling a sheet lined in red, he will enjoy filling one lined in blue, etc.

Experience has taught us to prepare a large number of the ten-bead bars; for the children will choose these from all the others, in order to count the tens in succession: 10, 20, 30, 40, etc. To this first bead material, therefore, we have added boxes filled with nothing but ten-bead bars. There are also small cards on which are written 10, 20, etc. The children put together two or more of the ten-bead bars to correspond with the number on the cards. This is an initial exercise which leads up to the multiples of 10. By superimposing these cards on that for the number 100 and that for the number 1000, such numbers as *1917* can be obtained.

The "bead work" became at once an established element in our method, scientifically determined as a conquest brought to maturity by the child in the very act of making it. Our success in amplifying and making more complex the early exercises with the rods has made the child's mental calculation more rapid, more certain, and more comprehensive. Mental calculation develops spontaneously, as if by a law of conservation tending to realize the "minimum of effort." Indeed, little by little the child ceases counting the beads and recognizes the numbers by their color: the dark blue he knows is 9, the yellow 4, etc. Almost without realizing it he comes now to count by *colors* instead of by *quantities* of beads, and thus performs actual operations in mental arithmetic. As soon as the child becomes conscious of this power, he joyfully announces his transition to the higher plane, exclaiming, "I can count in my head and I can do it more quickly!" This declaration indicates that he has conquered the first bead material.

## TENS, HUNDREDS, AND THOUSANDS

MATERIAL: I have had a chain made by joining ten ten-bead bars end to end. This is called the "hundred chain." Then, by means of short and very flexible connecting links I had ten of these "hundred chains" put together, making the "thousand chain."

These chains are of the same color as the ten-bead bars, all of them being constructed of orange-colored beads. The difference in their reciprocal length is very striking. Let us first put down a single bead; then a ten-bead bar, which is about seven centimeters long; then a hundred-bead chain, which is about seventy centimeters long; and finally the thousand-bead chain, which is about seven meters long. The great length of this thousand-bead chain leads directly to another idea of quantity; for whereas the 1, the 10, and the 100 can be placed on the table for convenient study, the entire length of the room will hardly suffice for the thousand-bead chain! The children find it necessary to go into the corridor or an adjoining room; they have to form little groups to accomplish the patient work of stretching it out into a straight line. And to examine the whole extent of this chain, they have to walk up and down its entire length. The realization they thus obtain of the relative values of quantity is in truth an event for them. For days at a time this amazing "thousand chain" claims the child's entire activity.

The flexible connections between the different hundred lengths of the thousand-bead chain permit of its being folded so that the "hundred chains" lie one next to the other, forming in their entirety a long rectangle. The same quantity which formerly impressed the child by its length is now, in its broad, folded form, presented as a *surface* quantity.

Now all may be placed on a small table, one below the other: first the single bead, then the ten-bead bar, then the "hundred chain," and finally the broad strip of the "thousand chain."

Any teacher who has asked herself how in the world a child may be taught to express in numerical terms quantitative proportions perceived through the eye, has some idea of the problem that confronts us. However, our children set to work patiently counting bead by bead from 1 to 100. Then they gathered in two's and three's about the "thousand chain," as if to help one another in counting it, undaunted by the arduous undertaking. They counted one hundred; and after one hundred, what? One hundred one. And finally two hundred, two hundred one. One day they reached seven hundred. "I am tired," said the child. "I'll mark this place and come back to-morrow."

"Seven hundred, seven hundred — Look!" cried another child. "There are seven — *seven* hundreds! Yes, yes; count the chains! Seven hundred, eight hundred, nine hundred, one thousand. Signora, signora, the 'thousand chain' has ten 'hundred chains'! Look at it!" And other children, who had been working with the "hundred chain," in turn called the attention of *their* comrades: "Oh, look, look! The 'hundred chain' has ten ten-bead bars!"

Thus we realized that the numerical concept of tens, hundreds, and thousands was given by presenting these chains to the child's intelligent curiosity and by respecting the spontaneous endeavors of his free activities.

And since this was our experience with most of the children, one easily can see how simple a suggestion would be necessary if the deduction did not take place in the case of some exceptional child. In fact, to make the idea of decimal relations apparent to a child, it is sufficient to direct his attention to the material he is handling. The teacher experienced in this method knows how to wait; she realizes that the child needs to exercise his mind constantly and slowly; and if the inner maturation takes place naturally, "intuitive explosions" are bound to follow as a matter of course. The more we allow the children to follow the interests which have claimed their fixed attention, the greater will be the value of the results.

## COUNTING-FRAMES

The direct assistance of the teacher, her clear and brief explanation, is, however, essential when she presents to the child another new material, which may be considered "symbolic" of the decimal relations. This material consists of two very simple bead counting-frames, similar in size and shape to the dressing-frames of the first material. They are light and easily handled and may be included in the individual possessions of each child. The frames are easily made and are inexpensive.

One frame is arranged with the longest side as base, and has four parallel metal wires, each of which is strung with ten beads. The three top wires are equidistant but the fourth is separated from the others by a greater distance, and this separation is further emphasized by a brass nail-head fixed on the left hand side of the frame. The frame is painted one color above the nail-head and another color below it; and on this side of the frame, also, numerals corresponding to each wire are marked. The numeral opposite the top wire is 1, the next 10, then 100, and the lowest, 1000.

We explain to the child that each bead of the first wire is assumed to stand for one, or unity, as did the separate beads they have had before; but each bead of the second wire stands for ten (or for one of the ten-bead bars); the value of each bead of the third wire is one hundred and represents the "hundred chain"; and each bead on the last wire (which is separated from the others by the brass nail-head) has the same value as a "thousand chain." [1]

At first it is not easy for the child to understand this symbolism, but it will be less difficult if he previously has worked over the chains, counting and studying them without being hurried. When the concept of the relationship between unity, tens, hundreds, and thousands has matured spontaneously, he more readily will be able to recognize and use the symbol.

Specially lined paper is designed for use with these frames. This paper is divided lengthwise into two equal parts, and on both sides of the division are vertical lines of different colors: to the right a green line, then a blue, and next a red line. These are parallel and equidistant. A vertical line of dots separates this group of three lines from another line which follows. On the first three lines from right to left are written respectively the units, tens, and hundreds; on the inner line the thousands.

The right half of the page is used entirely and exclusively to clarify this idea and to show the relationship of written numbers to the decimal symbolism of the counting-frame.

[1] It would, perhaps, be better in this first counting-frame to have the beads not only of different colors, but of different sizes, according to the value of the wires, as was suggested to me by a Portuguese professor who had been taking my course.

With this object in view, we first count the beads on each wire of the frame; saying for the top wire, one unit, two units, three units, four units, five units, six units, seven units, eight units, nine units, ten units. The ten units of this top wire are equal to one bead on the second wire.

The beads on the second wire are counted in the same way: one ten, two tens, three tens, four tens, five tens, six tens, seven tens, eight tens, nine tens, ten tens. The ten ten-beads are equal to one bead on the third wire.

The beads on this third wire then are counted one by one: one hundred, two hundreds, three hundreds, four hundreds, five hundreds, six hundreds, seven hundreds, eight hundreds, nine hundreds, ten hundreds. These ten hundred-beads are equal to one of the thousand-beads.

There also are ten thousand-beads: one thousand, two thousands, three thousands, four thousands, five thousands, six thousands, seven thousands, eight thousands, nine thousands, ten thousands. The child can picture ten separate "thousand chains"; this symbol is in direct relation, therefore, to a tangible idea of quantity.

Now we must transcribe all these acts by which we have in succession counted, ten units, ten tens, ten hundreds, and ten thousands. On the first vertical line to the extreme right (the green line) we write the units, one beneath the other; on the second line (blue) we write the tens; on the third line (red) the hundreds; and, finally, on the line beyond the dots we write the thousands. There are sufficient horizontal lines for all the numbers, including one thousand.

Having reached 9, we must leave the line of the units and pass over to that of the tens; in fact, ten units make one ten. And, similarly, when we have written 9 in the tens line we must of necessity pass to the hundreds line, because ten tens equal one hundred. Finally, when 9 in the hundreds line has been written, we must pass to the thousands line for the same reason.

The units from 1 to 9 are written on the line farthest to the right; on the next line to the left are written the tens (from 1 to 9); and on the third line, the hundreds (from 1 to 9). Thus always we have the numbers 1 to 9; and it cannot be otherwise, for any more would cause the figure itself to change position. It is this fact that the child must quietly ponder over and allow to ripen in his mind.

It is the nine numbers that change position in order to form all the numbers that are possible. Therefore, it is not the number in itself but its *position* in respect to the other numbers which gives it the value now of one, now of ten, now of one hundred or one thousand. Thus we have the symbolic translation of those real values which increase in so prodigious a way and which are almost impossible for us to conceive. One line of ten thousand beads is seventy meters long! Ten such lines would be the length of a long street! Therefore we are forced to have recourse to symbols. How very important this *position* occupied by the number becomes!

How do we indicate the position and hence the value of a certain number with reference to other numbers? As there are not always vertical lines to indicate the relative position of the figure, *the requisite number of zeros are placed to the right of the figure!*

The children already know, from the "Children's House," that zero has no value and that it can give no value to the figure with which it is used. It serves merely to show the position and the value of the figure written at its left. Zero does not give value to 1 and so make it become 10: the zero of the number 10 indicates that the figure 1 is not a unit but is in the next preceding position — that of the tens — and means therefore one ten and not one unit. If, for instance, 4 units followed the 1 in the tens position, then the figure 4 would be in the units place and the 1 would be in the tens position.

The " Children's House " child already knows how to write ten and even one hundred; and it is now very easy for him to write, with the aid of zeros, and *in columns,* from 1 to 1000: 1, 2, 3, 4, 5, 6, 7, 8, 9; 10, 20, 30, 40, 50, 60, 70, 80, 90; 100, 200, 300, 400, 500, 600, 700, 800, 900; 1,000. When the child has learned to count well in this manner, he can easily read any number of four figures.

Let us now make up a number on the counting-frame; for example, 4827. We move four beads to the left on the thousands-wire, eight on the hundreds-wire, two on the tens-wire, and seven on the units-wire; and we read, four thousand eight hundred and twenty-seven. This number is written by placing the numbers *on the same line* and in the mutually relative order determined by the symbolic positions for the decimal relations, 4827.

We can do the same with the date of our present year, writing the figures on the left-hand side of the paper as indicated: 1917.

Let us compose 2049 on the symbolic number frame. Two of the thousand-beads are moved to the left, four of the ten-beads, and nine of the unit-beads. On the hundreds-wire there is nothing. Here we have a good demonstration of the function of zero, which is to occupy the places that are empty on this chart.

Similarly, to form the number 4700 on the frame, four

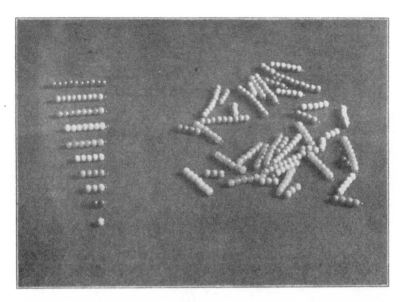

The bead material used for addition and subtraction. Each of the nine
numbers is of different colored beads.

Counting and calculating by means of the bead chains. (*A Montessori
School in Italy.*)

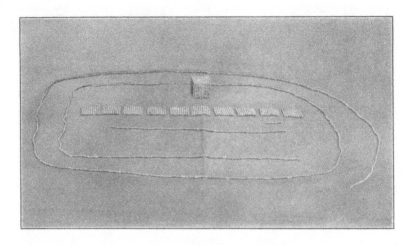

The bead cube of 10; ten squares of 10; and chains of 10, of 100, and of 1000 beads.

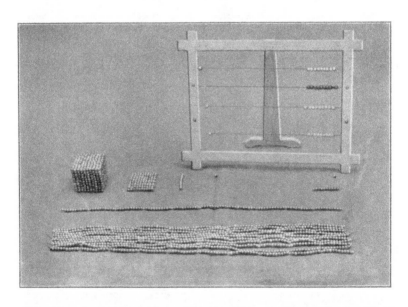

This shows the first bead frame which the child uses in his study of arithmetic. The number formed at the left on the frame is 1,111.

thousand-beads are moved to the left and seven hundred-beads, the tens-wire and the units-wire remaining empty. In transcribing this number, these empty places are filled by zeros — a figure of no value in itself.

When the child fully understands this process he makes up many exercises of his own accord and with the greatest interest. He moves beads to the left at random, on one or on all of the wires, then interprets and writes the number on the sheets of paper purposely prepared for this. When he has comprehended the position of the figures and performed operations with numbers of several figures he has mastered the process. The child need only be left to his auto-exercises here in order to attain perfection.

Very soon he will ask to go beyond the thousands. For this there is another frame, with seven wires representing respectively units, tens, and hundreds; units, tens and hundreds of the thousands; and a million.

This frame is the same size as the other one but in this the shorter side is used as the base and there are seven wires instead of four. The right-hand side is marked by three different colors according to the groups of wires. The units, tens and hundreds wires are separated from the three thousands wires by a brass tack, and these in turn are separated in the same manner from the million wire.

The transition from one frame to the other furnishes much interest but no difficulty. Children will need very few explanations and will try by themselves to understand as much as possible. The large numbers are the most interesting to them, therefore the easiest. Soon their copybooks are full of the most marvelous numbers; they have now become dealers in millions.

For this frame also there is specially prepared paper.

On the right-hand side the child writes the numbers corresponding to the frame, counting from one to a million: 1, 2, 3, 4, 5, 6, 7, 8, 9; 10, 20, 30, 40, 50, 60, 70, 80, 90; 100, 200, 300, 400, 500, 600, 700, 800, 900; 1,000, 2,000, 3,000, 4,000, 5,000, 6,000, 7,000, 8,000, 9,000; 10,000, 20,000, 30,000, 40,000, 50,000, 60,000, 70,000, 80,000, 90,000; 100,000, 200,000, 300,000, 400,000, 500,-000, 600,000, 700,000, 800,000, 900,000; 1,000,000.

After this the child, moving the beads to the left on one or more of the wires, tries to read and then to write on the left half of the paper the numbers resulting from these haphazard experiments.   For example, on the counting-frame he may have the number 6,206,818, and on the paper the numbers 1,111, 111; 8,640,850; 1,500,000; 3,780,000; 5,840,714; 720,000; 500,000; 430,000; 35,840; 80,724; 15,229; 1,240.

When we come to add and subtract numbers of several figures and to write the results in column, the facility resulting from this preparation is something astonishing.

## II

## THE MULTIPLICATION TABLE

MATERIAL: The material for the multiplication table is in several parts. There is a square cardboard with a hundred sockets or indentures (ten rows, ten in a row), and into each of these indentures may be placed a bead. At the top of the square and corresponding to each vertical line of indentures are printed the numbers 1, 2, 3, 4, 5, 6, 7, 8, 9, 10. At the left is an opening into which may be slipped a small piece of cardboard upon which are printed in red the numbers from 1 to 10. This cardboard serves as the multiplicand; and it can be changed, for there are ten of these slips, bearing the ten different numbers. In the upper left-hand corner is a small indenture for a little red marker, but this detail is merely secondary. This arithmetic board is a white square with a red border; and with it comes an attractive box containing a hundred loose beads.

The exercise which is done with this material is very simple. Suppose that 6 is to be multiplied by the numbers in turn from 1 to 10: $6 \times 1$; $6 \times 2$; $6 \times 3$; $6 \times 4$; $6 \times 5$; $6 \times 6$; $6 \times 7$; $6 \times 8$; $6 \times 9$; $6 \times 10$. Opposite the sixth horizontal line of indentures, in the small opening at the left is slipped the card bearing the number 6. In multiplying the 6 by 1, the child performs two operations: first, he puts the red marker above the printed 1 at the top of the board, and then he puts six beads (cor-

responding to the number 6) in a vertical column underneath the number 1.   To multiply 6 by 2, he places the red
marker over the printed 2, and adds six more beads, placed
in a column under number 2.   Similarly, multiplying 6
by 3, the red marker must be placed over the 3, and six
more beads added in a vertical line under that number.
In this manner he proceeds up to 6 × 10.

The shifting of the little red marker serves to indicate
the multiplier and requires constant attention on the part
of the child and great exactness in his work.

While the child is doing these operations he is writing
down the results.   For this purpose there is specially prepared paper with an attractive heading which the child can
place at the right of his multiplication board.   There are
ten sets of this paper in a series and ten series in a set,

**3**

| MULTIPLICATION TABLE |
| :---: |
| COMBINATION OF<br>**THREE**<br>WITH THE NUMBERS 1 TO 10 |
| 3 × 1 = ......................<br>3 × 2 = ......................<br>3 × 3 = ......................<br>3 × 4 = ......................<br>3 × 5 = ......................<br>3 × 6 = ......................<br>3 × 7 = ......................<br>3 × 8 = ......................<br>3 × 9 = ......................<br>3 × 10 = ...................... |

making a hundred sheets with each set of multiplication material. The accompanying cut shows a sheet prepared for the multiplication of number 3.

Everything is ready on the printed sheet; the child has only to write the results which he obtains by adding the beads in columns of three each. If he makes no error he will write: 3, 6, 9, 12, 15, 18, 21, 24, 27, 30.

In this way he will work out and write down the whole series from 1 to 10; and as there are ten copies of each sheet, he can repeat each exercise ten times.

Thus the child learns by memory each of these multiplications. And we find that he helps himself to memorize even in other ways. He walks up and down holding the multiplication sheet, which he looks at from time to time. It is a sheet which he himself has filled, and he may be memorizing seven times six, forty-two; seven times seven, forty-nine; seven times eight, fifty-six, etc.

This material for the multiplication table is one of the most interesting to the children. They fill six or seven sets, one after the other, and work for days and weeks on this one exercise. Almost all of them ask to take it home with them. With us, the first time the material was presented a small uprising took place, for they all wished to carry it away with them. As this was not permitted the children implored their mothers to buy it for them, and it was with difficulty that we made them understand that it was not on the market and therefore could not be purchased. But the children could not give up the idea. One older girl headed the rebellion. "The Dottoressa wants to try an experiment with us," she said. "Well, let's tell her that unless she gives us the material for the multiplication table we won't come to school any more."

This threat in itself was impolite, and yet it was interesting; for the multiplication table, the bug-bear of all children, had become so attractive and tempting a thing that it had made wolves out of my lambs!

When the children have repeatedly filled a whole series of these blanks, with the aid of the material, they are given a test-card by means of which they may compare their work for verification, and see whether they have made any errors in their multiplication. Table by table, number by number, they do the work of comparing each result with the number which corresponds to it in each one of the ten columns. When this has been done carefully, the children possess their own series, the accuracy of which they are able to guarantee themselves.

### MULTIPLICATION TABLE
PRESENTING THE COMBINATIONS OF NUMBERS IN THE
PROGRESSIVE SERIES FROM 1 TO 10

| | | | | |
|---|---|---|---|---|
| $1 \times 1 = 1$ | $2 \times 1 = 2$ | $3 \times 1 = 3$ | $4 \times 1 = 4$ | $5 \times 1 = 5$ |
| $1 \times 2 = 2$ | $2 \times 2 = 4$ | $3 \times 2 = 6$ | $4 \times 2 = 8$ | $5 \times 2 = 10$ |
| $1 \times 3 = 3$ | $2 \times 3 = 6$ | $3 \times 3 = 9$ | $4 \times 3 = 12$ | $5 \times 3 = 15$ |
| $1 \times 4 = 4$ | $2 \times 4 = 8$ | $3 \times 4 = 12$ | $4 \times 4 = 16$ | $5 \times 4 = 20$ |
| $1 \times 5 = 5$ | $2 \times 5 = 10$ | $3 \times 5 = 15$ | $4 \times 5 = 20$ | $5 \times 5 = 25$ |
| $1 \times 6 = 6$ | $2 \times 6 = 12$ | $3 \times 6 = 18$ | $4 \times 6 = 24$ | $5 \times 6 = 30$ |
| $1 \times 7 = 7$ | $2 \times 7 = 14$ | $3 \times 7 = 21$ | $4 \times 7 = 28$ | $5 \times 7 = 35$ |
| $1 \times 8 = 8$ | $2 \times 8 = 16$ | $3 \times 8 = 24$ | $4 \times 8 = 32$ | $5 \times 8 = 40$ |
| $1 \times 9 = 9$ | $2 \times 9 = 18$ | $3 \times 9 = 27$ | $4 \times 9 = 36$ | $5 \times 9 = 45$ |
| $1 \times 10 = 10$ | $2 \times 10 = 20$ | $3 \times 10 = 30$ | $4 \times 10 = 40$ | $5 \times 10 = 50$ |
| $6 \times 1 = 6$ | $7 \times 1 = 7$ | $8 \times 1 = 8$ | $9 \times 1 = 9$ | $10 \times 1 = 10$ |
| $6 \times 2 = 12$ | $7 \times 2 = 14$ | $8 \times 2 = 16$ | $9 \times 2 = 18$ | $10 \times 2 = 20$ |
| $6 \times 3 = 18$ | $7 \times 3 = 21$ | $8 \times 3 = 24$ | $9 \times 3 = 27$ | $10 \times 3 = 30$ |
| $6 \times 4 = 24$ | $7 \times 4 = 28$ | $8 \times 4 = 32$ | $9 \times 4 = 36$ | $10 \times 4 = 40$ |
| $6 \times 5 = 30$ | $7 \times 5 = 35$ | $8 \times 5 = 40$ | $9 \times 5 = 45$ | $10 \times 5 = 50$ |
| $6 \times 6 = 36$ | $7 \times 6 = 42$ | $8 \times 6 = 48$ | $9 \times 6 = 54$ | $10 \times 6 = 60$ |
| $6 \times 7 = 42$ | $7 \times 7 = 49$ | $8 \times 7 = 56$ | $9 \times 7 = 63$ | $10 \times 7 = 70$ |
| $6 \times 8 = 48$ | $7 \times 8 = 56$ | $8 \times 8 = 64$ | $9 \times 8 = 72$ | $10 \times 8 = 80$ |
| $6 \times 9 = 54$ | $7 \times 9 = 63$ | $8 \times 9 = 72$ | $9 \times 9 = 81$ | $10 \times 9 = 90$ |
| $6 \times 10 = 60$ | $7 \times 10 = 70$ | $8 \times 10 = 80$ | $9 \times 10 = 90$ | $10 \times 10 = 100$ |

The children should write down on the following form, in the separate columns, their verified results: under the 2, the column of the 2's; under the 3, the column of the 3's; under the 4, the column of the 4's, etc.

| 1 | 2 | 3 | 4 | 5 | 6 | 7 | 8 | 9 | 10 |
|---|---|---|---|---|---|---|---|---|----|
| 2 | | | | | | | | | |
| 3 | | | | | | | | | |
| 4 | | | | | | | | | |
| 5 | | | | | | | | | |
| 6 | | | | | | | | | |
| 7 | | | | | | | | | |
| 8 | | | | | | | | | |
| 9 | | | | | | | | | |
| 10 | | | | | | | | | |

Then they get the following table, which is identical with the test cards included in the material. It is a summary of the multiplication table — the famous Pythagorean table.

THE MULTIPLICATION TABLE

| 1 | 2 | 3 | 4 | 5 | 6 | 7 | 8 | 9 | 10 |
|---|---|---|---|---|---|---|---|---|----|
| 2 | 4 | 6 | 8 | 10 | 12 | 14 | 16 | 18 | 20 |
| 3 | 6 | 9 | 12 | 15 | 18 | 21 | 24 | 27 | 30 |
| 4 | 8 | 12 | 16 | 20 | 24 | 28 | 32 | 36 | 40 |
| 5 | 10 | 15 | 20 | 25 | 30 | 35 | 40 | 45 | 50 |
| 6 | 12 | 18 | 24 | 30 | 36 | 42 | 48 | 54 | 60 |
| 7 | 14 | 21 | 28 | 35 | 42 | 49 | 56 | 63 | 70 |
| 8 | 16 | 24 | 32 | 40 | 48 | 56 | 64 | 72 | 80 |
| 9 | 18 | 27 | 36 | 45 | 54 | 63 | 72 | 81 | 90 |
| 10 | 20 | 30 | 40 | 50 | 60 | 70 | 80 | 90 | 100 |

The child has built up his multiplication table by a long series of processes each incomplete in itself. It will now be easy to teach him to read it as a "multiplication table," for he already knows it by memory. Indeed, he will be able to fill the blanks from memory, the only difficulty being the recognition of the square in which he must write the number, which must correspond both to the multiplicand and to the multiplier.

We offer ten of these blank forms in our material. When the child, left free to work as long as he wishes on these exercises, has finished them all, he has certainly learned the multiplication table.

# III

## DIVISION

MATERIAL: The same material may be used for division, except the blanks, which are somewhat different.

Take any number of beads from the box and count them. Let us suppose that we have twenty-seven. This number is written in the vacant space at the left-hand side of the division blank.

| DIVISION | | REMAINDER |
|---|---|---|
| : 2 = ............. | | .................. |
| : 3 = ............. | | .................. |
| : 4 = ............. | | .................. |
| : 5 = ............. | | .................. |
| 27 : 6 = ............. | | .................. |
| : 7 = ............. | | .................. |
| : 8 = | 3 | 3 |
| : 9 = | 3 | |
| : 10 = | 2 | 7 |

Then taking the box of beads and the arithmetic board with the hundred indentures we proceed to the operation.

Let us first divide 27 by 10. We place ten beads in a vertical line under the 1; then in the next row ten more beads under the 2. The beads, however, are not sufficient to fill the row under the 3. Now on the paper prepared for division we write 2 on a line with the 10 to the left of the vertical line, and to the right of the same vertical line we write the remainder 7.

To divide 27 by 9, nine beads are counted out in the first row, then nine in the second row under the 2, and still another nine under the 3. There are no beads left over. So the figure 3 is written after the equal-sign (=) on a line with 9.

To divide 27 by 8 we count out eight beads, place them in a row under the 1, and then fill like rows under the 2 and the 3; in the fourth row there are only three beads. They are the remainder. And so on.

A package of one hundred division blanks comes in an attractive dark green cover tied with a silk ribbon. The multiplication blanks, with their tables for comparison and summary tables, come in a parchment envelope tied with leather strings.

| DIVISION | REMAINDER |
|---|---|
| : 2 = | .............................. |
| : 3 = | .............................. |
| : 4 = | .............................. |
| : 5 = | .............................. |
| : 6 = | .............................. |
| : 7 = | .............................. |
| : 8 = | .............................. |
| : 9 = | .............................. |
| : 10 = | .............................. |

# IV

## OPERATIONS IN SEVERAL FIGURES

By this time the child can easily perform operations with numbers of two or more figures, for he possesses all the materials necessary and is already prepared to make use of them.

For this work we have for the first three operations, addition, subtraction, and multiplication, a counting-frame; and for division a more complicated material which will be described later on.

### ADDITION

Addition on the counting frame is a most simple operation, and therefore is very attractive. Let us take, for example, the following:

$$1320 +$$
$$\underline{435}$$
$$=$$

First we slide over the beads to represent the first number: 1 on the thousands-wire, 3 on the hundreds-wire, and 2 on the tens-wire. Then we place next to them the beads representing the second number: 4 on the hundreds-wire, 3 on the tens-wire, and 5 on the units-wire. Now there remains nothing to be done except to write the number shown by the beads in their present position: 1755.

When the problem is a more complicated one, the beads for any one wire amounting to more than 10, the solution is still very easy.  In that case the entire ten beads would be returned to their original position and in their stead one corresponding bead of the next lower wire would be slipped over.  Then the operation is continued. Take, for example:

$$390 \: + $$
$$482$$
$$=$$

We first place the beads representing 390: that is, 3 on the hundreds-wire and 9 on the tens-wire; or, vice versa, beginning with the units, we would first place the 9 tens and then the 3 hundreds.  For the second number we place 4 beads for the hundreds and then we begin to place the 8 tens.  But when we have placed only one ten, the wire is full; so the ten tens are returned to their original position and to represent them we move over another bead on the hundreds-wire; then we continue to place the beads of the tens which now, after having converted 10 of them into 1 hundred, remain but 7.  Or we can begin the addition by placing the beads for the units before we place those for the hundreds; and in that case we move on the hundreds-wire first the bead representing the ten beads on the wire above, and then the 4 hundreds which must be added.  Finally we write down the sum as now indicated by the position of the beads: 872.

With a larger counting-frame it is possible to perform in this manner very complicated problems in addition.

This shows the second counting-frame used in arithmetic. The child is
writing the number she has just formed on her frame. (*The Rivington
Street Montessori School, New York.*)

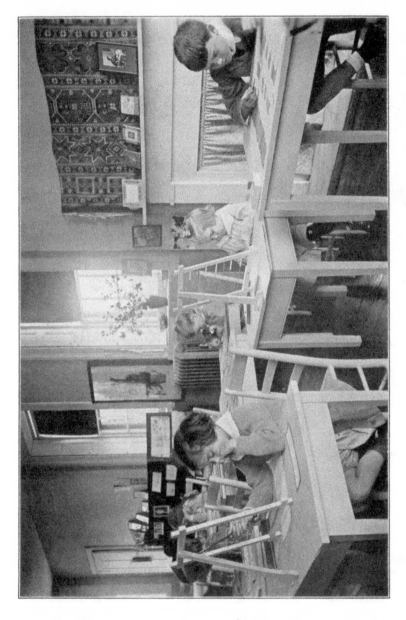

The two little girls are working out problems in seven figures. (*The Washington Montessori School, Washington, D. C.*)

The counting-frame lends itself equally well to problems in subtraction. Let us take, for example, the following:

$$8947 -$$
$$6735$$
$$=$$

We place the beads representing the first number; then from them we take the beads representing the second number. The beads remaining indicate the difference between the two numbers; and this is written: 2212.

Then comes the more complicated problem where it is necessary to borrow from a higher denomination. When the beads of one wire are exhausted, we move over the entire ten and take to represent them one bead from the lower wire; then we continue the subtraction. For example:

$$8954 -$$
$$7593$$
$$=$$

We move the beads representing the first number; then we take 3 beads from the units. Now we begin to subtract the tens. We wish to take away 9 beads; but when we have moved five the wire is empty, and there are still four more to be moved. We take away one bead from the hundreds-wire and replace the entire ten on the tens-wire; and then we continue to move beads on the tens-wire until we have taken a total of nine — that is, we now move the other four. On the hundreds-wire there remain but 8 beads, and from them we take the 5, etc. Our final remainder is 1361.

It is easy to see how familiar and clear to the child the technique of " borrowing " becomes.

## MULTIPLICATION

When there is a number to be multiplied by more than one figure, the child not only knows the multiplication table but he easily distinguishes the units from the tens, hundreds, etc., and he is familiar with their reciprocal relations.  He knows all the numbers up to a million and also their positions in relation to their value.  He knows from habitual practise that a unit of a higher order can be exchanged for ten of a lower order.

To have the child attack this new difficulty successfully one need only tell him that each figure of the multiplier must multiply in turn each figure of the multiplicand and that the separate products are placed in columns and then added.  The analytical processes hold the child's attention for a long period of time; and for this reason they have too great a formative value not to be made use of in the highest degree.  They are the processes which lead to that inner maturation which gives a deeper realization of cognitions and which results in bursts of spontaneous synthesis and abstraction.

The children, by rapidly graduated exercises, soon become accustomed to writing the analysis of each multiplication (according to its factors) in such a way that, once the work of arranging the material is finished, nothing is left for them to do but to perform the multiplications which they already have learned in the simple multiplication table.

Here is an example of the analysis of a multiplication with three figures appearing in both the multiplicand and the multiplier: $356 \times 742$.

$$742 = \begin{cases} 2 \text{ units} \\ 4 \text{ tens} \\ 7 \text{ hundreds} \end{cases} \qquad 356 = \begin{cases} 6 \text{ units} \\ 5 \text{ tens} \\ 3 \text{ hundreds} \end{cases}$$

Each of the first numbers is combined with the three figures of the other number in the following manner:

$$\begin{matrix} \text{u. } 6 \\ \text{t. } 5 \\ \text{h. } 3 \end{matrix} \Bigg\} \times \text{u. } 2 = \begin{cases} 12 \text{ } units \\ 10 \text{ tens} \\ 6 \text{ hundreds} \end{cases} \qquad \begin{matrix} \text{u. } 6 \\ \text{t. } 5 \\ \text{h. } 3 \end{matrix} \Bigg\} \times \text{t. } 4 = \begin{cases} 24 \text{ } tens \\ 20 \text{ hundreds} \\ 12 \text{ thousands} \end{cases}$$

$$\begin{matrix} \text{u. } 6 \\ \text{t. } 5 \\ \text{h. } 3 \end{matrix} \Bigg\} \times \text{h. } 7 = \begin{cases} 42 \text{ } hundreds \\ 35 \text{ thousands} \\ 21 \text{ tens of thousands} \end{cases}$$

When this analysis is written down, the work on the counting-frames begins. Here the operations are performed in the following manner: $2 \times 6$ units necessitate the bringing forward of the ten beads on the first wire. However, even those do not suffice. So they are slid back and one bead on the second wire is brought forward, to represent the ten replaced, and on the first wire two beads are brought forward (12).

Next we take $2 \times 5$ tens. There is already one bead on the tens-wire and to this should be added ten more, but instead we bring forward one bead on the hundreds-wire. At this point in the operation the beads are distributed on the wires in this manner:

2

1

1

Now comes $2 \times 3$ hundreds, and six beads on the corresponding wire are brought forward. When the multiplication by the units of the multiplier is finished, the beads on the frame are in the following order:

2

1

7

We pass now to the tens: $4 \times 6 = 24$ tens. We must therefore bring forward four beads on the tens-wire and two on the hundreds-wire:

2

5

9

$4 \times 5 = 20$ hundreds, therefore two thousands:

2

5

9

2

$4 \times 3$ thousands $= 12$ thousands; so we bring forward two beads on the thousands-wire and one on the ten-thousands-wire:

2

5

9

4

1

Now we take the hundreds: $7 \times 6$ hundreds are 42 hundreds; therefore we slide four beads on the thousands-wire and two on the hundreds-wire. But there already were nine beads on this wire, so only one remains and the other ten give us instead another bead on the thousands-wire:

2

5

1

9

1

5 × 7 thousands = 35 thousands, which is the same as
five thousands and three ten-thousands.    Three beads on
the fifth wire and five on the fourth are brought forward;
but on the fourth wire there already were nine beads, so
we leave only four, exchanging the other ten for one bead
on the fifth wire:

2

5

1

4

5

Finally 7 × 3 ten-thousands = 21 ten-thousands.    One
bead is brought forward on the fifth wire and two on the
hundred-thousands-wire.

At the end of the operation the beads will be distributed
as follows:

2 beads on the first    wire (units)
5    "      "    "   second    "     (tens)
1    "      "    "   third      "     (hundreds)
4    "      "    "   fourth    "     (thousands)
6    "      "    "   fifth       "     (tens of thousands)
2    "      "    "   sixth      "     (hundreds of thousands)

This distribution translated into figures gives the following number: 264,152.    This may be written as a result
right after the factors without the partial products: that
is, 742 × 356 = 264,152.

Although this discription may sound very complicated,
the exercise on the counting-frame is an easy and most in-

teresting arithmetic game. And this game, which contains the secret of such surprising results, not only is an exercise which makes more and more clear the decimal relations of reciprocal value and position, but also it explains the manner of procedure in abstract operations.

In fact, in the multiplication as commonly performed:

$$
\begin{array}{r}
356 \times \\
742 \\
\hline
712 \\
1424 \\
2492 \\
\hline
264152
\end{array}
$$

the same operations are involved; but the figures, once written down, cannot be modified as is possible on the frame by moving the beads and substituting beads of

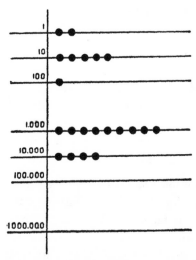

Fig. 1.  The disposition of the beads for the number 49,152.

higher value for those of lower value when the ten beads
of one wire, as a mechanical result of the structure of
the frame, are all used. As multiplication is ordinarily
written, such substitutions cannot be made; but the partial
products must be written down in order, placed in
column according to their value, and finally added. This
is a much longer piece of work, because the act of writing a figure is more complicated than that of moving a
bead which slides easily on the metal wire. Again, it is
not so clear as the work with the beads, once the child
is accustomed to handling the frame and no longer has
any doubt as to the position of the different values, and
when it has become a sort of routine to substitute one
bead of the lower wire for the ten beads of the upper
wire which have been exhausted. Furthermore, it is much
easier to add new products without the possibility of making a mistake. Let us go back to the point in the operation where the beads on the frame read thus:

2

5

1

9

1

and it was necessary to add 35 thousands — five beads
to the thousands-wire and three beads to the ten-thousands-
wire. The three beads on the fifth wire can be brought
forward without any thought as to what will happen on
the wire above when the five are added to the nine. Indeed, what takes place there does not make any difference, for it is not necessary that the operation on the higher
wire precede that on the lower wire.

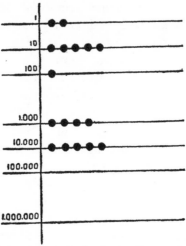

**Fig. 2.** The disposition of the beads for the number 54,152; after adding 5 thousands to the number 49,152.

In adding the five beads to the nine beads only four remain on the fourth wire, since the other ten are substituted by a bead on the lower wire; this bead may be brought forward even after the three for the ten-thousands have been placed.

By the use of the frame the child acquires remarkable dexterity and facility in calculating, and this makes his work in multiplication much more rapid. Often one child, working out an example on paper, has finished only the first partial multiplication when another child, working at the frame, has completed the problem and knows the final product. It is interesting even among adults to watch two compete in the same problem, one at the frame and the other using the ordinary method on paper.

It is very interesting, also, not to work out on the frame the individual products in the sequence indicated in analyzing the factors, but to work them out by chance. Indeed, it does not matter whether the beads are moved in the order of their alignment or at random. The beads on the ten-thousands-wire may be moved first, then the hundreds, the units, and finally the thousands.

These exercises, which give such a deep understanding of the operations of arithmetic, would be impossible with the abstract operation which is performed only by means of figures. And it is evident that the exercises can be amplified to any extent as a pleasing game.

### MULTIPLYING ON RULED PAPER

Take, for example, 8640 × 2531. We write the figures of the multiplicand one under the other but in their relative positions; this also can be written by filling in the vacant spaces with zeros.

In this way we repeat the multiplicand as many times as there are figures in the multiplier; but instead of writing beside these figures the words units, tens, etc., we indicate this with zeros, which, for the sake of clearness, we fill in till they resemble large dots.

The child already knows, from his previous exercises, that zero indicates the position of a figure and that multiplying by ten changes this position. Therefore zeros in the multiplier would cause a corresponding change of position in the figures of the multiplicand.

The accompanying figure shows clearly what it is not so easy to explain in words.

We are now ready for the usual procedure of multiplication. A child of seven years reaches this stage very easily after having done our preliminary exercises, and then it does not matter to him how many figures he has to use. Indeed, he is very fond of working with numbers of unheard of figures, as is shown in the following

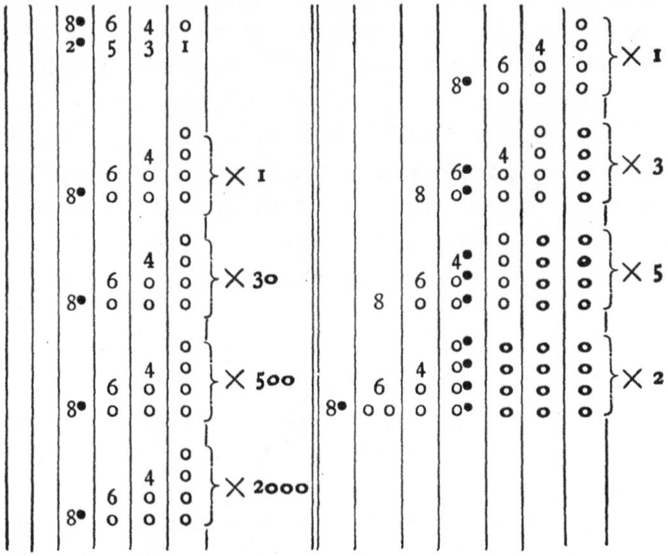

Fig. 3.

example — one of the usual exercises done by the children, who of themselves choose the multiplicand and the
multiplier; the teacher would never think of giving such
enormous numbers. They can now perform the operation

$$22,364,253 \times 345,234,611$$

```
              22364253 ×
             345234611
             ─────────
              22364253
              22364253
             134185518
              89457012
              67092759
              44728506
             111821265
              89457012
              67092759
             ──────────
             7720914184760583
```

without analysis of factors and without help from the frames but by the method commonly used. This may be seen by the way in which the example is written out and then done by the child.

### LONG DIVISION

Not only is it possible to perform long division with our bead material, but the work is so delightful that it becomes an arithmetical pastime especially adapted to the child's home activities. Using the beads clarifies the different steps of the operation, creating almost a *rational arithmetic* which supersedes the common empirical methods, that reduce the mechanism of abstract operations to a simple *routine*. For this reason, these pastimes prepare the way for the rational processes of mathematics which the child meets in the higher grades.

The bead frame will no longer suffice here. We need the square arithmetic board used for the first partial multiplications and for short division. However, we require several such boards and an adequate provision of beads. The work is too complicated to be described clearly, but in practise it is easy and most interesting.

It is sufficient here to suggest the method of procedure with the material. The units, tens, hundreds, etc., are expressed by different-colored beads: *units,* white; *tens,* green; *hundreds,* red. Then there are racks of different colors: *white* for the simple units, tens, and hundreds; *gray* for the thousands; *black* for the millions. There also are boxes, which on the outside are white, gray, or black, and on the inside white, green, or red. And for each box there is a corresponding rack containing ten tubes with ten beads in each.

Suppose we must divide 87,632 by 64. Five of the

boxes are put in a row, arranged from left to right according to the value of their color, as follows: two gray boxes — one green inside and the other white — and three white boxes with the inside respectively red, green, and white. In the first box to the left we put 8 green beads; in the second box 7 white beads; in the third, 6 red beads; in the fourth 3 green beads; and in the fifth box 2 white beads. Back of each box is one of the racks with ten tubes filled with beads of corresponding colors. These beads — ten in each tube — are used in exchanging the units of a higher denomination for those of a lower.

There are two arithmetic boards, one next to the other, placed below the row of boxes. In the one to the left, the little cardboard with the figure 6 is inserted in the slot we have described, and in the other to the right the figure 4.

Now to divide 87,632 by 64, place the first two boxes at the left (containing 8 and 7 beads respectively) above the two arithmetic boards. On the first board the eight beads are arranged in rows of six, as in the more simple division. On the second board the seven beads are arranged in rows of four, corresponding to the number indicated by the red figure. The two quotients must be reduced with reference to the quotient in the first arithmetic board. All the other is considered as a remainder. The quotient in this case is 1 and the remainders are 2 on the first board and 3 on the second.

When this is finished, the boxes are moved up one place and then the first box is out of the game, its place having been taken by the second box; so the gray-green box is no longer above the first board but the gray-white one instead, and above the second board we must place the box with the red beads.

The child here is solving a problem in long division. (*Montessori School, Barcelona, Spain.*)

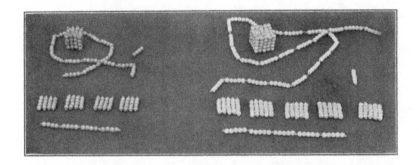

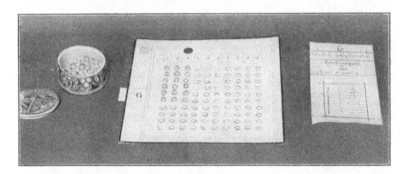

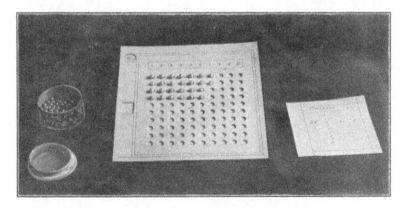

The illustration at the top shows the square and the cube of 4 and of 5. That in the middle shows the arithmetic-board being used for multiplication. In the photograph at the bottom a problem in division is being worked out on the arithmetic-board: $26 \div 4 = 6$ and 2 remainder.

Now the beads must be adjusted.   The two beads that
are left over on the card marked with the number 6 are
green but the box above this card is the gray-white one.
We must therefore change the green beads into white
beads, taking for each one of them a tube of ten white
beads.   The white beads which were left over on the other
card must be brought to the card above which the white
box is now placed.   We have only to arrange the white
beads now in rows of six while the other box of red beads
is emptied on to the second board in rows of four, as in
simple division.

With the material arranged in this way according to
color, we proceed to the reduction, which is done by
exchanging one bead of a higher denomination for
ten of a lower.   Thus, for example, in the present case we
have twenty-three white beads distributed on the first
board in rows of six, which gives a quotient of three and
a remainder of five.   On the second board there are six
red beads distributed in rows of four, giving a quotient
of one with a remainder of two.   Now the work of reduction begins.   This consists in taking one by one the
beads from the board to the left — in this case the white
— and exchanging them for ten red beads, which in turn
are placed in rows of four on the other board until the
quotients on the two cards are alike.   What is left
over is the remainder.   In this case it is necessary to
change only the one white bead so as to have the other
quotient reach three with a remainder of four.

The same process is continued until all the boxes are
used.

The final remainder is the one to be written down with
the quotient.

The exercise requires great patience and exactness, but

it is most interesting and might be called an excellent game of solitaire for children for home use. There is no intellectual fatigue but much movement and much intense attention. The quotients and remainders may be written on a prepared sheet of paper, so as to be verified by the teacher.

When the child has performed many of these exercises he comes spontaneously to try to foresee the result of an operation without having to make the material exchange and arrangement of the beads; hence to shorten the mechanical process. When at length he can " see " the situation at a glance, he will be able to do the most difficult division by the ordinary processes without experiencing any fatigue, or without having been obliged to endure tiring progressive lessons and humiliating corrections. Not only will he have learned how to perform long divisions but he will have become a master of their mechanism. He will realize each step, in ways that the children of ordinary secondary schools possibly never will be able to understand, when through the usual methods of rational mathematics they approach the incomprehensible operations which they have performed for several years without considering the reasons for them.

# V

## EXERCISES WITH NUMBERS

### Multiples, Prime Numbers, Factoring

When the child, by the aid of all this material, has had a chance to grasp the fundamental ideas relating to the four operations and has passed on to the execution of them in the abstract, he is ready to continue on the numerical processes which will lead to a more profound study preparatory to the more complex problems that await him in the secondary schools.

These studies are, however, a means of helping him to remember the things he already knows and to enlarge upon them. They come to him as a pastime, as an agreeable manner of thinking over either in school or at home the ideas which he already has gained.

One of the first exercises is that of continuing the multiplication of each number by the series of 1 to 10 which was begun by the exercises on the multiplication tables. This should be done in the abstract: that is, without recourse to the material. Let us, however, set some limit — we will stop when each product has reached 100. In order that these series of exercises may each be in one column the first exercises will stop with 50 and another can be used for the numbers from 51 to 100.

The two following tables (A and B) are the result. These are prepared in this manner in our material so that the child may compare his work with them.

## TABLE A

| | | | | | | | | |
|---|---|---|---|---|---|---|---|---|
| 2×1 = 2 | 3×1 = 3 | 4×1 = 4 | 5×1 = 5 | 6×1 = 6 | 7×1 = 7 | 8×1 = 8 | 9×1 = 9 | 10×1 = 10 |
| 2×2 = 4 | 3×2 = 6 | 4×2 = 8 | 5×2 = 10 | 6×2 = 12 | 7×2 = 14 | 8×2 = 16 | 9×2 = 18 | 10×2 = 20 |
| 2×3 = 6 | 3×3 = 9 | 4×3 = 12 | 5×3 = 15 | 6×3 = 18 | 7×3 = 21 | 8×3 = 24 | 9×3 = 27 | 10×3 = 30 |
| 2×4 = 8 | 3×4 = 12 | 4×4 = 16 | 5×4 = 20 | 6×4 = 24 | 7×4 = 28 | 8×4 = 32 | 9×4 = 36 | 10×4 = 40 |
| 2×5 = 10 | 3×5 = 15 | 4×5 = 20 | 5×5 = 25 | 6×5 = 30 | 7×5 = 35 | 8×5 = 40 | 9×5 = 45 | 10×5 = 50 |
| 2×6 = 12 | 3×6 = 18 | 4×6 = 24 | 5×6 = 30 | 6×6 = 36 | 7×6 = 42 | 8×6 = 48 | | |
| 2×7 = 14 | 3×7 = 21 | 4×7 = 28 | 5×7 = 35 | 6×7 = 42 | 7×7 = 49 | | | |
| 2×8 = 16 | 3×8 = 24 | 4×8 = 32 | 5×8 = 40 | 6×8 = 48 | | | | |
| 2×9 = 18 | 3×9 = 27 | 4×9 = 36 | 5×9 = 45 | | | | | |
| 2×10 = 20 | 3×10 = 30 | 4×10 = 40 | 5×10 = 50 | | | | | |
| 2×11 = 22 | 3×11 = 33 | 4×11 = 44 | | | | | | |
| 2×12 = 24 | 3×12 = 36 | 4×12 = 48 | | | | | | |
| 2×13 = 26 | 3×13 = 39 | | | | | | | |
| 2×14 = 28 | 3×14 = 42 | | | | | | | |
| 2×15 = 30 | 3×15 = 45 | | | | | | | |
| 2×16 = 32 | 3×16 = 48 | | | | | | | |
| 2×17 = 34 | | | | | | | | |
| 2×18 = 36 | | | | | | | | |
| 2×19 = 38 | | | | | | | | |
| 2×20 = 40 | | | | | | | | |
| 2×21 = 42 | | | | | | | | |
| 2×22 = 44 | | | | | | | | |
| 2×23 = 46 | | | | | | | | |
| 2×24 = 48 | | | | | | | | |
| 2×25 = 50 | | | | | | | | |

**TABLE B**

| | | | | | | | | |
|---|---|---|---|---|---|---|---|---|
| 2×26 = 52 | 3×17 = 51 | 4×13 = 52 | 5×11 = 55 | 6× 9 = 54 | 7× 8 = 56 | 8× 7 = 56 | 9× 6 = 54 | 10× 6 = 60 |
| 2×27 = 54 | 3×18 = 54 | 4×14 = 56 | 5×12 = 60 | 6×10 = 60 | 7× 9 = 63 | 8× 8 = 64 | 9× 7 = 63 | 10× 7 = 70 |
| 2×28 = 56 | 3×19 = 57 | 4×15 = 60 | 5×13 = 65 | 6×11 = 66 | 7×10 = 70 | 8× 9 = 72 | 9× 8 = 72 | 10× 8 = 80 |
| 2×29 = 58 | 3×20 = 60 | 4×16 = 64 | 5×14 = 70 | 6×12 = 72 | 7×11 = 77 | 8×10 = 80 | 9× 9 = 81 | 10× 9 = 90 |
| 2×30 = 60 | 3×21 = 63 | 4×17 = 68 | 5×15 = 75 | 6×13 = 78 | 7×12 = 84 | 8×11 = 88 | 9×10 = 90 | 10×10 = 100 |
| 2×31 = 62 | 3×22 = 66 | 4×18 = 72 | 5×16 = 80 | 6×14 = 84 | 7×13 = 91 | 8×12 = 96 | 9×11 = 99 | |
| 2×32 = 64 | 3×23 = 69 | 4×19 = 76 | 5×17 = 85 | 6×15 = 90 | 7×14 = 98 | | | |
| 2×33 = 66 | 3×24 = 72 | 4×20 = 80 | 5×18 = 90 | 6×16 = 96 | | | | |
| 2×34 = 68 | 3×25 = 75 | 4×21 = 84 | 5×19 = 95 | | | | | |
| 2×35 = 70 | 3×26 = 78 | 4×22 = 88 | 5×20 = 100 | | | | | |
| 2×36 = 72 | 3×27 = 81 | 4×23 = 92 | | | | | | |
| 2×37 = 74 | 3×28 = 84 | 4×24 = 96 | | | | | | |
| 2×38 = 76 | 3×29 = 87 | 4×25 = 100 | | | | | | |
| 2×39 = 78 | 3×30 = 90 | | | | | | | |
| 2×40 = 80 | 3×31 = 93 | | | | | | | |
| 2×41 = 82 | 3×32 = 96 | | | | | | | |
| 2×42 = 84 | 3×33 = 99 | | | | | | | |
| 2×43 = 86 | | | | | | | | |
| 2×44 = 88 | | | | | | | | |
| 2×45 = 90 | | | | | | | | |
| 2×46 = 92 | | | | | | | | |
| 2×47 = 94 | | | | | | | | |
| 2×48 = 96 | | | | | | | | |
| 2×49 = 98 | | | | | | | | |
| 2×50 = 100 | | | | | | | | |

## TABLE C

| | |
|---|---|
| 1 | 51 |
| 2 | 52 |
| 3 | 53 |
| 4 | 54 |
| 5 | 55 |
| 6 | 56 |
| 7 | 57 |
| 8 | 58 |
| 9 | 59 |
| 10 | 60 |
| 11 | 61 |
| 12 | 62 |
| 13 | 63 |
| 14 | 64 |
| 15 | 65 |
| 16 | 66 |
| 17 | 67 |
| 18 | 68 |
| 19 | 69 |
| 20 | 70 |
| 21 | 71 |
| 22 | 72 |
| 23 | 73 |
| 24 | 74 |
| 25 | 75 |
| 26 | 76 |
| 27 | 77 |
| 28 | 78 |
| 29 | 79 |
| 30 | 80 |
| 31 | 81 |
| 32 | 82 |
| 33 | 83 |
| 34 | 84 |
| 35 | 85 |
| 36 | 86 |
| 37 | 87 |
| 38 | 88 |
| 39 | 89 |
| 40 | 90 |
| 41 | 91 |
| 42 | 92 |
| 43 | 93 |
| 44 | 94 |
| 45 | 95 |
| 46 | 96 |
| 47 | 97 |
| 48 | 98 |
| 49 | 99 |
| 50 | 100 |

## TABLE D

1
2
3
4 = 2 × 2
5
6 = 2 × 3 = 3 × 2
7
8 = 2 × 4 = 4 × 2
9 = 3 × 3
10 = 2 × 5 = 5 × 2
11
12 = 2 ×6 = 3 × 4 = 4 × 3 = 6 × 2
13
14 = 2 × 7 = 7 × 2
15 = 3 × 5 = 5 × 3
16 = 2 × 8 = 4 × 4 = 8 × 2
17
18 = 2 ×9 = 3 × 6 = 6 × 3 = 9 × 2
19
20 = 2 × 10 = 4 × 5 = 5 × 4 =
 10 × 2
21 = 7 × 3 = 3 × 7
22 = 2 × 11
23
24 = 2 × 12 = 3 × 8 = 4 × 6 =
 6 × 4 = 8 × 3
25 = 5× 5
26 = 2 × 13
27 = 3 × 9 = 9 × 3
28 = 2 × 14 = 4 × 7 = 7 × 4
29
30 = 2 × 15 = 3 × 10 = 5 × 6 =
 6 × 5 = 10 × 3
31
32 = 2 × 16 = 4 × 8 = 8 × 4
33 = 3 × 11
34 = 2 × 17
35 = 5 × 7 = 7 × 5
36 = 2 × 18 = 3 × 12 = 4 × 9 =
 6 × 6 = 9 × 4
37
38 = 2 × 19
39 = 3 × 13
40 = 2 × 20 = 4 × 10 = 5 × 8 =
 8 × 5 = 10 × 4
41
42 = 2 × 21 = 3 × 14 = 6 × 7 =
 7 × 6
43
44 = 2 × 22 = 4 × 11
45 = 3 × 15 = 5 × 9 = 9 × 5
46 = 2 × 23
47
48 = 2 × 24 = 3 × 16 = 4 × 12 =
 6 × 8 = 8 × 6
49 = 7 × 7
50 = 2 × 25 = 5 × 10 = 10 × 5
51 = 3 × 17
52 = 2 × 26 = 4 × 13

53
54 = 2 × 27 = 3 × 18 = 6 × 9 =
 9 × 6
55 = 5 × 11
56 = 2 × 28 = 4 × 14 = 7 × 8 =
 8 × 7
57 = 3 × 19
58 = 2 × 29
59
60 = 2 × 30 = 3 × 20 = 4 × 15 =
 5 × 12 = 6 × 10 = 15 × 4
61
62 = 2 × 31
63 = 3 × 21 = 7 × 9 = 9 × 7
64 = 2 × 32 = 4 × 16 = 8 × 8
65 = 5 × 13
66 = 2 × 33 = 3 × 22 = 6 × 11
67
68 = 2 × 34 = 4 × 17
69 = 3 × 23
70 = 2 × 35 = 5 × 14 = 7 × 10 =
 10 × 7
71
72 = 2 × 36 = 3 × 24 = 4 × 18 =
 6 × 12 = 8 × 9 = 9 × 8
73
74 = 2 × 37
75 = 3 × 25 = 5 × 15
76 = 2 × 38 = 4 × 19
77 = 7 × 11
78 = 2 × 39 = 3 × 26 = 6 × 13
79
80 = 2 × 40 = 4 × 20 = 5 × 16 =
 8 × 10 = 10 × 8
81 = 3 × 27 = 9 × 9
82 = 2 × 41
83
84 = 2 × 42 = 3 × 28 = 4 × 21 =
 6 × 14 = 7 × 12
85 = 5 × 17
86 = 2 × 43
87 = 3 × 29
88 = 2 × 44 = 4 × 22 = 8 × 11
89
90 = 2 × 45 = 3 × 30 = 5 × 18 =
 6 × 15 = 9 × 10 = 10 × 9
91 = 7 × 13
92 = 2 × 46 = 4 × 23
93 = 3 × 31
94 = 2 × 47
95 = 5 × 19
96 = 2 × 48 = 3 × 32 = 4 × 24 =
 6 × 16 = 8 × 12
97
98 = 2 × 49 = 7 × 14
99 = 3 × 33 = 9 × 11
100 = 2 × 50 = 4 × 25 = 5 × 20 =
 10 × 10

To read over a column of the results of each number is to learn them by heart, and it impresses upon the child's memory the series of multiples of each number from 1 to 100.

With these tables a child can perform many interest-ing exercises. He has sheets of long narrow paper. On the left are written the series of numbers from 1 to 50 and from 51 to 100. He compares the numbers on these sheets with the same numbers in the tables, series by series, and writes down the different factors which he thus finds; for example, $6 = 2 \times 3$; $8 = 2 \times 4$; $10 = 2 \times 5$. Then finding the same number in the second column and the other columns his result will read, $6 = 2 \times 3 = 3 \times 2$; $18 = 2 \times 9 = 3 \times 6 = 6 \times 3 = 9 \times 2$.

In this comparison the child will find that some num-bers cannot be resolved into factors and their line is blank. By this means he gets his first intuition of prime num-bers (Tables C and D).

When the child has filled in this work from 1 to 50 and from 51 to 100 and has reduced the numbers to factors and prime numbers he may pass on to some exercises with the beads.

The children now meditate, using the material, on the results that they have obtained by comparing these tables. Let us consider, for example, $6 = 2 \times 3 = 3 \times 2$. The child takes six beads, and first makes two groups of three beads and then three groups of two.

And so on for each number he chooses. For example:

$$18 = 2 \times 9 = \bullet\bullet\bullet\bullet\bullet\bullet\bullet\bullet\bullet$$
$$= 9 \times 2 = \bullet\ \bullet\ \bullet\ \bullet\ \bullet\ \bullet\ \bullet\ \bullet\ \bullet$$

$= 6 \times 3 =$

$= 3 \times 6 =$

The child will try in every way to make other combinations and he will try also to divide the prime numbers into factors.

This intelligent and pleasing game makes clear to the child the " divisibility " of numbers. The work that he does in getting these factors by multiplication is really a way of dividing the numbers. For example, he has divided 18 into 2 equal groups, 9 equal groups, 6 equal groups, and 3 equal groups. Previously he has divided 6 into 2 equal groups and then into 3 equal groups. Therefore when it is a question of multiplying the two factors there is no difference in the result whether he multiplies 2 by 3 or 3 by 2; for the inverted order of the factors does not change the product. But in division the object is to arrange the number in equal parts and any modification in this equal distribution of objects changes the character of the grouping. Each separate combination is a different way of dividing the number.

The idea of division is made very clear to the child's mind: $6 \div 3 = 2$, means that the 6 can be divided into three groups, each of which has two units or objects; and $6 \div 2 = 3$, means that the 6 also can be divided into but two equal groups, each group made up of three units or objects.

The relations between multiplication and division are very evident since we started with $6 = 3 \times 2$; $6 = 2 \times 3$. This brings out the fact that multiplication may be used to prove division; and it prepares the child to understand the practical steps taken in division. Then some day when he has to do an example in long division, he will find no difficulty with the mental calculation required to determine whether the dividend, or a part of it, is divisible by the divisor. This is not the usual preparation for division, though memorizing the multiplication table is indeed used as a preparation for multiplication.

From the above exercises (Table D) others might be derived involving further analysis of the same numbers. For example, one of the possible factor groups for the number 40 is $2 \times 20$. But $20 = 2 \times 10$; and $10 = 2 \times 5$. Bringing together the smaller figures into which the larger numbers have been broken, we get $40 = 2 \times 2 \times 2 \times 5$; in other words $40 = 2^3 \times 5$.

This is the result for 60:

$$60 = 2 \times 30 = 2 \times 2 \times 15 = 2 \times 2 \times 3 \times 5 = 2^2 \times 3 \times 5$$

For these two numbers we get accordingly the prime factors: $2^3 \times 5$; and $2^2 \times 3 \times 5$. What then have the two larger numbers, 40 and 60 in common? The $2^2$ is included in the $2^3$; the series therefore may be written: $2^2 \times 2 \times 5$; and $2^2 \times 3 \times 5$. The common element (the greatest common divisor) is $2^2 \times 5 = 20$. The proof consists in dividing 60 and 40 by 20, something which will not be possible for any number higher than 20.

We have test sheets where the numbers from 1 to 100 are arranged in rows of 10, forming a square. Here the child's exercise consists in underlining, in different squares, the multiples of 2, 3, 4, 5, 6, 7, 8, 9, 10. The numbers so underlined stand out like a design in such a way that the child easily can study and compare the tables. For instance, in the square where he underlines the multiples of 2 all the even numbers in the vertical columns are marked; in the multiple of 4 we have the same linear

## TABLE E

1 **2** 3 4 5 6 7 8 9 **10**
11 **12** 13 14 15 **16** 17 **18** 19 **20**
21 **22** 23 **24** 25 **26** 27 **28** 29 30
31 **32** 33 **34** 35 **36** 37 **38** 39 40
41 **42** 43 **44** 45 46 47 **48** 49 50
51 **52** 53 **54** 55 **56** 57 **58** 59 60
61 **62** 63 **64** 65 **66** 67 **68** 69 70
71 **72** 73 **74** 75 **76** 77 **78** 79 **80**
81 **82** 83 **84** 85 **86** 87 **88** 89 **90**
91 **92** 93 **94** 95 **96** 97 **98** 99 **100**

1 2 3 **4** 5 6 7 **8** 9 10
11 **12** 13 14 15 **16** 17 18 19 **20**
21 22 23 **24** 25 26 27 **28** 29 30
31 **32** 33 34 35 **36** 37 38 39 40
41 42 43 **44** 45 46 47 **48** 49 50
51 **52** 53 54 55 **56** 57 58 59 **60**
61 62 63 **64** 65 66 67 **68** 69 70
71 **72** 73 74 75 **76** 77 78 79 **80**
81 82 83 **84** 85 86 87 **88** 89 90
91 **92** 93 94 95 **96** 97 98 99 100

---

1 2 **3** 4 5 **6** 7 8 **9** 10
11 **12** 13 14 **15** 16 17 **18** 19 20
**21** 22 23 **24** 25 26 **27** 28 29 **30**
31 32 **33** 34 35 **36** 37 38 **39** 40
41 **42** 43 44 **45** 46 47 **48** 49 50
**51** 52 53 **54** 55 56 **57** 58 59 **60**
61 62 **63** 64 65 **66** 67 68 **69** 70
71 **72** 73 74 **75** 76 77 **78** 79 80
**81** 82 83 **84** 85 86 **87** 88 89 **90**
91 92 **93** 94 95 **96** 97 98 **99** 100

1 2 3 4 **5** 6 7 8 9 **10**
11 12 13 14 **15** 16 17 18 19 **20**
21 22 23 24 **25** 26 27 28 29 **30**
31 32 33 34 **35** 36 37 38 39 **40**
41 42 43 44 **45** 46 47 48 49 **50**
51 52 53 54 **55** 56 57 58 59 60
61 62 63 64 **65** 66 67 68 69 **70**
71 72 73 74 **75** 76 77 78 79 **80**
81 82 83 84 **85** 86 87 88 89 **90**
91 92 93 94 **95** 96 97 98 99 **100**

---

1 2 3 4 5 **6** 7 8 9 10
11 **12** 13 14 15 16 17 **18** 19 20
21 22 23 **24** 25 26 27 28 29 **30**
31 32 33 34 35 **36** 37 38 39 40
41 **42** 43 44 45 46 47 **48** 49 50
51 52 53 **54** 55 56 57 58 59 **60**
61 62 63 64 65 **66** 67 68 69 70
71 **72** 73 74 75 76 77 **78** 79 80
81 82 83 **84** 85 86 87 88 89 **90**
91 92 93 94 95 **96** 97 98 99 100

1 2 3 4 5 6 **7** 8 9 10
11 12 13 **14** 15 16 17 18 19 20
**21** 22 23 24 25 26 27 **28** 29 30
31 32 33 34 **35** 36 37 38 39 40
41 **42** 43 44 45 46 47 48 **49** 50
51 52 53 54 55 **56** 57 58 59 60
61 62 **63** 64 65 66 67 68 69 **70**
71 72 73 74 75 76 **77** 78 79 80
81 82 83 **84** 85 86 87 88 89 90
**91** 92 93 94 95 96 97 **98** 99 100

```
 1  2  3  4  5  6  7  8  9 10     1  2  3  4  5  6  7  8  9 10
11 12 13 14 15 16 17 18 19 20    11 12 13 14 15 16 17 18 19 20
21 22 23 24 25 26 27 28 29 30    21 22 23 24 25 26 27 28 29 30
31 32 33 34 35 36 37 38 39 40    31 32 33 34 35 36 37 38 39 40
41 42 43 44 45 46 47 48 49 50    41 42 43 44 45 46 47 48 49 50
51 52 53 54 55 56 57 58 59 60    51 52 53 54 55 56 57 58 59 60
61 62 63 64 65 66 67 68 69 70    61 62 63 64 65 66 67 68 69 70
71 72 73 74 75 76 77 78 79 80    71 72 73 74 75 76 77 78 79 80
81 82 83 84 85 86 87 88 89 90    81 82 83 84 85 86 87 88 89 90
91 92 93 94 95 96 97 98 99 100   91 92 93 94 95 96 97 98 99 100
```

```
 1  2  3  4  5  6  7  8  9 10
11 12 13 14 15 16 17 18 19 20
21 22 23 24 25 26 27 28 29 30
31 32 33 34 35 36 37 38 39 40
41 42 43 44 45 46 47 48 49 50
51 52 53 54 55 56 57 58 59 60
61 62 63 64 65 66 67 68 69 70
71 72 73 74 75 76 77 78 79 80
81 82 83 84 85 86 87 88 89 90
91 92 93 94 95 96 97 98 99 100
```

grouping — a vertical line — but the numbers marked
are alternate numbers; in 6 the same vertical grouping
continues, but one number is marked and two are skipped;
and again in the multiples of 8 the same design is repeated with the difference that every fourth number is
underlined. On the square marked off for the multiples
of 3 the numbers marked form oblique lines running from
right to left and all the numbers in these oblique lines are
underlined. In the multiples of 6 the design is the same
but only the alternating numbers are underlined. The
6 therefore, partakes of the type of the 2 and of the 3;
and both of these are indeed its factors.

# VI

## SQUARE AND CUBE OF NUMBERS

Let us take two of the two-bead bars (green) which were used in counting in the first bead exercises. Here, however, these form part of another series of beads. Along with these two bars there is a small chain: ●● — ●● By joining two like bars, the chains represent 2 × 2. There is another combination of these same objects — the two bars are joined together not in a chain but in the form of a square: ●● ●●

They represent the same thing: that is to say, as numbers they are 2 × 2; but they differ in position — one has the form of a line, the other of a square. It can be seen from this that if as many bars as there are beads on a bar are placed side by side they form a square.

In the series in fact we offer squares of 3 × 3 pink beads; 4 × 4 yellow beads; 5 × 5 pale blue beads; 6 × 6 gray beads; 7 × 7 white beads; 8 × 8 lavender beads; 9 × 9 dark blue beads; and 10 × 10 orange beads; thus reproducing the same colors as were used at the beginning in counting.

For every number there are as many bars as there are beads for the number, 3 bars for the 3, 4 for the 4, etc.; in addition there is a chain consisting of an equal number of bars, 3 × 3; 4 × 4; and, as we have seen, there is a square containing another equal quantity.

The child not only can count the beads of the chains

and squares, but he can reproduce them by placing the corresponding single bars either in a horizontal line or laying them side by side in the shape of a square. The number repeated as many times as the unit it contains is really the multiplication of the number by itself.

For example, taking the small square of four the child can count four beads on each side; multiplying 4 by 4 we have the number of beads in the square, 16. Multiplying one side by itself (squaring one side) we have the area of the little square.

This can be continued for 5, 8, 9, etc. The square of 10 has ten beads on each side. Multiplying 10 by 10, in other words, " squaring " one side we get the entire number of beads forming the area of the square: 100.

However, it is not the form alone which gives these results; for if the ten bars which formed the square are placed end to end in a horizontal line, we get the " hundred chain." This can be done with each square; the chain 5 × 5, like the square 5 × 5, contains the same number of beads, 25. We teach the child to write the numbers with symbol for the square: $5^2 = 25$; $7^2 = 49$; $10^2 = 100$, etc.

Our material here is manufactured with reference to the numbers 2, 3, 4, 5, 6, 7, 8, 9, 10. It is " offered " to the child, beginning with the smaller numbers. Given the material and freedom, the idea will come of itself and the child will " work " it into his consciousness on them.

In this same period we take up also the cubes of the numbers, and there is a similar material for this: that is, the chain of the cube of the number is made up of chains of the square of that number joined by several links which permit of its being folded. There are as many squares for a number as there are units in that number — four

squares for number 4, six squares for 6, ten squares for 10
— and a cube of the beads is formed by placing the necessary number of squares one on top of the other.

Let us consider the cube of four. There is a chain
formed by four chains each representing the square of
four. They are joined by small links so that the chain

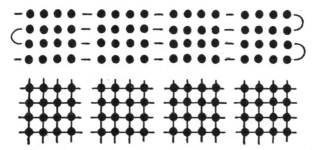

can be rolled up lengthwise. The chain of the cube, when
thus rolled, gives four squares similar to the separate
squares, which, when drawn out again, form a straight
line.

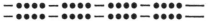

Fig. 5.—This shows only part of the entire chain for 4³.

The quantity is always the same: four times the square
of four. $4 \times 4 \times 4 = 4^2 \times 4 = 4^3$.

The cube of four comes with the material; but it can
be reproduced by placing four loose squares one on top of
the other. Looking at this cube we see that it has all its
edges of four. Multiplying the area of a square by the
number of units contained in the side gives the volume
of the cube: $4^2 \times 4$.

In this way the child receives his first intuitions of the
processes necessary for finding a surface and volume.

With this material we should not try to teach a great

deal but should leave the child free to ponder over his own observations — observing, experimenting, and meditating upon the easily handled and attractive material.

\* \* \*

Little by little we shall see the slates and copybooks filled with exercises of numbers raised to the square or cube independently of the rich series of objects which the material itself offers the child. In his exercises with the square and cube of the numbers he easily will discover that to multiply by ten it suffices to change the position of the figures — that is to say, to add a zero. Multiplying unity by ten gives 10; ten multiplied by ten is equal to 100; one hundred multiplied by ten is equal to 1,000, etc.

Before arriving at this point the child will often either have discovered this fact for himself or have learned it by observing his companions.

Some of the fundamental ideas acquired only through laborious lessons by our common school methods are here learned intuitively, naturally, and spontaneously. An interesting study which completes that already made with the "hundred chain" and the "thousand chain" is the comparison of the respective square chain and cube chain. Such differing relations showing the increasing length are most illustrative and make a marked impression upon the child. Furthermore, they prepare for knowledge that is to be used later. Some day when the child hears of "geometric progressions" or "linear squares" he will understand immediately and clearly.

It is interesting to build a small tower with the bead cubes. Though it will resemble the pink tower, this tower, which seems to be built of jewels, gives a profound notion of the relations of quantity.   By this time these cubes are no longer recognized superficially through sensorial impressions, but their minutest details are known to the child through the progressively intelligent work which they have occasioned.

# PART IV

# GEOMETRY

# I

## PLANE GEOMETRY

The geometric insets used for sensorial exercises in the " Children's House " made it possible for the child to become familiar with many figures of plane geometry: the square, rectangle, triangle, polygon, circle, ellipse, etc. By means of the third series of corresponding cards, where the figures are merely outlined, he formed the habit of recognizing a geometric figure represented merely by a line. Furthermore, he has used a series of iron insets reproducing some of the geometric figures which he previously had learned through the use of wooden geometric insets. He used these iron insets to draw the outline of a figure, which he then filled in with parallel lines by means of colored pencils (an exercise in handling the instruments of writing).

The geometric material here presented to the elementary classes supplements that used in the " Children's House." It is similar to the iron insets; but in this material each frame is fastened to an iron foundation of exactly the same size as the frame. Since each piece is complete in itself, no rack is needed to hold them.

The frame of the inset is green, the foundation is white, and the inset itself — the movable portion — is red. When the inset is in the frame, the red surface and the green frame are in the same plane.

This material further differs from the other in that each

259

inset is composed not of a single piece, as in the first material, but of many pieces which, when put together on the white foundation, exactly reproduce the geometric figure there designated.

The use to which these modified insets may be put is most varied. The main purpose is to facilitate the child's auto-education through exercises in geometry and often through the solution of real problems. The fact of being able actually to "handle geometric figures," to arrange them in different ways, and to judge of the relations between them, commands the child's absorbed attention. The putting together of the insets, which deal with equivalent figures, reminds one of the "games of patience"— picture puzzles — which have been invented for children but which, while amusing them, have no definite educational aim. Here, however, the child leaves the exercises with "clear concepts" and not merely with general "notions" of the principles of geometry, a thing which is very hard to accomplish by the methods common to the older schools. The difference between like figures, similar figures, and equivalent figures, the possibility of reducing every regular plane figure to an equivalent rectangle, and finally the solution of the theorem of Pythagoras — all these are acquired eagerly and spontaneously by the child. The same may be said about work in fractions, which is made most interesting by the exercises with the circular insets. The real meaning of the word *fraction,* operations in fractions, the reduction of common fractions to decimal fractions — all of this is mastered and becomes perfectly clear in the child's mind.

These are formative conquests and at the same time a dynamic part of the child's intellectual activity. A child who works spontaneously and for a long period of time with this material not only strengthens his reasoning powers and his character but acquires higher and clearer cognitions, which increase his mental capacity. In his succeeding spontaneous flights into the abstract he will show ability for surprising progress. While a high school child is still wasting his mental effort in trying to understand the relation between geometrical figures, which it seems impossible for him to comprehend, our child in the primary grades is "finding it out for himself" and is so elated by his discovery that he immediately begins the search for other geometrical relations. Our children gallop freely along over a smooth road, urged on by the inner energy of their growing psychic organism, while many other children plod on barefooted and in shackles over stony paths.

Every positive conquest gained through objects with our method of freedom — allowing the child to exercise himself at the time when he is most ready for the exercise and permitting him to complete this exercise — results in spontaneous abstractions. How is it possible to lead a child to perform abstractions if his mind is not sufficiently mature and he is without adequate information? These two points of support are, as it were, the feet of the psychic man who is traveling toward his highest mental activities. We shall always see the repetition of this phenomenon. Every ulterior exercise of inner development, every ulterior cognition, will lead the child to new and ever higher flights into the realm of the abstract. It is well, however, to emphasize this principle: that the mind, in order to fly, must leave from some point of contact, just as the aeroplane starts from its hangar, and that it must have reached a certain degree of maturity, as is the case with the small bird when it tries its wings and starts on its first flight from the nest where it was born and gained its strength. An aeroplane of perpetual flight without a means of replenishing its supplies, and a bird with only an "instinct of flight" without the process of development that takes place from the egg to the first flight, are things that do not exist.

A machine flying perpetually without need of replenishing the fuel for its propelling energy, and an instinct without a corresponding organism, are pure fancies. The same is true of the flight of man's imagination, which soars through space and creates. Though this is the mind's "manner of being," its "highest instinct," yet it also needs to find support in reality, to organize its inner forces from time to time. The longer a material can claim and hold a child's attention, the greater promise it gives that an "abstract process," an "imaginative creation" will follow as the result of a developed potentiality. This creative imagination, which is ever returning to reality to gain inspiration and to acquire new energies, will not be a vain, exhaustible, and fickle thing, like the so-called imagination which our ordinary schools are trying to develop.

Without positive replenishment in reality there never will be a spontaneous flight of the mind; this is the unsurmountable difficulty of the common schools in their attempt to "develop the imagination" and to "lead to education." The child who without any impelling force from within is artificially "borne aloft" by the teacher, who forces him into the "abstract," can at most learn only how to descend slowly like a parachute. He can never learn to "lift himself energetically to dizzy heights." This is the difference; hence the necessity for considering the positive basis which holds the mind of the child to

systematic auto-exercises of preparation. After this it
suffices merely to grant freedom to the child's genius in
order that it may take its own flight.

I need not repeat that even in the period of replenishing,
freedom is the guide in finding the "particular moment"
and the "necessary time"; for I already have spoken
insistently and at length concerning this. It is well, however, to reaffirm here even more clearly that a material for
development predetermined by experimental research and
put into relation with the child (through lessons) ac-
complishes so complete a work by the psychic reactions
which it is capable of stimulating that marvelous phenomena of intellectual development may be obtained.
These geometric insets furnish rich materials for the application of this principle and respond wonderfully to the
"instinct for work" in the child mind.

The exercises with this material not only are exercises
of composition with the pieces of an inset or of the substitution of them into their relative metal plates; they are
also exercises in drawing which, because of the labor they
require, allow the child to take cognizance of every detail
and to meditate upon it.

The designing done with these geometric insets, as will
be explained, is of two kinds: geometric and artistic (mechanical and decorative). And the union of the two kinds
of drawings gives new ways of applying the material.

The geometric design consists in reproducing the figure
outlined by the corresponding insets. In this way the
child learns to use the different instruments of drawing —
the square, the ruler, the compass, and the protractor. In
these exercises he acquires, with the aid of the special portfolio which comes with the material, actual and real cognitions in geometry.

Artistic designs are made by combining the small pieces of the various geometric insets. The resulting figures are then outlined and filled in with colored pencils or water-colors. Such combinations on the part of the child are real esthetic creations. The insets are of such reciprocal proportions that their combination results in an artistic harmony which facilitates the development of the child's esthetic sense. With our insets we were able to repro-duce some of the classic decorations found in our master-pieces of art, such as decorations by Giotto.

A combination of geometric design and artistic design is formed by decorating the different parts of the geometric figure — as the center, the sides, the angles, the circum-ference, etc.; or by elaborating with free-hand details the decorations which have resulted from the combination of the insets. But a far better concept of all this will be gained as we pass on to explain our didactic material.

## II

## THE DIDACTIC MATERIAL USED FOR GEOMETRY

### Equivalent, Identical and Similar Figures

First Series of Insets: *Squares and Divided Figures.* This is a series of nine square insets, ten by ten centimeters, each of which has a white foundation of the same size as the inset.

One inset consists of an entire square; the others are made up in the following manner:

A square divided into two equal rectangles
"     "     "     "    four equal squares.
"     "     "     "    eight equal rectangles
"     "     "     "    sixteen equal squares
"     "     "     "    two equal triangles
"     "     "     "    four equal triangles
"     "     "     "    eight equal triangles
"     "     "     "    sixteen equal triangles

The child can take the square divided into two rectangles and the one divided into two triangles and interchange them: that is, he can build the first square with triangles and the second with rectangles. The two triangles can be superimposed by placing them in contact at the under side where there is no knob, and the same can be done with the rectangles, thus showing their equivalence by placing one on the other. But there also is a certain

265

relation between the triangles and the rectangles; indeed, they are each half of the same square; yet they differ greatly in form. Inductively the child gains an idea of equivalent figures. The two triangles are identical; the two rectangles also are identical; whereas the triangle and the rectangle are equivalents. The child soon makes comparisons by placing the triangle on the rectangle, and he notices at once that the small triangle which is left over on the rectangle equals the small triangle which remains uncovered on the larger triangle, and therefore that the triangle and the rectangle, though they do not have the same form, have the same area.

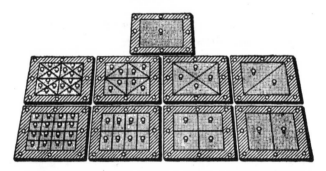

This exercise in observation is repeated in a like manner with all the other insets, which are divided successively into four, eight, and sixteen parts. The small square which is a fourth of the original square, resulting from the division of this latter by two medial lines, is equivalent to the triangle which was formed by dividing this same original square into four triangles by two diagonal lines. And so on.

By comparing the different figures the child learns the difference between *equivalent* figures and *identical* figures. The two rectangles are the result of dividing the large

square by a medial line and are identical; the two triangles are formed by dividing the original square by a diagonal line, etc. *Similar* figures, on the other hand, are
those which have the same form but differ in dimension.
For example, the rectangle which is half of the original
square and the one which is half of the smaller square —
that is, an eighth of the original square — are neither
identical nor equivalent but they are *similar* figures. The
same may be said of the large square and of the smaller
ones which represent a fourth, a sixteenth, etc.

Through these divisions of the square an idea of fractions is gained intuitively. However, this is not the material used for the study of fractions. For this purpose
there is another series of insets.

Second Series of Insets: *Fractions*. There are ten
metal plates, each of which has a circular opening ten centimeters in diameter. One inset is a complete circle; the
other circular insets are divided respectively into 2, 3, 4,
5, 6, 7, 8, 9, and 10 equal parts.

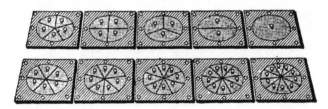

The children learn to measure the angles of each piece,
and so to count the degrees. For this work there is a circular piece of white card-board, on which is drawn in black
a semicircle with a radius of the same length as that of the
circular insets. This semicircle is divided into 18 sectors
by radii which extend beyond the circumference on to
the background; and these radii are numbered by tens

from 0° to 180°. Each sector is then subdivided into ten parts or degrees.

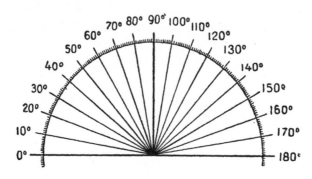

The diameter from 0° to 180° is outlined heavily and extends beyond the circumference, in order to facilitate the adjustment of the angle to be measured and to give a strict exactness of position. This is done also with the radius which marks 90°. The child places a piece of an inset in such a way that the vertex of the angle touches the middle of the diameter and one of its sides rests on the radius marked 0°. At the other end of the arc of the inset he can read the degrees of the angle. After these exercises, the children are able to measure any angle with a common protractor. Furthermore, they learn that a circle measures 360°, half a circle 180°, and a right angle 90°. Once having learned that a circumference measures 360° they can find the number of degrees in any angle; for example, in the angle of an inset representing the seventh of the circle, they know that 360° ÷ 7 = (approximately) 51°. This they can easily verify with their instruments by placing the sector on the graduated circle.

These calculations and measurements are repeated with all the different sectors of this series of insets where the circle is divided into from two to ten parts. The pro-tractor shows approximately that:

$$\frac{1}{3} \text{ circle } = 120° \quad \text{and} \quad 360° \div 3 = 120°$$

$$\frac{1}{4} \text{ '' } = 90° \quad \text{ '' } \quad 360° \div 4 = 90°$$

$$\frac{1}{5} \text{ '' } = 72° \quad \text{ '' } \quad 360° \div 5 = 72°$$

$$\frac{1}{6} \text{ '' } = 60° \quad \text{ '' } \quad 360° \div 6 = 60°$$

$$\frac{1}{7} \text{ '' } = 51° \quad \text{ '' } \quad 360° \div 7 = 51°$$

$$\frac{1}{8} \text{ '' } = 45° \quad \text{ '' } \quad 360° \div 8 = 45°$$

$$\frac{1}{9} \text{ '' } = 40° \quad \text{ '' } \quad 360° \div 9 = 40°$$

$$\frac{1}{10} \text{ '' } = 36° \quad \text{ '' } \quad 360° \div 10 = 36°$$

In this way the child learns to write fractions:

$$\frac{1}{2} \quad \frac{1}{3} \quad \frac{1}{4} \quad \frac{1}{5} \quad \frac{1}{6} \quad \frac{1}{7} \quad \frac{1}{8} \quad \frac{1}{9} \quad \frac{1}{10}$$

He has concrete impressions of them as well as an intuition of their arithmetical relationships.

The material lends itself to an infinite number of combinations, all of which are real arithmetical exercises in fractions. For example, the child can take from the circle the two half circles and replace them by four sectors of 90°, filling the same circular opening with entirely different pieces. From this he can draw the following conclusion:

$$\frac{1}{2} + \frac{1}{2} = \frac{1}{4} + \frac{1}{4} + \frac{1}{4} + \frac{1}{4}.$$

He also may say that two halves are equal to four fourths, and write accordingly:

$$\frac{2}{2} = \frac{4}{4}.$$

 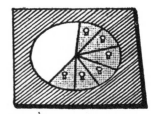

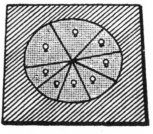

This is merely the expression of the same thing. Seeing the pieces, he has done an example mentally and then has written it out. Let us write it according to the first form, which is, in reality, an analysis of this example:

$$\frac{1}{2} + \frac{1}{2} = \frac{1}{4} + \frac{1}{4} + \frac{1}{4} + \frac{1}{4}.$$

When the denominator is the same, the sum of the fractions is found by adding the numerators:

$$\frac{1}{2}+\frac{1}{2}=\frac{2}{2};\quad\frac{1}{4}+\frac{1}{4}+\frac{1}{4}+\frac{1}{4}=\frac{4}{4}.$$

The two halves make an entire circle, as do the four fourths.

Now let us fill a circle with different pieces: for example, with a half circle and two quarter circles. The result is $1=\frac{1}{2}+\frac{2}{4}$. And in the inset itself it is shown that $\frac{1}{2}=\frac{2}{4}$. If we should wish to fill the circle with the largest piece $(\frac{1}{2})$ combined with the fewest number of pieces possible, it would be necessary to withdraw the two quarter sectors and replace them by another half circle; result:

$$1=\frac{1}{2}+\frac{1}{2}=\frac{2}{2}=1.$$

Let us fill a circle with three $\frac{1}{5}$ sectors and four $\frac{1}{10}$ sectors:

$$1=\frac{3}{5}+\frac{4}{10}.$$

If the larger pieces are left in and the circle is then filled with the fewest number of pieces possible, it would necessitate replacing the four tenths by two fifths. Result:

$$1=\frac{3}{5}+\frac{2}{5}=\frac{5}{5}=1.$$

Let us fill the circle thus: $\frac{5}{10}+\frac{1}{4}+\frac{2}{8}=1.$

Now try to put in the largest pieces possible by substituting for several small pieces a large piece which is

equal to them.   In the space occupied by the five tenths
may be placed one half, and in that occupied by the two
eighths, one fourth; then the circle is filled thus:

$$1 = \frac{1}{2} + \frac{1}{4} + \frac{1}{4} = \frac{1}{2} + \frac{2}{4}.$$

We can continue to do the same thing, that is to replace the smaller pieces by as large a sector as possible,
and the two fourths can be replaced by another half circle.
Result:

$$1 = \frac{1}{2} + \frac{1}{2} = \frac{2}{2} = 1.$$

All these substitutions may be expressed in figures thus:

$$\frac{5}{10} + \frac{1}{4} + \frac{2}{8} = \frac{1}{2} + \frac{1}{4} + \frac{1}{4} =$$

$$\frac{1}{2} + \frac{2}{4} = \frac{1}{2} + \frac{1}{2} = \frac{2}{2} = 1.$$

This is one means of initiating a child intuitively into
the operations used for the reduction of fractions to their
lowest terms.

Improper fractions also interest them very much.
They come to these by adding a number of sectors which
fill two, three, or four circles.   To find the whole numbers which exist under the guise of fractions is a little
like putting away in their proper places the circular insets which have been all mixed up.   The children mani-
fest a desire to learn the real operations of fractions.
With improper fractions they originate most unusual
sums, like the following:

$$\frac{\left[8+\left(\frac{7}{7}+\frac{18}{9}+\frac{24}{2}\right)+1\right]}{8}=$$

$$\frac{[8+(1+2+12)+1]}{8}=$$

$$\frac{8+15+1}{8}=\frac{24}{8}=3.$$

We have a series of commands which may be used as a guide for the child's work. Here are some examples:

— Take $\frac{1}{5}$ of 25 beads

— Take $\frac{1}{4}$ " 36 counters

— Take $\frac{1}{6}$ " 24 beans

— Take $\frac{1}{3}$ " 27 beans

— Take $\frac{1}{10}$ " 40 beans

— Take $\frac{2}{5}$ " 60 counters

In this last there are two operations:

$$60 \div 5 = 12; \ 12 \times 2 = 24; \ \text{or} \ 2 \times 60 = 120;$$
$$120 \div 5 = 24, \text{ etc.}$$

REDUCTION OF COMMON FRACTIONS TO DECIMAL FRAC-TIONS: The material for this purpose is similar to that of the circular insets, except that the frame is white and is marked into ten equal parts, and each part is then sub-divided into ten. In these subdivisions the little line which marks the five is distinguished from the others by its greater length. Each of the larger divisions is marked respectively with the numbers, 10, 20, 30, 40, 50, 60, 70, 80, 90, and 0. The 0 is at the top and there is a raised radius against which are placed the sectors to be measured.

To reduce a common fraction to a decimal fraction the sector is placed carefully against the raised radius, with the arc touching the circumference of the inset. Where the arc ends there is a number which represents *the hundredths* corresponding to the sector. For example, if the $\frac{1}{4}$ sector is used its arc ends at 25; hence $\frac{1}{4}$ equals 0.25.

Page 275 shows in detail the practical method of using our material to reduce common fractions to decimal fractions. In the upper figure the segments correspond to

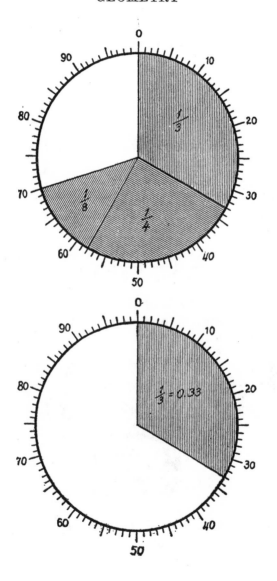

$\dfrac{1}{3}$, $\dfrac{1}{4}$, and $\dfrac{1}{8}$ of a circle are placed within the circle divided into hundredths.  Result:

$$\frac{1}{3} + \frac{1}{4} + \frac{1}{8} = 0.70.$$

The lower figure shows how the $\dfrac{1}{3}$ sector is placed:  $\dfrac{1}{3}$ $= 0.33$.

If instead we use the $\dfrac{1}{5}$ sector we have: $\dfrac{1}{5} = 0.20$, etc.

Numerous sectors may be placed within the circle; for example:

$$\frac{1}{4} + \frac{1}{7} + \frac{1}{9} + \frac{1}{10}.$$

In order to find the sum of the fraction reduced to decimals, it is necessary to read only the number at the outer edge of the last sector.

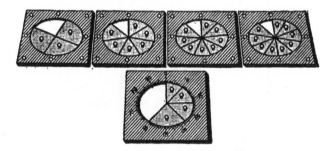

Using this as a basis, it is very easy to develop an arithmetical idea.  Instead of 1, which represents the whole circle, let us write 100, which represents its subdivisions when used for decimals, and let us divide the 100 into as many parts of a circle as there are sectors in the circle, and the reduction is made. All the parts which result are so many hundredths. Hence:

$$\frac{1}{4} = 100 \div 4 = 25 \text{ hundredths: that is, } \frac{25}{100} \text{ or } 0.25.$$

The division is performed by dividing the numerator by the demonator:

$$1 \div 4 = 0.25.$$

THIRD SERIES OF INSETS: *Equivalent Figures.* Two concepts were given by the squares divided into rectangles and triangles: that of fractions and that of equivalent figures.

There is a special material for the concept of fractions which, besides developing the intuitive notion of fractions, has permitted the solution of examples in fractions and of reducing fractions to decimals; and it has furthermore brought cognizance of other things, such as the measuring of angles in terms of degrees.

For the concept of equivalent figures there is still another material. This will lead to finding the area of different geometric forms and also to an intuition of some theorems which heretofore have been foreign to elementary schools, being considered beyond the understanding of a child.

MATERIAL: Showing that a triangle is equal to a rectangle which has one side equal to the base of the triangle, the other side equal to half of the altitude of the triangle.

In a large rectangular metal frame there are two white openings: the triangle and the equivalent rectangle. The pieces which compose the rectangle are such that they may fit into the openings of either the rectangle or the triangle. This demonstrates that the rectangle and the triangle are equivalent. The triangular space is filled by two pieces formed by a horizontal line drawn through the triangle parallel to the base and crossing at half the altitude. Taking the two pieces out and putting them one on top of the other the identity of the height may be verified.

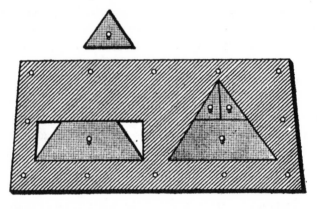

Already the work with the beads and the squaring of numbers has led to finding the area of a square by multiplying one side by the other; and in like manner the area of a rectangle is found by multiplying one side by the other. Since a triangle may be reduced to a rectangle, it is easy to find its area by multiplying the base by half the height.

MATERIAL: Showing that a rhombus is equal to a rectangle which has one side equal to one side of the rhombus and the other equal to the height of the rhombus.

The frame contains a rhombus divided by a diagonal line into two triangles and a rectangle filled with pieces which can be put into the rhombus when the triangles have been removed, and will fill it completely. In the material

there are also an entire rhombus and an entire rectangle.
If they are placed one on top of the other they will be

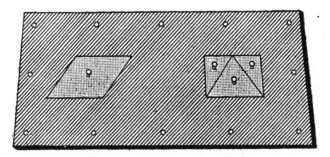

found to have the same height. As the equivalence of the
two figures is demonstrated by these pieces of the rectangle which may be used to fill in the two figures, it

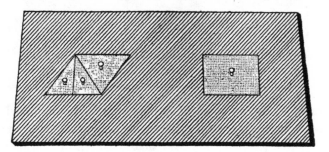

is easily seen that the area of a rhombus is found by multiplying the side or base by the height.

MATERIAL: To show the equivalence of a trapezoid
and a rectangle having one side equal to the sum of the
two bases and the other equal to half the height.

The child himself can make the other comparison: that
is, a trapezoid equals a rectangle having one side equal
to the height and the other equal to one-half the sum of

the bases. For the latter it is only necessary to cut the long rectangle in half and superimpose the two halves.

The large rectangular frame contains three openings: two equal trapezoids and the equivalent rectangle having one side equal to the sum of the two bases and the other side equal to half the height. One trapezoid is made of two pieces, being cut in half horizontally at the height of half its altitude; the identity in height may be proved by placing one piece on top of the other. The second

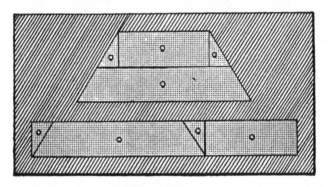

trapezoid is composed of pieces which can be placed in the rectangle, filling it completely. Thus the equivalence is proved and also the fact that the area of a trapezoid is found by multiplying the sum of the bases by half the height, or half the sum of the bases by the height.

With a ruler the children themselves actually calculate the area of the geometrical figures, and later calculate the area of their little tables, etc.

MATERIAL: To show the equivalence between a regular polygon and a rectangle having one side equal to the perimeter and the other equal to half of the hypotenuse.

In the material there are two decagon insets, one con-

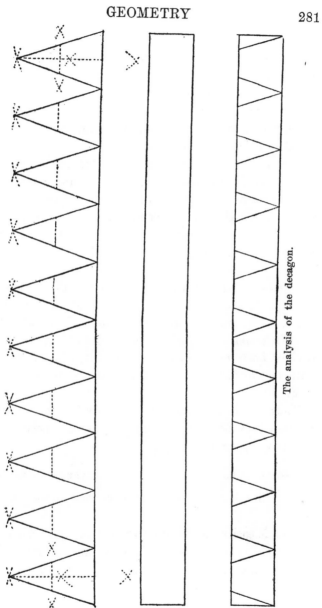

The analysis of the decagon.

sisting of a whole decagon and the other of a decagon divided into ten triangles.

Page 281 shows a table taken from our geometry portfolio, representing the equivalence of a decagon to a rectangle having one side equal to the perimeter and the other equal to half the hypotenuse.

The photograph shows the pieces of the insets — the decagon and the equivalent rectangle — and beneath each one there are the small equal triangles into which it can be subdivided. Here it is demonstrated that a rectangle equivalent to a decagon may have one side equal to the whole hypotenuse and the other equal to half of the perimeter.

Another inset shows the equivalence of the decagon and a rectangle which has one side equal to the perimeter of the decagon and the other equal to half of the altitude of each triangle composing the decagon. Small triangles divided horizontally in half can be fitted into this figure, with one of the upper triangles divided in half lengthwise.

Thus we demonstrate that the surface of a regular polygon may be found by multiplying the perimeter by half the hypotenuse.

### SOME THEOREMS BASED ON EQUIVALENT FIGURES

*A.* All triangles having the same base and altitude are equal.

This is easily understood from the fact that the area of a triangle is found by multiplying the base by half the altitude; therefore triangles having the same base and the same altitude must be equal.

For the inductive demonstration of this theorem we have the following material: The rhombus and the equiv-

The bead number cubes built into a tower.

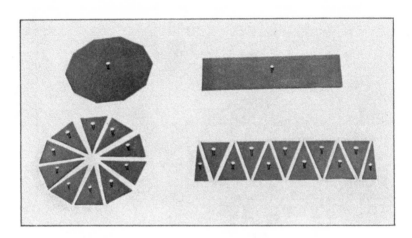

The decagon and the rectangle can be composed of the same triangular
insets.

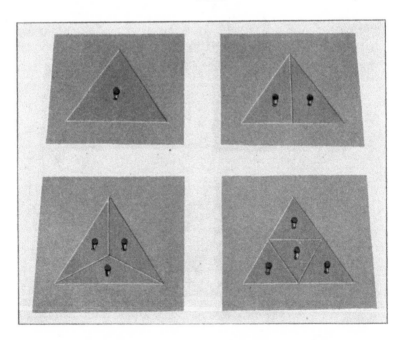

The triangular insets fitted into their metal plates.

alent rectangle are each divided into two triangles. The triangles of the rhombus are different, for they are divided by opposite diagonal lines. The three different triangles resulting from these divisions have the same base (this can be actually verified by measuring the bases of the different pieces) and fit into the same long rectangle which is found below the first three figures. Therefore, it is demonstrated that the three triangles have the same altitude. They are equivalent because each one is the half of an equivalent figure.,

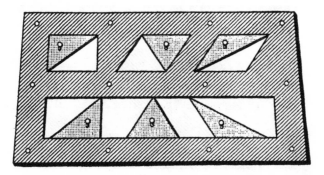

B. The Theorem of Pythagoras: In a right-angled triangle the square of the hypotenuse is equal to the sum of the squares of the two sides.

Material: The material illustrates three different cases:

> First case: In which the two sides of the triangle are equal.
> Second case: In which the two sides are in the proportion of 3:4.
> Third case: General.

*First case:* The demonstration of this first case affords an impressive induction.

In the frame for this, shown below, the squares of the
two sides are divided in half by a diagonal line so as to
form two triangles and the square of the hypotenuse is
divided by two diagonal lines into four triangles. The
eight resulting triangles are all identical; hence the triangles of the squares of the two sides will fill the square
of the hypotenuse; and, vice versa, the four triangles of
the square of the hypotenuse may be used to fill the two
squares of the sides. The substitution of these different

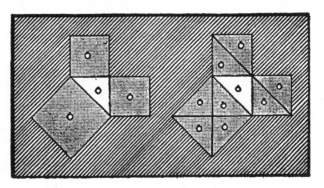

pieces is very interesting, and all the more because the triangles of the squares of the sides are all of the same color,
whereas the triangles formed in the square of the hypotenuse are of a different color.

*Second case:* Where the sides are as the proportion
of $3:4$.

In this figure the three squares are filled with small
squares of three different colors, arranged as follows: in
the square on the shorter side, $3^2 = 9$; in that on the
larger side, $4^2 = 16$; in that on the hypotenuse, $5^2 = 25$.

The substitution game suggests itself. The two
squares formed on the sides can be entirely filled by
the small squares composing the square on the hypotenuse,

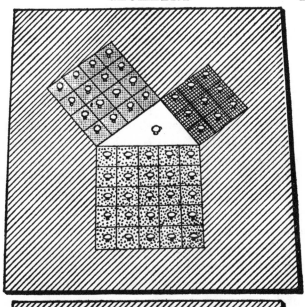

Second Case

so that they are both of the same color; while the square
formed on the hypotenuse can be filled with varied designs
by various combinations of the small squares of the sides
which are in two different colors.

*Third case:* This is the general case.

The large frame is somewhat complicated and difficult
to describe. It develops a considerable intellectual exercise. The entire frame measures 44 × 24 cm. and may
be likened to a chess-board, where the movable pieces are
susceptible of various combinations. The principles already proved or inductively suggested which lead to the
demonstration of the theorem are:

(1) That two quadrilaterals having an equal base and
equal altitude are equivalent.

(2) That two figures equivalent to a third figure are
equivalent to each other.

In this figure the square formed on the hypotenuse is
divided into two rectangles. The additional side is determined by the division made in the hypotenuse by
dropping a perpendicular line from the apex of the triangle to the hypotenuse. There are also two rhomboids
in this frame, each of which has one side equal respectively to the large and to the small square of the sides
of the triangle and the other side equal to the hypotenuse.

The shorter altitude of the two rhomboids, as may be
seen in the figure itself, corresponds to the respective alti-
tudes, or shorter sides, of the rectangles. But the longer
side corresponds respectively to the side of the larger and
of the smaller squares of the sides of the triangle.

It is not necessary that these corresponding dimensions
be known by the child. He sees red and yellow pieces of
an inset and simply moves them about, placing them in
the indentures of the frame. It is the fact that these

movable pieces actually fit into this white background which gives the child the opportunity for reasoning out the theorem, and not the abstract idea of the corresponding relations between the dimensions of the sides and the different heights of the figures. Reduced to these terms the exercise is easily performed and proves very interesting.

This material may be used for other demonstrations:

DEMONSTRATION A: *The substitution of the pieces.* Let us start with the frame as it should be filled originally. First take out the two rectangles formed on the hypotenuse; place them in the two lateral grooves, and lower the triangle. Fill the remaining empty space with the two rhomboids.

The same space is filled in both cases with:

A triangle plus two rectangles, and then
A triangle plus two rhomboids.

Hence the sum of the two rectangles (which form the square of the hypotenuse) is equal to the sum of the two rhomboids.

In a later substitution we consider the rhomboids instead of the rectangles in order to demonstrate their respective equivalence to the two squares formed on the sides of the triangle. Beginning, for example with the larger square, we start with the insets in the original position and consider the space occupied by the triangle and the larger square. To analyze this space the pieces are all taken out and then it is filled successively by:

The triangle and the large square in their original positions.
The triangle and the large rhomboid.

DEMONSTRATION B:   *Based on Equivalence.*   In this second demonstration the relative equivalence of the rhomboid, the rectangles, and the squares is shown outside the figure by means of the parallel indentures which are on both sides of the frame.   These indentures, when the pieces are placed in them, show that the pieces have the same altitude.

This is the manner of procedure:   Starting again with the original position, take out the two rectangles and place them in the parallel indentures to the left, the larger in the wider indenture and the smaller in the narrower indenture.   The different figures in the same indenture have the same altitude; therefore the pieces need only to be placed together at the base to prove that they are equal — hence the figures are equal in pairs: the smaller rectangle equals the smaller rhomboid and the larger rectangle equals the larger rhomboid.

Starting again from the original position you proceed analogously with the squares.   In the parallel indentures to the right the large square may be placed in the same indenture with the large rhomboid, which, however, must be turned in the opposite direction (in the direction of its greatest length); and the smaller square and the smaller rhomboid fit into the narrower indenture.   They have the same altitude; and that the bases are equal is easily verified by putting them together; therefore here is proof that the squares and the rhomboids are respectively equivalent.

Rectangles and squares which are equivalent to the same rhomboids are equivalent to each other.   Hence the theorem is proved.

·       ·       ·       ·       ·       ·       ·       ·

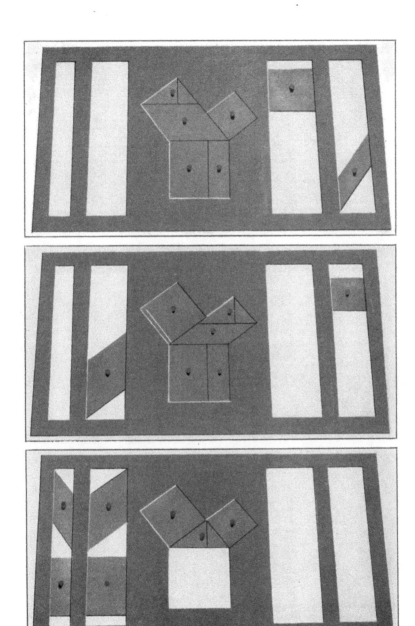

Showing that the two rhomboids are equal to the two rectangles.

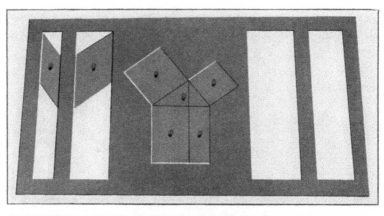

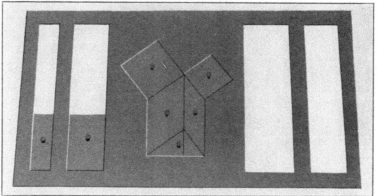

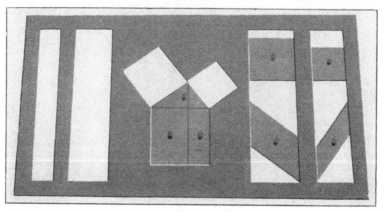

Showing that the two rhomboids are equal to the two squares.

This series of geometric material is used for other purposes, but they are of minor importance.

FOURTH SERIES OF INSETS: *Division of a Triangle.* This material is made up of four frames of equal size, each containing an equilateral triangle measuring ten centimeters to a side. The different pieces should fill the triangular spaces exactly.

One is filled by an entire equilateral triangle.

One is filled by two rectangular scalene triangles, each

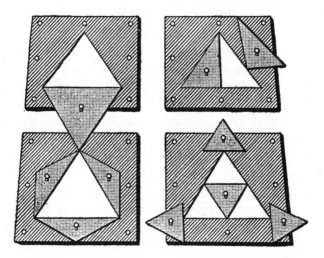

equal to half of the original equilateral triangle, which is bisected by dropping a line perpendicularly to the base.

The third is filled by three obtuse isosceles triangles, formed by lines bisecting the three angles of. the original triangle.

The fourth is divided into four equilateral triangles which are similar in shape to the original triangle.

With these triangles a child can make a more exact analytical study than he made when he was observing the triangles of the plane insets used in the "Children's House." He measures the degrees of the angles and learns to distinguish a right angle (90°) from an acute angle (<90°) and from an obtuse angle (>90°).

Furthermore he finds in measuring the angles of any triangle that their sum is always equal to 180° or to two right angles.

He can observe that in equilateral triangles all the angles are equal (60°); that in the isosceles triangle the two angles at the opposite ends of the unequal side are equal; while in the scalene triangle no two angles are alike. In the right-angled triangle the sum of the two acute angles is equal to a right angle. A general definition is that those triangles are similar in which the corresponding angles are equal. )

MATERIAL FOR INSCRIBED AND CONCENTRIC FIGURES: In this material, which for the most part is made up of that already described, and which is therefore merely an application of it, inscribed or concentric figures may be placed in the white background of the different inset frames. For example, on the white background of the large equilateral triangle the small red equilateral triangle, which is a fourth of it, may be placed in such a way that each vertex is tangent to the middle of each side of the larger triangle.

There are also two squares, one of 7 centimeters on a side and the other 3.5. They have their respective frames with white backgrounds. The 7 centimeters square may be placed on the background of the 10 centimeters square in such a way that each corner touches the middle of each side of the frame. In like manner the 5 centimeters square, which is a fourth of the large square, may be put in the 7 centimeters square; the 3.5 centimeters square in the 5 centimeters square; and finally the tiny square, which is $\frac{1}{16}$ part of the large square, in the 3.5 centimeters square.

There is also a circle which is tangent to the edges of the large equilateral triangle. This circle may be placed on the background of the 10 centimeters circle, and in that case a white circular strip remains all the way round (concentric circles). Within this circle the smaller equilateral triangle ($\frac{1}{4}$ of the large triangle) is perfectly inscribed. Then there is a small circle which is tangent to the smallest equilateral triangle.

Besides these circles which are used with the triangles there are two others tangent to the squares: one to the 7 centimeters square and the other to the 3.5 centimeters square. The large circle, 10 centimeters in diameter, fits exactly into the 10 centimeters square; and the other circles are concentric to it.

These corresponding relations make the figures easily adaptable to our artistic composition of decorative design (see following chapter).

Finally, together with the other material, there are two stars which are also used for decorative design. The two stars, or " flowers," are based on the 3.5 centimeters square. In one the circle rests on the side as a semi-circle (simple flower); and in the other the same circle goes around the vertex and beyond the semi-circle until it meets the reciprocal of four circles (flower and foliage).

# III

## SOLID GEOMETRY

Since the children already know how to find the area of ordinary geometric forms it is very easy, with the knowledge of the arithmetic they have acquired through work with the beads (the square and cube of numbers), to initiate them into the manner of finding the volume of solids. After having studied the cube of numbers by the aid of the cube of beads it is easy to recognize the fact that the volume of a prism is found by multiplying the area by the altitude.

In our didactic material we have three objects for solid geometry: a prism, a pyramid having the same base and altitude, and a prism with the same base but with only one-third the altitude. They are all empty. The two prisms have a cover and are really boxes; the uncovered pyramid can be filled with different substances and then emptied, serving as a sort of scoop.

These solids may be filled with wheat or sand. Thus we put into practise the same technique as is used to calculate capacity, as in anthropology, for instance, when we wish to measure the capacity of a cranium.

It is difficult to fill a receptacle completely in such a way that the measured result does not vary; so we usually put in a scarce measure, which therefore does not correspond to the exact volume but to a smaller volume.

One must know how to fill a receptacle, just as one

must know how to do up a bundle, so that the various objects may take up the least possible space. The children like this exercise of shaking the receptacle and getting in as great a quantity as possible; and they like to level it off when it is entirely filled.

The receptacles may be filled also with liquids. In this case the child must be careful to pour out the contents without losing a single drop. This technical drill serves as a preparation for using metric measures.

By these experiments the child finds that the pyramid has the same volume as the small prism (which is one-third of the large prism); hence the volume of the pyramid is found by multiplying the area of the base by one-third the altitude. The small prism may be filled with clay and the same piece of clay will be found to fill the pyramid. The two solids of equal volume may be made of clay. All three solids can be made by taking five times as much clay as is needed to fill the same prism.

. . . . . . . .

Having mastered these fundamental ideas, it is easy to study the rest, and few explanations will be needed.

In many cases the incentive to do original problems may be developed by giving the children definite examples: as, how can the area of a circle be found? the volume of a cylinder? of a cone? Problems on the total area of some solids also may be suggested. Many times the children will risk spontaneous inductions and often of their own accord proceed to measure the total surface area of all the solids at their disposal, even going back to the materials used in the " Children's House."

The material includes a series of wooden solids with a base measurement of 10 cm.:

A quadrangular parallelopiped (10 × 10 × 20 cm.)
A quadrangular parallelopiped equal to ⅓ of above
A quadrangular pyramid (10 × 10 × 20 cm.)
A triangular prism (10 × 20 cm.)
A triangular prism equal to ⅓ of above
The corresponding pyramid (10 × 20 cm.)
A cylinder (10 cm. diameter, 20 altitude)
A cylinder equal to ⅓ of above
A cone (10 cm. diameter, 20 altitude)
A sphere (10 cm. diameter)
An ovoid (maximum diameter 10 cm.)
An ellipsoid (maximum diameter 10 cm.)
  Regular Polyhedrons
Tetrahedron
Hexahedron (cube)
Octahedron
Dodecahedron
Icosahedron
(The faces of these polyhedrons are in different colors.)

APPLICATIONS: *The Powers of Numbers.*

MATERIAL: Two equal cubes of 2 cm. on a side; a prism twice the size of the cubes; a prism double this preceding prism; seven cubes 4 cm. on a side.
The following combinations are made:

The two smaller cubes are placed side by side = 2.
In front of these is placed the prism which is twice as large as the cube = $2^2$.
On top of these is placed the double prism, making a cube with 4 cm. on a side = $2^3$.
One of the seven cubes is put beside this = $2^4$.

In front are placed two more of the seven cubes $= 2^5$.

On top are put the remaining four equal cubes $= 2^6$.

In this way we have made a cube measuring 8 cm. on a side. From this we see that:

2$^3$, 2$^6$ have the form of a cube.
2$^2$, 2$^5$ have the form of a square.
2 , 2$^4$ have a linear form.

*The Cube of a Binomial:* $(a + b)^3 = a^3 + b^3 + 3a^2b + 3b^2a.$

MATERIAL: A cube with a 6 cm. edge, a cube with a 4 cm. edge; three prisms with a square base of 4 cm. on a side and 6 cm. high; three prisms with a square base of 6 cm. to a side and 4 cm. high. The 10 cm. cube can be made with these.

These two combinations are in special cube-shaped boxes into which the 10 cm. cube fits exactly.

.    .    .    .    .    .    .    .

*Weights and Measures:* All that refers to weights and measures is merely an application of similar operations and reasonings.

The children have at their disposal and learn to handle many of the objects which are used for measuring both in commerce and in every-day life. In the " Children's House" days they had the long stair rods which contain the meter and its decimeter subdivisions. Here they have a tape-measure with which they measure floors, etc., and find the area. They have the meter in many forms: in the anthropometer, in the ruler. Then, too, they use the metal tape, the dressmaker's tape measure, and the meterstick used by merchants.

The twenty centimeter ruler divided into millimeters they use constantly in design; and they love to calculate the area of the geometric figures they have designed or of the metal insets. Often they calculate the surface of the white background of an inset and that of the different pieces which exactly fit this opening, so as to verify the former. As they already have some preparation in decimals it is no task for them to recognize and to remember that the measures increase by tens and take on new names each time. The exercises in grammar have greatly facilitated the increase in their vocabulary.

They calculate the reciprocal relations between length, surface, and volume by going back to the three sets which first represented "long," "thick," and "large."

The objects which differ in length vary by 10's; those differing in areas vary by 100's; and those which differ in volume vary by 1000's.

The comparison between the bead material and the cubes of the pink tower (one of the first things they built) encourages a more profound study of the sensory objects which were once the subject of assiduous application.

By the aid of the double decimeter the children make the calculations for finding the volume of all the different objects graded by tens, such as the rods, the prisms of the broad stair, the cubes of the pink tower.

By taking the extremes in each case they learn the relations between objects which differ in one dimension, in two dimensions, and in three dimensions. Besides, they already know that the square of 10 is 100, and the cube of 10 is 1000.

. . . . . . . . .

Hollow geometric solids, used for determining equivalence by measuring sand, sugar, etc.

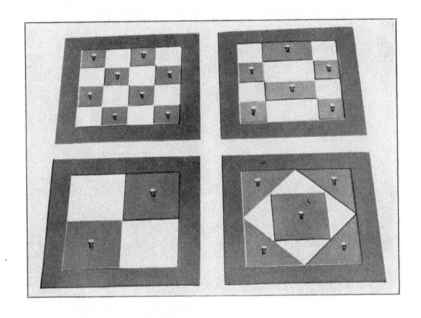

Designs formed by arranging sections of the insets within the frames.

The children make use of various scientific instruments: thermometers, distillers, scales, and, as previously stated, the principal measures commonly used.

By filling an empty metal cubical decimeter, which like the geometric solids is used for the calculation of volume, they have a liter measure of water, which may be poured into a glass liter bottle. All the decimal multiples and subdivisions of the liter are easily understood. Our children spent much time pouring liquids into all the small measures used in commerce for measuring wine and oil.

They distil water with the distiller. They use the thermometer to measure the temperature of water in ebullition and the temperature of the freezing mixture. They take the water which is used to determine the weight of the kilogram, keeping it at the temperature of 4° C.

The objects which serve to measure capacity also are at the disposal of the children.

There is no need to go into more details upon the multitudinous consequences resulting from both a methodical preparation of the intellect and the possibility of actually being in contact with real objects.

A great number of problems given by us, as well as problems originated by the children themselves, bear witness to the ease with which external effects may be spontaneously produced when once the inner *causes* have been adequately stimulated.

PART V

DRAWING

# I

## LINEAR GEOMETRIC DESIGN DECORATION

I already have mentioned the fact that the material of the geometric insets may be applied also to design.

It is through design that the child may be led to ponder on the geometric figures which he has handled, taken out, combined in numerous ways, and replaced. In doing this he completes an exercise necessitating much use of the reasoning faculties. Indeed, he reproduces all of the figures by linear design, learning to handle many instruments — the centimeter ruler, the double decimeter, the square, the protractor, the compass, and the steel pen used for line ruling. For this work we have included in the geometric material a large portfolio where, together with the pages reproducing the figures, there are also some illustrative sheets with brief explanations of the figures and containing the relative nomenclature. Aside from copying designs the child may copy also the explanatory notes and thus reproduce the whole geometry portfolio. These explanatory notes are very simple. Here, for example, is the one which refers to the square:

"Square: The side or base is divided into 10 cm. All the other sides are equal, hence each measures 10 cm. The square has four equal sides and four equal angles which are always right angles. The number 4 and the identity of the sides and angles are the distinguishing characteristics of the square."

The children measure paper and construct the figure

301

with attention and application that are truly remarkable. They love to handle the compasses and are very proud of possessing a pair.

One child asked her mother for a Christmas gift of "one *last* doll and a box of compasses," as if she were ending one epoch of her life and beginning another. One little boy begged his mother to let him accompany her when she went to buy the compass for him. When they were in the store the salesman was surprised to find that so young a child was to use the compass and gave them a box of the simplest kind. "Not those," protested the little fellow; "I want an engineer's compass;" and he picked out one of the most complicated ones. This was the very reason why he was so anxious to go with his mother.

As the children draw, they learn many particulars concerning the geometric figures: the sides, angles, bases, centers, median lines, radii, diameters, sectors, segments, diagonals, hypotenuses, circumferences, perimeters, etc. They do not, however, learn all this as so much dry information nor do they limit themselves to reproducing the designs in the geometry portfolio. Each child adds to his own portfolio other designs which he chooses and sometimes originates. The designs reproduced in the portfolio are drawn on plain white drawing paper with China inks, but the children's special designs are drawn on colored paper with different colored inks and with gildings (silver, gold). The children reproduce the geometric figures and then they fill them in with decorations made either with pen or water-colors. These decorations serve especially to emphasize, in a geometric analysis, the various parts of the figure, such as center, angles, circumference, medians, diagonals, etc.

The decorated motif is selected or else invented by the child himself. He is allowed the same freedom of choice in his backgrounds as he enjoys for his inks or water-colors. The observation of nature (flowers and their different parts — pollen, leaves, a section of some part observed under the microscope, plant seeds, shells, etc.) serves to nourish the child's æsthetic imagination. The children also have access to artistic designs, collections of photographs reproducing the great masterpieces, and Haeckel's famous work, *Nature's Artistic Forms,* all of which equipment is so interesting and delightful to a child.

The children work many, many hours on drawing. This is the time we seize for reading to them (see above p. 197) and almost all their history is learned during this quiet period of copy and simple decoration which is so conducive to concentration of thought.

Copying some design, or drawing a decoration which has been directly inspired by something seen; the choice of colors to fill in a geometric figure or to bring out, by small and simple designs, the center or side of the figure; the mechanical act of mixing a color, of dissolving the gildings, or of choosing one kind of ink from a series of different colors; sharpening a pencil, or getting one's paper in the proper position; determining through tentative means the required extension of the compass — all this is a complex operation requiring patience and exactitude. But it does not require great intellectual concentration. It is, therefore, a work of application rather than of inspiration; and the observation of each detail, in order to reproduce it exactly, clarifies and rests the mind instead of rousing it to the intense activity demanded by the labor of association and creation. The child is busy with his hands rather than with his mind; but yet his mind is sufficiently stimulated by this work as not easily to wander away into the world of dreams.

These are quiet hours of work in which the children use only a part of their energies, while the other part is reaching out after something else; just as a family sits quietly by the fireside in long winter evenings engaged in light manual labors requiring little intelligence, watching the flames with a sense of enjoyment, willing to pass in this way many peaceful hours, yet feeling that a certain side of their needs is not satisfied. This is the time chosen for story telling or for light reading. Similarly this is the best time for our little children to listen to reading of all kinds.

During these hours they listened to the reading of books like *The Betrothed* (of Manzoni), psychological books like Itard's *Education of the Savage of Aveyron,* or historical narratives. The children took a deep interest in the reading. Each child may be occupied with his own design as well as with the facts which he is hearing described. It seems as though the one occupation furnishes the energy necessary for perfection in the other. The mechanical attention which the child gives to his design frees his mind from idle dreaming and renders it more capable of completely absorbing the reading that is going on; and the pleasure gained from the reading which, little by little, penetrates his whole being seems to give new energy to both hand and eye. His lines become most exact and the colors more delicate.

When the reading has reached some point of climax we hear remarks, exclamations, applause or discussions, which animate and lighten the work without interrupting it. But there are times when, with one accord, our children abandon their drawing so as to act out some humorous selection or to represent an historical fact which has touched them deeply; or, indeed, as happened during the reading of the *Savage of Aveyron,* their hands remained almost unconsciously raised in the intensity of their emotion, while on their faces was an expression of ecstasy, as if they were witnessing wonderful unheard-of things. Their actions seemed to interpret the well-known sentiment: "Never have I seen woman like unto this."

ARTISTIC COMPOSITION WITH THE INSETS: Our geometric insets, which are all definitely related to one another in dimensions and include a series of figures which can be contained one within the other, lend themselves to very beautiful combinations. With these the children make real creations and often follow out their artistic ideas for days and even weeks. By moving the small pieces or by combining them in different ways on the white background, these very insets produce various decorations. The ease with which the child may form designs by arranging the little pieces of iron on a sheet of paper and then outlining them, and the harmony which is thus so easily obtained, affords endless delight. Really wonderful pieces of work are often produced in this way.

During these periods of creative design, as indeed during the periods of drawing from life, the child is deeply and wholly concentrated. His entire intellect is at work and no kind of instructive reading would be at all fitting while he is engaged in drawing or designing of this nature.

With the insets, as we have said, we have reproduced some of the classic decorations so greatly admired in the

Italian masterpieces; for instance, those of Giotto in Florentine Art. When the children try with the insets to reproduce these classic decorations from photographs they are led to make most minute observations, which may be considered a real study of art. They judge the relative proportions of the various figures in such a way that their eye learns to appreciate the harmony of the work. And thus, even in childhood, a fine æsthetic enjoyment begins to engage their minds on the higher and more noble planes.

## II

## FREE-HAND DRAWING—STUDIES FROM LIFE

All the preceding exercises are "formative" for the art of drawing. They develop in the child the manual ability to execute a geometric design and prepare his eye to appreciate the harmony of proportions between geometric figures. The countless observations of drawings, the habit of minute examination of natural objects, constitute so many preparatory drills. We can, however, say that the whole method, educating the eye and the hand at the same time and training the child to observe and execute drawings with intense application, prepares the mechanical means for design, while the mind, left free to take its flight and to create, is ready to produce.

It is by developing the individual that he is prepared for that wonderful manifestation of the human intelligence, which drawing constitutes. The ability *to see reality* in form, in color, in proportion, to be master of the movements of one's own hand — that is what is necessary. Inspiration is an individual thing, and when a child possesses these formative elements he can give expression to all he happens to have.

There can be no "graduated exercises in drawing" leading up to an artistic creation. That goal can be attained only through the development of mechanical technique and through the freedom of the spirit. That

307

is our reason for not teaching drawing directly to the child. We prepare him indirectly, leaving him free to the mysterious and divine labor of reproducing things according to his own feelings. Thus drawing comes to satisfy a need for expression, as does language; and almost every idea may seek expression in drawing. The effort to perfect such expression is very similar to that which the child makes when he is spurred on to perfect his language in order to see his thoughts translated into reality. This effort is spontaneous; and the real drawing teacher is in the inner life, which of itself develops, attains refinement, and seeks irresistibly to be born into external existence in some empirical form. Even the smallest children try spontaneously to draw outlines of the objects which they see; but the hideous drawings which are exhibited in the common schools, as "free drawings" "characteristic" of childhood, are not found among our children. These horrible daubs so carefully collected, observed, and catalogued by modern psychologists as "documents of the infant mind" are nothing but monstrous expressions of intellectual lawlessness; they show only that the eye of their child is uneducated, the hand inert, the mind insensible alike to the beautiful and to the ugly, blind to the true as well as to the false. Like most documents collected by psychologists who study the children of our schools, they reveal not the soul but the errors of the soul; and these drawings, with their monstrous deformities, show simply what the uneducated human being is like.

Such things are not "free drawings" by children. *Free drawings* are possible only when we have a *free child* who has been left free to grow and perfect himself in the assimilation of his surroundings and in mechanical reproduction; and who when left free to create and express himself actually does create and express himself.

The sensory and manual preparation for drawing is nothing more than an alphabet; but without it the child is an illiterate and cannot express himself. And just as it is impossible to study the writing of people who cannot write, so there can be no psychological study of the drawings of children who have been abandoned to spiritual and muscular chaos. All psychic expressions acquire value when the inner personality has acquired value by the development of its formative processes. Until this fundamental principle has become an absolute acquisition we can have no idea of the psychology of a child as regards his creative powers.

Thus, unless we know how a child should develop in order to unfold his natural energies, we shall not know how drawing as a natural expression is developed. The universal development of the wondrous language of the hand will come not from a " school of design " but from a " school of the new man " which will cause this language to spring forth spontaneously like water from an inexhaustible spring. To confer the gift of drawing we must create an eye that sees, a hand that obeys, a soul that feels; and in this task the whole life must cooperate. In this sense life itself is the only preparation for drawing. Once we have lived, the inner spark of vision does the rest.

Leave to man then this sublime gesture which transfers to the canvas the marks of creative divinity. Leave it free to develop from the very time when the tiny child takes a piece of chalk and reproduces a simple outline on the blackboard, when he sees a leaf and makes his first reproduction of it on the white page. Such a child is in

Designs formed by the use of the geometry squares, circles, and equilateral triangle, modified by free-hand drawing. In the design on the right the "flower" within the cross is made with compasses; the decorative detail in the arms of the cross and the circle in the center are free-hand. The design on the left is similar to a decoration in the Cathedral at Florence, in the windows round the apse.

310

Decorations formed by the use of the geometry insets. That on the right is
a copy of the design by Giotto shown below the picture of the Madonna
in the Upper Church of St. Francis d'Assisi (Umbria).

search of every possible means of expression, because
no one language is rich enough to give expression to the
gushing life within him. He speaks, he writes, he draws,
he sings like a nightingale warbling in the springtime.

Let us consider, then, the "elements" which our children have acquired in their development with reference
to drawing: they are observers of reality, knowing how to
distinguish the *forms* and *colors* they see there.

Children are peculiarly sensitive in their appreciation
of color. This sensibility began to grow in the sensory
exercises in the early years. Their hands have been
trained to the most delicate movements and the children
have been masters of them since the days of the "Children's House." When they begin to draw outlines they
copy the most diverse objects — not only flowers but
everything which interests them: vases, columns and even
landscapes. Their attempts are spontaneous; and they
draw both on the blackboard and on paper.

As regards colors, it should be recalled that while still
in the "Children's House" the children learned to prepare the different shades, mixing them themselves and
making the various blends. This always held their
eager interest. Later the care with which they seek to
get shades corresponding exactly to natural colorings is
something truly remarkable.[1] Over and over again the
children try to mix the most diverse colors, diluting or
saturating them until they have succeeded in reproducing
the desired shade. It is surprising also to see how often
their eye succeeds in appreciating the finest differences

---

[1] We give to the children first only tubes containing the three fundamental colors, red, yellow, and blue; and with these they produce a
large number of shades.

Making decorative designs with the aid of geometric insets. (*The Washington Montessori School, Washington, D. C.*)

Water-color paintings from nature, showing spontaneous expression resulting from work in natural science.

of color and in reproducing them with striking accuracy.

The study of natural science proved to be a great help in drawing. Once I tried to show some children how a flower should be dissected, and for this purpose I provided all the necessary instruments: the botanist's needle, pincers, thin glass plates, etc., just as is done at the university for the experiments in natural science. My only aim was to see whether the preparations which university students make for botanical anatomy were in any way adaptable to the needs of little children. Even at the time when I studied in the botanical laboratory at the university I felt that these exercises in the preparation of material might be put to such use. Students know how difficult it is to prepare a stem, a stamen, an epithelium, for dissection, and how only with difficulty the hand, accustomed for years exclusively to writing, adapts itself to this delicate work. Seeing how skilful our children were with their little hands I decided to give them a complete scientific outfit and to test by experiment whether the child mind and the characteristic manual dexterity shown by children were not more adapted to such labors than the mind and hand of a nineteen-year-old student.

My suspicion proved correct. The children with the keenest interest dissected a section of the violet with remarkable accuracy, and they quickly learned to use all the instruments. But my greatest surprise was to find that they did not despise or throw away the dissected parts, as we older students used to do. With great care they placed them all in attractive order on a piece of white paper, as if they had in mind some secret purpose. Then with great joy they began to draw them; and they were accurate, skilled, tireless, and patient, as they are in everything else. They began to mix and dilute their colors to obtain the correct shades. They worked up to the last minute of the school session, finishing off their designs in watercolor: the stem and leaves green, the in-

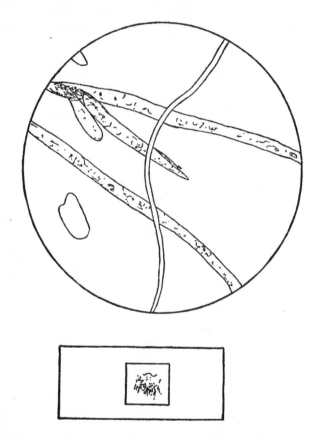

dividual petals violet, the stamens — all in a row — yellow, and the dissected pistil light green. The following day a little girl brought me a charmingly vivacious written composition, in which she told of her enthusiasm over the new work, describing even the less noticeable details of the little violet.

These two expressions — drawing and composition — were the spontaneous manifestations of their happy entrance into the realms of science.

Encouraged by this great success, I took some simple microscopes to school. The children began to observe the pollen and even some of the membrane coverings of the flower. By themselves they made some splendid cross-sections of the stems, which they studied most attentively.

They "drew everything they saw." Drawing seemed to be the natural complement of their observation work.

In this way the children learned to draw and paint *without a drawing teacher*. They produced works which, in geometric designs as well as in studies from life, were considered far above the average drawings of children.

PART VI

MUSIC

# I

## THE SCALE

Since the publication of my first volume on the education of small children, considerable progress has been made in the matter of musical education. Miss Maccheroni, who came to Rome to work with me on experiments looking to the continuation of the methods used with primary classes, was successful in establishing a number of tests which constituted our first steps into this important field of education. We are under great obligations to the Tronci firm of Pistoja, which took charge of the manufacture of materials and gave us the most sympathetic cooperation.

We had already prepared at the time of that first publication an equipment of bells to be used in training the ear to perceive differences between musical sounds. The methods of using this material were considerably modified and perfected again after the publication of my *Own Handbook* (New York, Stokes, 1914), in which for the first time appeared a treatise on musical method. The foundation of the system consists of a series of bells representing the whole tones and semi-tones of one octave. The material follows the general characteristics of that used in the sensorial method, that is, the objects differ from each other in one and only one quality, the one which concerns the stimulation of the sense under education. The bells, for instance, must be *apparently identical* in

319

dimensions, shape, etc., but they must *produce different sounds.* The basic exercise is to have the child recognize " identities." He must pair off the bells which give the same sound.

The bell system is constructed as follows: We have a very simple support, made of wood (of course any other material might be used) 115 cm. long and 25 cm. wide. On this the bells rest. The board is wide enough to hold

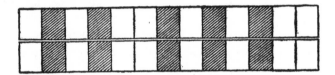

two bells placed lengthwise and end to end across it. The board is marked off into black and white spaces, each wide enough to hold one bell. The white spaces represent whole tones, the black spaces semi-tones. Though the apparent purpose of this board is to serve as a support, it is in reality a *measure,* since it indicates the regular position of the notes in the simple diatonic scale. The combination of white and black rectangles indicates the interval between the various notes in the scale: in other words, a semi-tone between the third and fourth and between the seventh and eighth, and a whole tone between the others. Bells showing the value of each rectangle are fixed in proper order in the upper portion of the support. These bells are not all of the same size, but vary in dimension regularly from the bottom to the top of the scale. This permits considerable saving in manufacture; for, to get a different sound from bells of the same size, different thicknesses are required, and this entails more labor for construction and consequently greater cost. But in addition the child here sees a material variation corresponding to the differences in quality of sound. On the other hand, the other bells on which the child is to perform his critical exercises are of *identical dimensions.*

In the exercise the child strikes with a small mallet one of the bells fixed on the support. Then, from among the others scattered at random on the table, he finds one which gives the same sound and places it on the board in front of the fixed bell corresponding to it. In the most elementary exercises, only the whole tone bells corresponding to the white spaces are used. Later, the semitones are brought in. This first exercise in sense percep-, tion corresponds to the pairing practised in other sensory exercises (color, touch, etc.) The next step is for the child to distinguish differences, and at the same time, gradations of stimuli (like the exercises with the color charts, hearing, etc.) In this case the child mixes at random the eight bells, all of the same size, which give the whole tones of the scale. He is to find *do,* then *re,* and so on through the octave one note after the other, placing the bells in order in their proper places. Nomenclature is taught step by step as in the other sensorial exercises. To familiarize the child with the names, *do, re, mi, fa, sol, la, si,* we use small round disks, the circular form serving to suggest the head of the written note. On each disk the name of the note is written. The disks are to be placed on the bases of the bells that correspond to them. The exercises in naming the notes may be begun with the fixed bells, in order (with children who already know how to read) to associate the sounds with their names in the first exercise of pairing. Later, when the child comes to the exercise of putting the bells in gradation, he can place the corresponding disk on each bell as he finds it.

Some individuals, commenting on this material, have solemnly protested their native inability to understand music, insisting that music reveals its secrets only to a chosen few. We may point out in reply that, so far, our principal object is simply to distinguish notes so widely different from each other that the different number of vibrations can easily be measured with instruments. It is a question of a material difference which any normal ear can naturally detect without any miraculous aptitude of a musical character. One might as well claim that it is the privilege only of genius to distinguish one color from another somewhat like it. Particular aptitude for music is determined by conditions of a quite different and a much higher order, such as intuition of the laws of harmony and counterpoint, inspiration for composition, and so on.

In actual practise, we found that when the material was used with some restrictions by forty children between three and six years of age, only six or seven proved capable of filling out the major scale by ear. But when the material was freely placed at their disposal, they all progressed along the same lines and showed about the same rate of improvement, as was the case in our experiments with reading, writing, etc. When individual differences appeared, it was by no means due to the *possibility* of performing these tasks, but rather to the amount of *interest* taken in the exercises, for which some children showed actual enthusiasm. Eagerness for surmounting difficulties and for high attainment is much more frequently found in children than we, judging by our own experience as adults, easily suspect. In any event, actual performance is the only guide to the revelation of particular aptitude, of personal calling.

When one of the larger children spreads on the table the eight bells of similar size to make up the scale by ear, the little ones pick up a single bell, sometimes reaching out for it with the greatest eagerness. They beat it with the mallet for a long time, they feel of it, examining it carefully, making it ring more and more slowly. The older children take special interest in the pairing, often repeating the same exercise many times; but an unusual charm is found in the successive sounds of the eight bells when placed in order; in other words, in hearing the scale. Nennella, one of the children of the " Children's House " of Via Giusti, played the scale over two hundred times in succession, one hundred for the ascending scale and one hundred back again. The whole class is sometimes interested in listening, the children following with absolute silence the classic beauty of this succession of sounds. Another child, Mario, used to go to the very end of the table — as far away as possible, and resting his elbows on the table with his head in his hands, he would remain without stirring in the silence of the darkened room, showing his extraordinary interest in the exercise in every detail of demeanor and facial expression.

At a certain moment, interest in reproducing the note vocally appears. The children accompany the scale with their voices. They strive for the exact reproduction of the sound which the bell gives. Their voices become soft and musical in this exercise, showing nothing of that shrillness, so characteristic of children's voices in the usual popular songs. In the classes of Via Trionfale it happened that some children asked permission to accompany vocally the scale that a child was playing softly on the bells. The interest taken in this exercise was of a higher order than that shown by children in the singing of songs. It was easy to see that songs with their capricious intervals between widely separated notes and calling for pronunciation of words, musical expression, differences in time, etc., are unadapted to the most elementary exercises in singing.

It was possible to test the absolute memory of the child for the different notes without any set exercise. After a long series of experiments in pairing, the children begin - to make scales, using only one series of bells, and they repeat this exercise many times and in different ways. Sometimes, for instance, a child always looks for the lowest note, *do,* then for the next above it, *re,* etc. Again, a child will take any bell at random, looking next for the note immediately above or immediately below, and so on. It also happens that on picking up some bell or other, the child will exclaim on hearing its sound, this is *mi,* this is *do,* and so on. One child had made a splendid demonstration of the use of the bells before her Majesty, the Queen Mother. This was in the month of May. Although he had had no further access to the materials in his " Children's House " of Via Giusti, in the November following he was asked to use some musical pipes,[1] which he had hardly seen before, and which happened to be in great disorder since they had just arrived from the factory. There were sixteen pipes mixed at random, comprising a double diatonic scale. He took one of the pipes, struck it and said, " This is *si,*" and immediately hung it on the appropriate hook of the support. On ringing the next one, he said, this is *mi,* and again put the pipe

[1] The pipes are an equipment parallel to the bells. They are to be recommended for schools, which can afford a more sumptuous outlay.

in the right place. So he went on and arranged the sixteen pipes in accurate order on the two parallel frames. He had had a good deal of exercise during the preceding year and had preserved an absolutely accurate memory of the notes.

As is the case with colors, geometrical shapes, etc., the children begin at this point to explore the environment. One will come to the teacher at the piano and say, striking a key, " This is *ste*," meaning that the note corresponds to the first syllable of the first word in some song he knows (Stella, Stellina). It happens that the key struck by the child is a *do,* the very note corresponding to the syllable *ste* in the song. We had many touching examples of this musical exploration of the environment.

## II

## THE READING AND WRITING OF MUSIC

Material: In "The Children's House" the musical staff is introduced by means of a board painted green with the lines in bas relief. On each line and in each space representing the octave to which the sounds of the bells respectively correspond, is a small circular indenture, or socket, into which the disk for each note may be inserted. Inside each indenture is written a number: 1, 2, 3, 4, 5, 6, 7. The disks used in this exercise have a number written on the lower face and the name of a note on the upper: for instance, 1, *do;* 2, *re;* 3, *mi;* 4, *fa;* 5, *sol;* 6, *la;* 7, *si:*

*do - re - mi - fa - sol - la - si - do.*

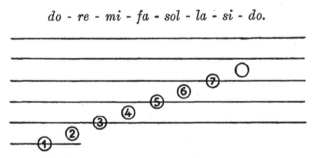

This device enables the child to place the notes on their respective lines without making any mistakes and to examine their relative positions. The indentures are so arranged as to show an empty space wherever a semi-tone appears:

*do, re, mi, fa, sol, la, si, do.*

326

In the semi-tone spaces black counters are to be placed.
At a later stage of this exercise the staff is represented by
a wooden board similar to the one described above, but
without the indentures. The child has at his disposal a
great many disks with the notes written out in full on
one face. He can arrange thirty or forty of these disks
at random on the board, keeping them, however, in their

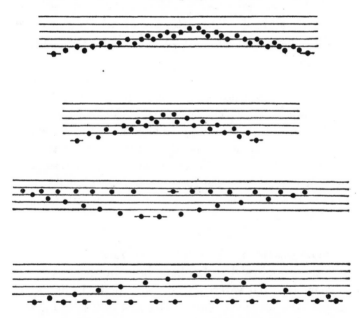

places according to the names of the notes; but each time
the surface showing the name of the note should be placed
downward on the board, so that on the line only disks
without names are visible. When a child has finished
this exercise, he is to turn the disks over without disar-
ranging them and so determine from their names whether
he has placed them properly. All the disks on a given
line or in a given space should have the same names.

Should any doubt arise as to the proper place of a note, the other board with the numbered indentures can be used as a check.

When a child has reached this stage of development, he can practice reading the musical script, ringing the bells according to the notes he is interpreting. The musical staffs are prepared on oblong cards about seventeen centimeters broad. The notes are about two centimeters in diameter. The cards are variously colored — blue, violet, yellow, red.

The next step is for the children to write notes themselves. For this purpose we have prepared little sheets which can be bound together into a book or album.

We offer also a few songs employing two or three notes so simple in character that the child can make them out by ear on his bells. When, after some practise, he is certain he can copy the song, he writes the notes on his staff and so becomes the editor of his own music.

### TREBLE AND BASS CLEFS

*Arrangement of the notes in the form of a rhombus:* All the exercises thus far have been in reference to the higher *clef*. However, no representation of this key has as yet been given the child. His first task is to learn the relative position of the notes on the two staffs. To supply this want, following the system of the Musical Conservatory of Milan, we have adopted the double staff.

A sheet on which the child writes his own music.

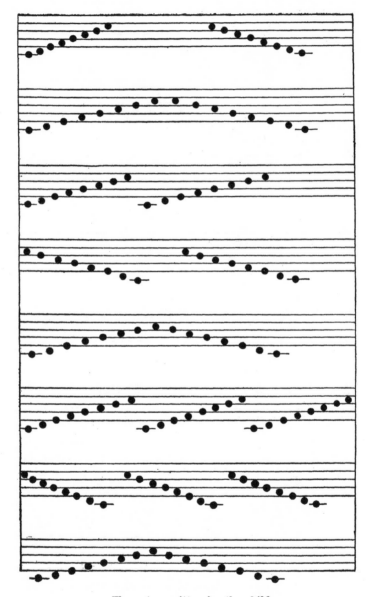

The notes written by the child.

The broken line (p. 328) indicates the position of
*do,* the point of departure for the scale. In fact, as the
notes pass from line to space and space to line, they form
the natural series:

*do, re, mi, fa, sol, la, si, do.*

The same situation develops as they go down the scale:

*do, si, la, sol, fa, mi, re, do.*

When the position of *do* has been determined, the other
notes above and below it are easily found. From the
*do* on the left the child can find his way to the *do* on the

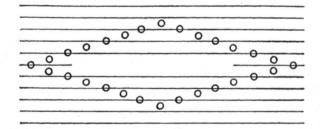

next octave higher and come down again. Likewise from
the same point on the right (*do*) he can go down to the
*do* of the lower octave and then go up the scale again.
When these notes are represented on the combined
staffs with the counters, the resulting design is a rhombus.

Separating the two staffs, the arrangement of the notes
in the higher and lower key (the C scale and bass) becomes apparent and the different significance of the two
series can be emphasized by placing to the left of the
staff the two clef signs, which have been prepared as special portions of our material.

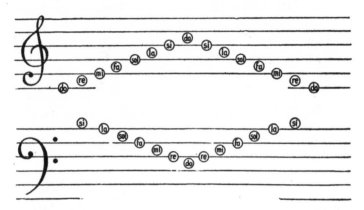

In this way the children have learned the scale in *do major* in the two keys.  The arrangement of the black and white spaces puts them in a position to recognize these notes even on the piano.  Our material, in fact, includes a diminutive keyboard where the keys are small enough to fit the size of a child's hand.  It can be used as an exercise for the finger muscles.  As each key is touched it raises a hammer marked with the name of the note struck, which the child can see through a glass. Thus while the child is practising his finger movements, he fixes his acquaintance with the arrangement of the notes on the keyboard.  This small piano makes no noise. However, a sort of organ-pipe mechanism can be fitted on above the hammers in such a way that each stroke, as the hammer rises, connects with a reed which gives a corresponding sound.

All the exercises thus far have been based upon sensory experience as the point of departure.  The child's ear has recognized the fundamental sounds and initiated him into real musical education.  All the rest, such as the music writing, etc., *is not music.*

# III

## THE MAJOR SCALES

We have developed additional material for the teaching of the scales. Here we show a chart somewhat suggesting the arrangement of the bell material used in the first exercises. That is, the relative intervals between the various notes of the scale are clearly indicated. The *scale* is, in fact, a series of eight sounds, the intervals between each being as indicated by the black marks in the design: whole tone, whole tone, semi-tone, whole tone, whole tone, whole tone, semi-tone.

In the *do major* scale the intervals are indicated as follows: a whole tone between *do* and *re*; *re* and *mi*; *fa* and *sol*; *sol* and *la*; *la* and *si*; and a semi tone between *mi* and *fa* and *si* and *do*. If, however, instead of beginning with *do,* the scale starts from some other note, the mutual intervals characterizing the scale remain unchanged. It is as though the whole scale with its characteristic construction as regards tone differences were moved along. Accordingly, as our plate shows, under the figure of the two octaves there is another figure. This latter is a movable piece of cardboard which shows the construction of the octave in black and white. This movable card is fastened to the large chart by a ribbon. Supposing now we slide this movable piece, as indicated in the figure, to the level of *mi*. The intervals between the tones of the *mi* scale are the same as in all the other scales. In other words, they remain as indicated on the small movable card. It is necessary, accordingly, to strike on the grand scale the notes corresponding to the white spaces of the movable slip: viz.,

*mi, fa* diesis, *sol* diesis, *la, si, do* diesis, *re* diesis.

This process may be repeated by sliding the movable card to all the notes in succession. In this way all the scales are gradually constructed. This becomes an interesting theoretical exercise, since the child discovers that he is able to build *all possible scales* by himself.

We have, however, for this purpose a real musical material, as appears from our design. Here on a wooden form like that used for the bells, but two octaves instead of one octave long, we have arranged prisms of equal dimensions but painted black and white according to the tones they represent. Each prism shows a rectangular plate exposed to view. The plates are identical in appearance on all the prisms. They are, however, really of different lengths according to the different prisms. When these plates are struck, they give the notes of two octaves, the prisms acting as sounding boards. The sounds are soft and mellow and unusually clear, so that we do not exaggerate in describing this mechanism as really a musical instrument (resembling the Xylophone). In our design each piece is arranged in its proper position in the *do major* scale.

Since the intervals between the tones are the same for all the scales without distinction, if the group of prisms is moved as a whole from right to left, sliding along the wooden form, some of the prisms will fall. The resulting effect is the same as that produced when the small card was moved over the larger chart (see above). No

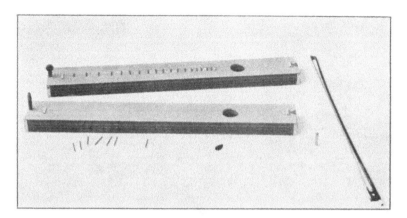

The monocord. In the first instrument the notes are indicated by frets. On the monocord in the foreground the child places the frets as he discovers the notes by drawing the bow across the string.

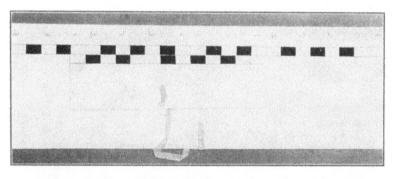

Material for indicating the intervals of the major scale and its transposition from one key to another.

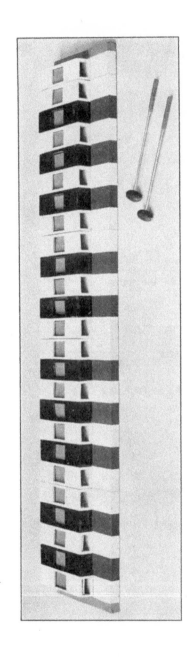

The upper cut shows the music bars arranged for the scale of C major. The lower cut shows the transposition of the scale, preserving, however, the same intervals.

matter how far the group of prisms is moved, the scale
can be obtained by striking all the prisms corresponding
to the white spaces on the wooden form.

For instance, let us take away the two first prisms, *do*
and *do diesis* on the left, and push the whole group of
prisms from right to left until *re* reaches the point formerly occupied by *do*. If, now, we strike the plates
which correspond to the notes of the major scale, we obtain the major scale in *re*. On examining the notes
which make up this scale, we find: *re, mi, fa diesis, sol,
la, si, do diesis, re.*

This brief description will indicate how interesting
this instrument is. It contains in very simple form and
expresses in a clear and delightful way the fundamental
principles of harmony. Its use can be made apparent
to teachers by the three following tables.

As the children derive in this way all the possible
scales, they should transfer them to their copy books,
making use of all the symbols of musical notation. The
copying of the scales should be developed progressively:
first the scale with one *diesis,* next the scale with two,
then the one with three *dieses,* etc. Fine opportunities
for observation are here offered. A child may see for
instance that a scale with two *dieses* has the same *diesis*
which appeared in the preceding scale; a scale with three
*dieses* has the two *dieses* of the preceding scales, and so
on. The *dieses* recur at intervals of five notes.

Since in using the first material, by changing the third
and sixth bell, the child was taught to recognize the har-
monic minor scale, to construct it and listen to it, it is
now an obviously simple matter for him to make up all
the minor scales.

We have thus developed exercises which prepare for

the recognition of the major and minor tones as well as for the recognition of the different tones. It also becomes an easy matter to play a simple *motif* in different keys. It is sufficient to move the series of plates, as has been indicated, and play them over according to the indications of the white and black spaces of the wooden form.

Here is a specimen of key transposition:

At this point children usually develop great keenness for producing sounds and scales on all kinds of instruments (stringed instruments, wind instruments, etc.)

One of the instruments which brings the child to producing and recognizing notes is the *monochord*. It is a simple, resonant box with one string. The first

Scale of C.

Scale with sharps.          Scale with flats.

exercise is in tuning. The string is made to correspond with one of the resonant prisms (*do*). This is
made possible by a key with which the string can be loos-
ened or tightened. The child may now be taught to handle the violin bow or mandolin plectrum, or he may be
instructed in the finger thrumming used for the harp
or banjo. On one of our monochords, the notes are indicated by fixed transversal frets, the name of each note
being printed in the proper space. These notes are, however, not written on the other monochord, where the child
must learn to discover by ear the proper distances at

which the notes are produced. In this case the child has
at his disposal movable frets with which he can indicate
the points he has discovered as producing a given note.
These frets should be left in position by the child to
serve as a check on his work. The children have shown
considerable interest also in little pitchpipes, which give
very pleasing tones.

. . . . . . . .

Thus in composing the scales and in listening to them
the child performs real exercises in musical education.
A given melody in the major scale is repeated in various
keys. In listening to it carefully, in repeating it, in
observing the notes which make it up, the child has an

C Pitch.

D Pitch.

E Pitch.

F Pitch.

exercise similar to the audition of the note, but an exercise of a far more advanced character.

This exercise is to be the starting point for *understanding* melody. To make the hearing of music an intelligent act and not like the mechanical process which appears when children read, in loud monotone, books which they cannot understand and of the meaning of which they have no idea, preparatory exercises are required. We get this preparation through various exercises in the audition of various scales for the recognition of key, and in exercises on the interpretation of rhythm.

# IV

## EXERCISES IN RHYTHM

One of our most successful exercises has proved to be that originally conceived as a help in teaching children to walk, viz., "walking the line." It will be remembered that among the exercises in motor education used at the outset of our method, appeared that of walking with one foot in front of the other on a line drawn on the floor, much as do tight-rope-walking acrobats. The purpose of this exercise was to stabilize equilibrium, to teach erect carriage and to make movement freer and more certain.

Miss Maccheroni began her exercises in rhythm by accompanying this walking of the children with piano music. In fact, the sound of the piano came to be the call signal for the children to take up this exercise. The teacher starts to play and immediately the children come of their own accord, and almost without exception, to take up their positions on the line. At the very beginning the music seems to be purely a signal, at best a pleasant accompaniment to the motor exercise. There is no apparent adaptation of the child's movements to the musical rhythm. However, as the same measure is repeated for a considerable period, the rudiments of this adaptation begin to appear. One of the children begins to keep step with the rhythm of the music. Individual differences in adaptation persist for some time; but if the same musical rhythm is kept up, almost all the children finally become sensible to it. In fact, these little people begin to develop general attitudes of body, in relation to the music, which are of the greatest interest. First of all, the children change their gait according to the music: the light walk, the war-like march, the run, develop on the impulse of the rhythmic movement. It is not that the teacher "teaches" the child to change his walk according to the music: the phenomenon arises of its own accord. The child begins to interpret the rhythm by moving in harmony with it. But to obtain this result the teacher must play perfectly, carefully noting all the details of musical punctuation. The creation of musical feeling in the children depends upon the teacher's own feeling and the rigorous accuracy of her own execution.

It will be useful to give here a few details on the execution of these first rhythmic exercises. The children begin, as we have said, by learning to walk on the line. They develop a passion for walking on that line, yielding to a fascination which grown-up people cannot conceive. They seem to put their whole souls into it. This is the moment for the teacher to sit down at the piano and without saying anything to play the first melody in our series. The children smile, they look at the piano and continue to walk, becoming more and more concentrated on what they are doing. The melody acts as a persuading voice; the children begin to consider the time of the music and little by little their tiny feet begin to strike the line in step with it. Some of our three-year-olders begin to keep step as early as the first or second trial. After a very few attempts a whole class of forty children will be walking in time. We must warn against the error of playing with special emphasis on the measure;

in other words, of striking more loudly than is required the note (thesis) which marks the inception of the rhythmic period. The teacher should be careful simply to bring out all the expression that the melody requires. She may be sure that the rhythmic cadence will become apparent from the tune itself. The playing of one note more loudly than the others, thus to emphasize the rhythmic accent (thesis), is to deprive the selection of all its value as melody and therefore of its power to cause the motory action corresponding to rhythm. It is necessary to play accurately and with feeling, giving an interpretation as real as possible. We get thus a " musical time " which, as every one knows, is not the "mechanical time " of the metronome. If it is certainly absurd to play a *Nocturne* of Chopin on the metronome, it is hardly less absurd and certainly quite as disagreeable to play a piece of dance music on that instrument. Even those people who have a great aptitude for feeling "time" and who play with special attention to exactness of measure, know that they cannot follow the metronome without positive discomfort. Children feel the rhythm of a piece of music if it is played with *musical feeling;* and not only do they follow the time with their footsteps, but, as the rhythmic periods vary, they adapt the whole attitude of their bodies to the melodic period, which is developed around the beats constituting the rhythm as around points of support. There is a vast difference between this exercise and that of having children march to the clapping of hands or to the time of *one, two, three,* etc., counted in a tone of command.

A child of ten years was dancing to the music of a Chopin waltz played with most generous concessions to the different colorations indicated in the text. She put into her movements a certain fullness of swing, to bring out the effect which a marked *rallentando* gives the notes. Of course this method of dancing demands on the part of the children a perfect and intimate identification of spirit with the music; but this is something which children, even when they are small, possess in a very special way, and which they develop in their long and uninterrupted walks on the line to the sounds of a tune often repeated. It is curious to see them assume a demeanor entirely in harmony with the expression of the music they are following. A little boy of three, during the playing of our first melody, held the palms of his hands turned parallel with the floor and as he walked he bent his knees slightly with each step. On passing from our first to our second tunes, he changed not only the rapidity of his footsteps, but the attitude of his whole body. Considered as something external this may be of slight importance, but considered as evidence of a mental state, the change in demeanor bears witness to a distinct artistic experience. The composer of the tune could well be proud of such a sincere response to his work, if the test of musical beauty be regarded as successful communication of feeling.

Our second tune is a rapid *andante* somewhat *staccato*. The first was slow and blending (*legato*). The children feel the *legato*, answering it with very reserved movements. The *staccato* lifts them from the floor. The *crescendo* makes them hurry and stamp their feet. The *forte* sometimes brings them to clap their hands, while *calando* restores them to the silent march, which turns, during the *piano*, to perfect silence. The completion of the musical period brings them to a halt and they stand there expectant until it is taken up again; or if it be the end of the whole tune, they suddenly stop.

Beppino, a little boy of three, used to keep time with the extended forefinger of his right hand. The music was a song in two parts repeated alternately, the one in *legato* and the other in *staccato;* with the *legato* he used a uniform regular movement; he followed the *staccato* with sudden spasmodic beats.

To-day forty children may be seen walking as softly as possible during a tune played *pianissimo*. These same children on the day when they first heard the *piano* kept calling to the teacher " play louder; we can't hear " and yet at that time the teacher was playing not *pianissimo,* but *mezzo forte!*

At first the children interested in the first tune are deaf to any other. The children in the St. Barnaba School in Milan got in step with the first tune. They did not notice that the teacher had changed to the second and kept their step so well that when the first tune was resumed, the teacher found them in perfect time, while on the faces of the children appeared a smile of recognition, as it were, of an old friend.

If the teacher is sufficiently cautious, she can discover without disturbing the children the moment when they have caught a new tune; and even if only a few succeed in following both of the first two melodies, the teacher can satisfy these few by alternating the tunes. This does not disturb the others who come, little by little, to notice the change in the music and to fall in with the new movement. In a public kindergarten at Perugia an attempt of this nature was made without warning by a lady, who, being a visitor, felt free to take this liberty. The children were invited into the large hall and left to themselves while the lady was playing on the piano our third melody, a march. The older children caught the movement at once. After they had been marching for some time a *galop* was played. Some hesitation appeared in a few pupils while others apparently were not aware of the change in the music. Suddenly two or three began to run, as though swept away by the rhythmic wave, as though borne along by the music. They hardly seemed to touch that floor to which, but a few moments previously, the march seemed to have glued them at every step! A portion of the children in this class had taken seats in the sloping auditorium around the room. They were the youngest children; and when the victorious charge broke out to the tune of the *galop,* they began to clap their hands enthusiastically. Some of the teachers felt alarmed, but certainly the spectacle was an inspiring one.

It follows that if we are to *tell* the children to " hop," " run," or " march," there is no use in our giving them music. We must take our choice: either *music* or *commands.* Even in our reading lessons with the slips, we do not tell the child the word that he must read. We must do without commands, without false accentuation of notes, without enforced positions. Music, if it be in reality an expressive language, suggests everything to children if they are left to themselves. Rhythmic interpretation of the musical thought is expressed by the attitude and movement of body and spirit.

Nannina, a girl four years old, would gracefully spread her skirt, and relax her arms along her body. She would bend her knees slightly, throw her head back and turning her pretty little face to one side, smile at those behind her as though extending her amiability in all directions.

Beppino, four and a half years old, stood with his feet

together motionless at the center of the ellipse drawn on the floor, on which the children were walking. He beat the time of the first tune with an outstretched arm, bowing from the waist in perfectly correct form at every measure. The time consumed in this bow of Beppino exactly filled the interval between one *thesis* and the next and was in perfect accord with the movement of the tune.

Nannina, the same pretty girl we mentioned above, always grew stiff when a military march was played; she would frown and walk heavily.

On the other hand, the intervention of the teacher to give some apposite lesson, tending to perfect certain movements, is something which gives the children extraordinary delight. Five of our little girls embraced each other rapturously and smothered the teacher with kisses when they had learned a few new movements of a rhythmic dance.

Otello, Vincenzino and Teresa had been taught to get a better effect from their tambourines, their steps and gestures. Each of them thanked the teacher for the profitable lesson in a special way. Vincenzino gave her a beaming smile whenever he marched past her; Teresa would furtively touch her with her hand; Otello was even more demonstrative — as he went by her he would leave the line, run to her and embrace her for a second or two.

If the spontaneity of every child has been respected; if, in other words, every child has been able to grow in his or her own way, listening to the tunes, following them with the footsteps and with free movements — interpreting them; if each child has been able to penetrate, without being disturbed by any one, into the heart of the beautiful fact which the understanding of music constitutes; then it is easy for the teacher who has forty children (between three and five and a half years of age) only one assistant, and preferably perhaps a whole apartment instead of a closed room, to sit down at the piano and teach eight children a long and intricate dance,— the lanciers in five parts. And then just like the orchestra leader who has prepared his pupils, the teacher with a minimum of effort gets the very effect in dancing, etc., which teachers generally are so anxious to obtain. Then we can get marches, counter marches, simultaneous movements, alternate movements, interweaving lines,— anything in fact, that we wish, and with perfect accuracy besides; since every movement in the children corresponds exactly with the development of the tune.

For instance, the children are marching two by two, holding each other's hand, during the playing of a short tune. At the end of this melody they slowly kneel, but in such a way that on the sound of the last note they are touching the floor very gently with their knees. There is something sweet about the accuracy and the perfect simultaneousness attained by the children, under the guidance of the tune. The effect of these exercises on them is to bring repose to their whole body and a sense of peace to their little souls.

On one occasion in a school just opened in Milan, 1908, the children re-acted to the piano by jumping about in confusion, waving their arms, moving their shoulders and legs. This was really an attempt to represent by a sort of chaos the complexity of the rhythmic movements they were hearing. They were actually making, without any assistance from others, a spontaneous attempt at musical interpretation. They soon grew tired of this, saying that "the thing was ugly." They had, however, divined the possibilities of an orderly motory action; and when they had become quiet again, they began to listen to the music with great interest waiting for the revelation of its deep secret. Then suddenly they began to walk again, this time regularly and according to the real measure.

One of the children, whose graph was somewhat as follows:

(pauses, that is, on the line of quiescence, with frequent excursions into the negative field), took no part in these rhythmic exercises. On the contrary, he was always breaking them up by pushing the other children out of line or making a noise. Finally, however, he did learn not to disturb others; in other words, to stay *quiet,* something which he had never known how to do before. It is a great conquest for a disorderly child to gain the ability to become quite motionless, in a gently placid state of mind. His next step was to learn to move delicately, with respect for other people; and he came to have a certain sensitiveness about his relations with his schoolmates. For example, he used to blush when they smiled at him and even when he took no part in what they were doing, he shared their activities with an affectionate attention. From this point on Riziero (that was the child's name) entered on a higher plane of existence — one of order, labor and politeness.

The fact also that children at times listen to the music, while remaining seated comfortably around the room, watching the other children dance and march, is in itself a pretty thing. The children who are seated become very self-controlled. They watch their schoolmates or exchange a few words cautiously with each other. At times, even, they let themselves go in interesting expressions of movement with their arms. The manifestations of placidity and interest here seen cannot be disjoined from a healthful, spiritual upbuilding,— a beautiful orderliness, which is being established within them. Obviously, a wonderful harmony springs up between the teacher, who plays with enthusiastic feeling and with all possible skill of hand and abundance of spirit simply because she feels the musical phenomena around her in the children, and the pupils who, little by little, are transformed under this influence, and show an understanding of the music, which becomes for them something more and more intimate, more and more complete. It is no longer a question of the *step,* but of the position of the whole body: arms, heads, chests *are moved* by the music.

Finally, many of the children beat time with their hands, and interpret correctly without ever having been taught distinctions between 3 and 4 time, etc. When a keen interest in " guessing " the time is awakened in them, the children look about for various objects — wands, tambourines, castagnettes, etc., and the class exercise is developed to perfection. The child comes to be " possessed " by the music. He obeys the musical command with his whole body and becomes more and more perfect in this obedience shown by his muscles.

Here is a pretty story which will show to what extent children can feel themselves dependent on the music which " makes them move." Once my father went into a room where a little Parisian girl whom he was very fond of was passionately marching to the rhythm of a tune played on the piano. The child usually ran to meet the old gentleman; but that day the moment she saw him she began to shout to Miss Maccheroni, who was playing, *"Arrête, arrête!"* She wanted to go and shake hands with my father, something she could not do as long as the music was continuing to *command* her to move with the rhythm. And in fact, it was not until Miss Maccheroni stopped playing that the little girl was able to run and deliver her greeting.

. . . . . . . .

We have prepared a series of tunes for this work and I think it will be useful to give here those which we finally selected because they have succeeded, whenever they were tried, in arousing in the children the phenomena above described. There are eight movements chosen from six well-known pieces of music. These few movements repeated over and over again and played with all possible accuracy, will surely, sooner or later, be felt in every rhythm by the children.

The transition from following the time by ones (that is, one beat for every rhythmic element) to the indication of simply the beginning of the measure (that is, one beat on the *thesis*) appeared for the first time in a "Children's House" directed by Miss Maccheroni. There, one morning when the children were following the music with great pleasure, marching about and beating on tambourines, it was a girl who first caught the strong beat (*thesis*). A little boy behind her made the conquest a second later; but while the little girl lost what she had gained almost immediately, the little boy developed it to perfection. Shortly after other children made the same progress, apparently as a saving of effort: they began, that is, by beating once on every step. This required a rapid movement and an endless succession of beats. All of a sudden they began to beat on the first note of a measure.

Here, for instance, is a case of 4/4 time:

The children at first marked the time without regard to the measure, thus:

| | | | | | | | | | | |

But the moment comes suddenly when they catch the measure: then they beat it as follows:

| • • • | • • • | • • •

In other words, their beats fall only on the first note of the measure.

Maria Louise, a little under four years of age, was walking to the sound of a 2/4 march, played rather lightly. Suddenly she called to the teacher: *"Regarde, regarde, comme je fais!"* She was making little skips, gracefully raising her arms on the first beat of the measure. Her invention was extraordinarily happy and graceful.

Usually in teaching the divisions of musical time, it has been the custom to play *forte* the time called theoretically *tempo forte:* in other words, to strike hard on the first note of every rhythmic measure. In fact, teachers of children or young people can often be heard playing a tune with special emphasis on the first note of every measure and playing the successive notes *pianissimo.* Naturally the motory action corresponds to this: it will be tense for the strong beats and light for the weak beats. But what value has all this in relation to the feeling of the rhythmic measure? What is called theoretic-

The children using the music bells and the wooden keyboards. (*The Washington Montessori School, Washington, D. C.*)

Analyzing the beat of a measure while walking on a line.  (*A Montessori School in Italy.*)

ally *tempo forte* has no relation to the meaning of the
words " strong " and " weak " in their ordinary sense.
It is a question of *emphasis* and *expression,* which derive
their nature from the laws of musical time and melodic
composition and certainly not from the wrist muscles of
the person playing. If this were not so, a person could
play the first, second or third note of a measure as *forte,*
whereas, in reality, it is the first that is always " strong."

In practise, children, to whom the six tunes we pro-
posed for the beginning of this study were played — and
played always with rigorous musical interpretation and
with expressiveness — succeeded in recognizing the first
beat of the measure as " strong," and went on thus to
divide into measures some thirty pieces of music of
varied rhythm. Even the following year, after the summer vacation, they kept asking for new pieces of music
just for the " fun " of working out the measure in them.
They would stand at the side of the teacher at the piano
and either with their hands or with soft playing on the
castagnettes or tambourines, accompany their new piece
of music. In general they would listen in silence to the
first measure and then fall in with their little beats like
any well-trained orchestra. They took the trouble no
longer to march to the music: they were interested in this
new form of study; while the smaller tots, delighted with
the new music, were still walking undisturbed along the
elliptical line on the floor which was to guide them to such
great conquests!

The strong beat (*thesis*) is the key that opens to the
higher laws of music. Sometimes it is played, for reasons of expression, very softly and always possesses the
solemnity of the note which dominates the rhythm. It
may even be syncopated or lacking entirely, just as when

the orator on reaching his climax pronounces in a very low voice the phrase which is to produce the great effect, or even pauses and is silent: this sentence rings powerfully in the ears of those who listen.

The same error which leads to heavy stress, in playing, on the first beat of every measure in order to attract the attention of the children to it, also leads to suggesting secondary movements in addition to the one which marks the *thesis*. The children, for instance, must make four movements for a 4/4 time: movements in the air for the secondary beats, and a more energetic movement for the *thesis*. The result is that interest in the succession of movements replaces attention to the fact of most importance, which is *to feel* the value of the first beat. Children who feel the first note because it is played "strong" and who proceed from one strong beat to the following strong beat guided by a succession of movements, are not, it is obvious, following the tune. One little girl who had been prepared by this method found herself, on having mistaken the beat, constantly persisting in her mistake under the guidance of her four movements. It is like presenting a cube or a triangle to children of three years with the teacher enumerating the sides, the angles, the apexes, etc. In reality the children do not get any notion of the triangle or the cube.

Our children come ultimately to represent the secondary beats with slight movements, as follows:

and then they count them. When we have gone thus far we reach the point which is exactly the *point of departure* for ordinary methods, namely, counting *one! two! three! four!* to keep step in time.

    •     •     •     •     •     •     •     •

As a practical application of the information already acquired in the division of time into measures, we next pass to the exercise of playing the scales in 2/4, 3/4 and 4/4 time and with the triplets. The scale, the classic type of the melody, lends itself beautifully to these interpretations of various measures. Every one must have passed hours at the piano playing simple scales and finding a delicious variety in the exercise. The *do* scale itself may be played, for instance, thus:

or thus:

or thus:

Our little piano may be of use in this exercise; but it is better first to use an exercise more easy for finger movement and for the position of the hand:

    •     •     •     •     •     •     •     •

Children who have succeeded in identifying and dividing the melody into measures and the measure itself into

2, 3, 4, understand very easily the time values of the
notes.   It is sufficient to let the child hear each exercise

*first* and he will repeat it with precision.   Thus all kinds
of dry explanation of musical *values* disappear.

The following notation

presents no special difficulty if the child has once heard it.

Our next step is to use some exercises for the analysis of the measure, for instance:

The children follow these exercises, marching so as to put one step on every note.  Even children of four years when prepared with the preceding exercises succeed in following these with the very greatest interest.  They are

especially delighted with the long note which keeps them
hanging in position with one foot in front of them on the
line and the other one behind them also on the line.  The
position is that of a person who stops before bringing up
the foot which is still behind him.

Since the children already know how to *read* music,
there is hung up before them a green chart (similar in dimensions to the musical staffs already familiar to them)
on which is written the exercise which is being played at
the piano by the teacher and which they execute on the
floor-line.

Examples:

Here is another:

We even give a simple tune like this one (composed by
Professor Jean Gibert of the Montessori Primary School
of Barcelona):

Of course, sooner or later children fix their attention on the varying form of the notes and discover that this difference in form bears a relation to differences in time-value of the notes:

This is the time to give in very brief explanation the lesson on the value of the notes. Thereafter the child may write from memory a simple melody which the teacher has first played on the piano. Almost always the child writes this down with accuracy, showing that he has control over the musical values appearing in the melody in question. The child uses for this purpose a large green chart containing various musical staffs on which movable notes may be fixed at pleasure. These notes are equipped with a pin which may be pushed into the wood. The simple exercises given for the analysis of the measures, transferred into various keys, can after some practise in playing them on the system of plates be put into their copy books by the children. These exercises for measure-analysis are so simple that the children themselves have sometimes learned to play them on the piano. It then has happened that the class went of its own accord into the piano room; one child began to play and the others followed the music on the floor-line. The children as they walk ultimately come to sing the scales and the easy tunes (of which they have recognized the notes) pronouncing the names of the notes; but in so pronouncing them they soften their voices to the point of attaining an expression which may be called even artistic. When the teacher plays, the music gains the added charm of harmony, since the teacher can give not only the simple scale, but the relative chords, and this gives the scale a vigorous and very sweet fullness.

These exercises in measure analysis have also been particularly useful in their application to gymnastic exercises. The children follow them with gymnastic movements, using especially the movements of Dalcroze, which are admirably adapted to the measures of ⅔, ¾, ¼, etc., and which have a real beauty. We discovered that these exercises proved to be complexly difficult for the children who had not practised sufficiently in the interpretation of the different note values. On the other hand, they were very easy for those who had come to have a clear feeling for these different values. This was proof to us that sensorial preparation must precede these exercises, and furthermore, that the only difficulty Dalcroze movements encounter in children arises from insufficient sensory preparation in the children themselves.

In the same way we illustrate the different details of musical writing: the dotted note,

the triplet:

the *legato,* the *staccato,* etc.

Here is an example of a *legato* effect:

(Sonnambula.   Quintet)

This example which derives all its expressive value
from the ties, also brings out the value of the note:

We need, accordingly, a collection of musical selections
in which the value of the notes is obvious and clear to such
an extent that the children come to recognize the different
values.   This recognition must be obtained by ear through
listening to the music, not by eye looking at the symbols
while the teacher explains.

The ¼ note always has a different musical content
from the ¹⁄₁₆ note.  A musical piece made up of the 16th
or 32d notes has a character of its own (joy or agitation);
and a piece made up of half or whole notes has likewise
its peculiar character (religious, sad, impressive).

The same may be said of every musical symbol, the
value of which is brought out by the note being played

with that value and in reference to that symbol. It has been held that in playing for children and in copying music for the use of children the expression-symbols should be suppressed. We should observe that these signs of expression bear to music the relation that punctuation bears to the written sentence; their suppression takes away all value from the notes. For example, the *legato* and symbols which indicate that difference ( ⏜ and • ) have therefore the very greatest value.

The children succeed quite easily in using and reading the accessory symbols of music. They already know their meaning through having heard them. We have not found it necessary to use such signs as *sense objects,* such as bars (to be placed on the wooden staff to divide measure from measure), time fractions, parentheses and so on. Although we had these manufactured, we ultimately abandoned them because we found that they were simply in the way.

On the other hand, we found considerable utility in our large colored cards with a single staff already described. On these are written various measures which the children read with a special pleasure and execute on their bells.

.    .    .    .    .    .    .    .

With all this a way has been opened to a really musical education. Once Miss Maccheroni, while executing her customary rhythmic tunes, reproduced a melodious religious movement, " *O Sanctissima,*" which the children heard for the first time. The children all left the line and gathered around the piano to listen. Two or three little girls kneeled on the floor and others remained mo-

tionless executing plastic poses with their arms. This revealed to us their sensitiveness to melody; they felt moved not to march but to pray and assume various poses.

We have not yet been able to push our experiments far enough precisely to define the musical material adapted to children of various ages. We have, however, made a very great number of successful attempts to bring children to enjoy melody and sentimental expression in music. The practicableness and utility of musical auditions, or, if you wish, of concerts for children, graduated in difficulty, executed on various instruments, but on one instrument at a time, are beyond all question; this applies above all to songs reproduced by the human voice, when a well-trained voice is available.

If a real artist should take up the task of analyzing for children the language of music, bringing them to enjoy it phrase by phrase and under different *timbres* (voice, strings, etc.), his new and scientific application of the art would prove to be a real benefaction to humanity. How many people capable of profound enjoyment of music would be produced in the future from these groups of little ones, so intelligent in music, who follow the most expressive tunes with so much passion and in a silence more absolute than any celebrated artist can dream of attaining in a meeting of adults! No one among these little hearers is cold, far away in thought. But on the faces of the children appears the interior working of a spirit, tasting a nectar essential to its very life.

How many times a plastic pose, a kneeling posture, an ecstatic face, will move the heart of the artist to a sense of joy greater than that which any applause of a throng of people often indifferent or inattentive, can possibly give him! Usually only those wounded at heart by the difficulty of being understood by others, or discouraged by the coldness or rudeness of other people, or oppressed by disillusion, or filled with a sense of painful loneliness or need of expansion in some other way, feel in music the voice which opens the doors of the heart and causes a health-giving flood of tears or raises the spirit to a lofty sense of peace. Only they can understand how necessary a companion for humanity music is. We know, of course, to-day that music is an indispensable stimulant for soldiers rushing forth to die. How much more truly would it then become a stimulant for all who are to live!

This conviction is already in the hearts of many people. In fact, attempts have already been made to reach the populace by concerts in the public squares and by making concert halls accessible to people of every class; but after all, do such attempts amount to more than putting the cheap editions of the classics into circulation among illiterates? Education is the prime requisite; without such education we have a people of deaf mutes forever barred from any music. The ear of the uneducated man cannot perceive the sublime sounds which music would bring within his reach. That is why though the music of Bellini and Wagner is being played in public squares, the saloons are just as full as before.

If, however, from these pupils of ours a whole people could grow up, it would be sufficient to go through the streets with a good piece of music and everybody would come out to hear. All those places where the rough and abandoned wrecks of humanity seek enjoyment, like homeless dogs looking for food in our ash-cans, would be emptied as if by magic. We would have an actual realization of the Allegory of Orpheus; for hearts which are to-day of stone would then be stirred and brought to life by a sublime melody.

### Singing

Singing began with the scale. The singing of a scale, first in accompaniment with the bells and later with the piano is a first and great delight to the children. They sing it in various ways, now in a low voice, now very loud, now all together in unison, now one by one. They sing divided into two groups, sharing the notes alternately between them. Among the songs which we offer to the children, the greatest favorite proved to be the syllabic Gregorian Chant. It is something like a very perfect form of speech. It has a conversational intonation, the softness of a sentence well pronounced, the full roundness of the musical phrase. The examples given here have almost the movement of the scale.

Many other verses of the Gregorian Chant have, like these, proved to be the delight of the Montessori Elementary School of Barcelona. There the children are especially keen about this very simple music which they like to play on the piano, on their plates (Xylophones) or on their monochords.

Ro - ra - te Cœ - li de su - per

et nu - bes plu - ant ju - stum

Pu - er na - tus in Beth - le - em, al - le - lu - ia.

Un - de gau - det Je - ru - sa - lem Al - le - lu -

ia Al - le - lu - ia In Cor - dis ju - bi - lo

Chri-stum na-tum a - do - re-mus, Cum no - vo Can - ti - co.

MUSICAL PHRASES FOR THE INITIAL RHYTHMIC
EXERCISES

We give here in complete form the musical phrases used
by us for the first rhythmic exercises. They are adequate
for giving the sensation of rhythm and for suggesting the
motory actions associated with the rhythm. This musical
material now forms in our schools part of the material
which is experimentally established.

*Works from which Selections are Taken*    *Motor Reactions*
*Provoked*

1. " Ancora un bacio," mazurka, Bastianelli. . Slow walk.
2. " Si j'étais roi," Adolphe Adam. . . . . . . . . . Accelerated walk.
3. " Eagle March," Wagner. . . . . . . . . . . . . . . March step.
4. " Galop," Strauss . . . . . . . . . . . . . . . . . . . . . Run.
5. " Italian folk-song " . . . . . . . . . . . . . . . . . . Hop.
6. " Pas des patineurs " . . . . . . . . . . . . . . . . . . Sedate walk.

## ANCORA UN BACIO
### (*Mazurka*)

Bastianelli.

## SI J'ÉTAIS ROI

Adolphe Adam.

## EAGLE MARCH

Wagner.

GALOP

Strauss.

ITALIAN FOLK SONG

PAS DES PATINEURS

## O SANCTISSIMA

# V

## MUSICAL AUDITIONS

The movement entitled "O Sanctissima," played by Miss Maccheroni one day by chance among the rhythmic exercises, is regarded by us as an introduction to *musical audition.* It will be recalled that the children had been accustomed to alter their style of marching on the floor-line according to changes in the music. It had never, however, occurred to them to leave the line. When this piece was played they all crowded around the piano, motionless, thoughtful, absorbed; while two or three little ones fell to their knees and assumed various poses. This experience suggested to us the idea of "musical auditions," if you wish "concerts for children."

Children, little by little to be sure, but no less admirably, enter into the spirit of music. After the numerous rhythmic exercises, as soon, that is, as they have mastered the problem of measure, almost any *sonata* is within their reach. They can handle not isolated movements merely, but whole pieces of music. The same is true of the auditions. At first, of course, it is better to select simple phrases; but gradually the children come to enjoy "the best music," joyfully recognizing the feeling which it expresses and which inspired it. Our pupils used to exclaim, for instance: "This piece is for weeping," "This is for prayer," "Now we must laugh," "Now we must shout," etc.

We cannot, however, insist too strongly on the need

376

for the greatest possible care in the execution of the selections used. A child audience is a very special one. It demands something more than is expected by the average "intelligent audience." It is one in which musical intelligence must be *developed*. Our object must be the creation not merely of higher and higher grades of understanding but also of higher and higher grades of *feeling*. In this sense, we can never *do too much* for the children. It is a task not beneath the dignity of the greatest composers, the most accomplished technicians. Indeed, any one of such might well esteem it a privilege some day to hear it said of his work that it aroused the first love for music in the hearts of one of these little ones. For thus music would have been made a companion, a consoler, a guardian angel of man! It is of course not the lot of all of us to attain the exalted position of greatness whether as artists or technicians. We must content ourselves with assuming an obligation: with *giving* all the soul and all the skill we possess. We must conceive of ourselves as transmitters of the largess of music to our children. We must deeply feel our calling as bestowers of a divine gift.

The following titles were all used successfully by us in our experiments. They are supplements to the "O Sanctissima" and a "Pater Noster."

A. NARRATIVES.

> *Trovatore:* "Tacea la notte placida."
> *Lucrezia Borgia:* "Nella fatal di Rimini e memorabil guerra."
> *Lucia di Lamermoor:* "Regnava nel silenzio."
> *Trovatore:* "Racconto di Azucena."
> *Sonnambula:* "A fosco cielo, a notte bruna."
> *Rigoletto:* "Tutte le feste al tempio."
> *Fra Diavolo:* "Quell'uom dal fiero aspetto."

B. DESCRIPTION.

> *Beethoven:* "Moonlight."
> *Bohème:* "Nevica; qualcuno passe e parla" (Act II, prelude).
> *Aida,* prelude as far as "Cieli azzurri."
> *Aida,* "Marcia trionfale" (containing the motive of the scene to which it belongs).

C. SENTIMENT AND PASSION:

> *Gaiety:*
>> *Traviata:* "Libiam nei lieti calici."
>> *Sonnambula:* "In Elvezia non v'ha rosa fresca e bella al par d'Alina."
>> *Traviata:* "Sempre libera deggi' io folleggiar."
>> *Faust:* Peasant song, "La vaga pupilla."

> *Contentment:*
>> *Aida:* "Rivedrò le foreste imbalsamate."

> *Passion:*
>> *Traviata:* "Amami Alfredo."
>> *Lucrezia Borgia:* "Era desso il figliuol mio."

> *Anguish:*
>> *Lucrezia Borgia:* "Mio figlio, ridate a me il mio figlio."
>> "       "       "Infelice, il veleno bevesti."

> *Threat:*
>> *Cavalleria Rusticana:* "Bada, Santuzza, schiavo non son."

> *Allurement:*
>> *Barbiere di Siviglia:* "La calunnia è un venticello."
>> *Iris:* "La Piovra."

> *Comic:*
>> *Barbiere di Siviglia:* "Pace e gioia sia con voi."
>> *Fra Diavolo:* "Grazie al ciel per una serva."

*Invitation:*

    *Faust:* " Permetteresti a me."

    *Bohème:* song of Rudolph, " Che gelida manina."

*Anger:*

    *Sonnambula:* " Ah perchè non posso odiarti."

*Sorrow of sacrifice:*

    *Bohème:* " Vecchia zimarra senti."

*Meditation:*

    Mendelsohn: Romances.

    Mozart.

    Chopin.

D. FOLK SONGS AND DANCES.

# PART VII
# METRICS

# I

## THE STUDY OF METRICS IN ELEMENTARY SCHOOLS

One of the novelties included in our experiments was the teaching of metrics, hitherto reserved for high schools. The love shown by children for poetry, their exquisite sensitiveness to rhythm, led me to suspect that the native roots of poetry might be present in little children. I suggested to Miss Maria Fancello, a teacher of literature in the high schools and my colleague, to attempt such an experiment. She began with children of different ages, and, together, we succeeded in discovering a highly interesting department of education, the object of which might be to give the mass of the people, prepared for life in the primary schools, the basic elements of literary appreciation, thus opening a new source of pleasure calculated also to increase general enlightenment. A populace capable of enjoying poetry, of judging the beauty of verse, and hence of coming in contact with the spirits of our greatest poets, would be something quite different to the masses we now know. To find the like we have to imagine the people of ancient story, who talked in poetry and moved their bodies to the rhythm, thus laying the foundations of refined civilization.

It is not our intention to describe in detail all we did in these experiments. It will be sufficient to summarize the results, which may suggest useful material and methods to others.

As soon as the children are somewhat advanced in reading, poetry, which they loved so much in the " Children's House," may be included in the materials offered in partial satisfaction of their insatiable desire to read. It is best to begin with poems composed of stanzas of different lengths, the stanzas being printed at easily noticeable intervals from each other. The lines may be counted, in teaching the two new words " stanza " and " line." The process involved is a recognition of " objects," suggesting the first exercise in reading, where the children put *names* on things; though here the situation is much simpler. At the same time we have the exercise of counting the lines. In short, it is a review exercise of the greatest simplicity.

The counting of the lines leads at once to the identification of such groups as the couplet, quatrain, octave, etc. But little time is spent on such a crude detail. The little ones almost immediately become interested in the rhyme. The first step is the recognition of rhyming syllables which are underlined with colored pencils, using a different color for each rhyme. Seven-year-olders take the greatest delight in this work, which is too simple to arouse interest in children of eight or nine. Those of seven do such work about as quickly as those of ten, the speed of the younger children being due apparently to their enthusiasm, the slowness of the older to their lack of interest. We may note in passing that these exercises furnish tests of absolute exactness as to rapidity of work. Children of eight are able to go one step beyond marking the rhymes with colored pencils. They can use the more complicated device of marking lines with the letters of the alphabet: aa, bb, cc, etc. Marking with numbers to the left the lines in their order, and the rhymes with letters to the right, we get a specimen result as follows:

| | |
|---|---|
| 1° Rondinella pellegr*ina* | a |
| 2° Che ti posi sul ver*one* | b |
| 3° Ricantando ogni matt*ina* | a |
| 4° Quella flebile canz*one* | b |
| 5° Che vuoi dirmi in tua fav*ella* | c |
| 6° Pellegrina rondin*ella*? | c |

(Translation: "Wandering swallow, as you sit there on my balcony each morning, singing to me your tearful song, what is it you are trying to tell me in your language, wandering swallow?")

This brings out the difference between the alternating rhyme (a, b, a, b) and the couplet (c, c), as well as the morphology of the stanza.

. . . . . . . .

In reading the lines over and over again to work out the rhyme scheme, the children spontaneously begin to catch the tonic accents. Their readiness in this respect is a matter of common observation. In fact, in ordinary schools, the teachers are continually struggling against the " sing-song " developed by children in reading poetry. This " sing-song " is nothing more nor less that stress on the rhythmic movement.

On one occasion, one of our children, a little boy, had been spending some time over a number of decasyllabic lines. While waiting in the corridor for the doors to open at dismissal time, he suddenly began to walk up and down " right-about-facing " at every three steps and saying aloud: " tatatá, tatatá, tatatátta," right-about-face, then " tatatá, tatatá, tatatátta." Each step was accompanied by a gesture in the air with his little clenched fist. This tot was marching to the verse rhythm, just as he would have marched to music. It was a case of perfectly interpretative "gymnastic rhythm." His gestures fell on the three tonic accents of the Italian decasyllable, the right-about marked the end of the "verse"— the "turn" in the line, which he indicated by "turning" himself around to begin over again.

When the children have reached such a stage of sensory development, they have no difficulty in recognizing the tonic accents. For this purpose, we have prepared sheets with poems written in a clear hand. The children mark with a neatly drawn accent the letter on which the rhythmic accent falls. The material should be systematically presented. We found from experience that the children first discover the accents in *long* lines made up of *even-numbered* syllables (parisyllabic lines), where the accents recur at regular intervals and are clearly called for both by sense, word accent and rhythm. We were able to establish the following sequence for various Italian lines, which present a graduated series of difficulties to the child in recognizing the accents:

1. Decasyllables: example:

> S'ode a déstra uno squíllo di trómba
> A sinístra rispónde uno squíllo:
> D'ambo i láti calpésto rimbómba
> Da caválli e da fánti il terrén.
> Quinci spunta per l'ária un vessíllo:
> Quindi un áltro s'avánza spiegáto:
> Ecco appáre un drappéllo schieráto;
> Ecco un áltro che incóntro gli vién.
>
> (MANZONI, *La battaglia di Maclodio*.)

(Translation: "A trumpet call sounds to the right; a trumpet calls answers to the left; all around the earth shakes with the charge of horses and men. Here a standard is broken out to the breeze; there another advances waving; here a line of troops appears, there another rushing against it.")

2. Dodecasyllables: example:

> Ruéllo, Ruéllo, divóra la vía,
> Portáteci a vólo, bufére del ciél.
> È présso alla mórte la vérgine mía,
> Galóppa, galóppa, galóppa Ruél.
>
> (Prati, *Galoppo notturno.*)

(Translation: "Ruello, Ruello, as fast as you can! O storm-winds of heaven, lend us your wings; my loved one is lying near death; onward, onward, onward, Ruello!")

3. Eight syllable lines (*ottonario*): example:

> Solitário bosco ombróso,
> A te viéne afflitto cór,
> Per trovár qualche ripóso
> Fra i silénzi in quest'orrór.
>
> (Rolli, *La lontananza.*)

(Translation: "O deserted wood! To your shade the sorrowing heart comes to find some rest in your cool silence.")

4. Six syllable lines (*senario*): example:

> Pur báldo di spéme
> L'uom última giúnto
> Le céneri préme
> D'un móndo defúnto;
> Incálza di sécoli
> Non ánco matúri
> I fúlgidi augúri.
>
> (Zanella, *La conchiglia fossile.*)

(Translation: "Radiant with hope, the latest comer treads on the ashes of a dead world, pursuing the glowing aspirations of ages not yet ripe.")

Note: In the above selections the vowels in broad-faced

type have been marked with an accent by the child, to indicate the rhythmic beat.

We found, on the other hand, that greater difficulty is experienced by the children in lines where the syllables are in odd-numbers (imparisyllabics), the hardest of the Italian lines being the hendecasyllable, which is a combination of the seven syllable and the five syllable line, fused together with all their great varieties of movement.

We established the following gradation of difficulties:

1. Seven syllable line (*settenario*): example:

> Già riéde Prímavéra
> Col súo fioríto aspétto,
> Già il gráto zéffirétto
> Schérza fra l'érbe e i fiór.
>
> (METASTASIO, *Primavera*.)

(Translation:  "Now already flowery Spring returns; again the lovely zephyrs dance amidst the grass and blossoms.")

2. Five syllable line (*quinario*): example:

> Viváce símbolo
> Dé la famíglia,
> Le diè la trémula
> Mádre a la fíglia,
> Le diè la suócera
> Buóna a la nuóra
> Ne l'últim' óra.
>
> (MAZZONI, *Per un mazzo di chiavi*.)

(Translation:  "As a vivid symbol of the home, they were passed on by the dying mother to her daughter or to her son's wife."

3. Nine syllable line (*novenario*): example:

> Te tríste!   Che a válle t'aspéttano
> I giórni di cántici prívi;
> Ah nó, non dai mórti che t'ámano,
> Ti guárda, fratéllo, dai vívi.
>
> (CAVALLOTTI, *Su in alto*.)

(Translation: "Alas, for thee, O brother! Yonder, songless days await thee. Ah no, have no fear of the dead: they love thee! The living only shouldst thou fear!")

4. Hendecasyllable: example:

> Per me si vá nella cittá dolénte,
> Per me si vá nell' etérno dolóre,
> Per me si vá tra la perdúta génte.
> (DANTE, *Divina Commedia, Inferno.*)

(Translation: "Through me ye enter the city of sorrow; through me ye enter the realm of eternal grief; through me ye enter the regions of the damned").

The typical ending of these various lines is the trochee (— ∪, *verso piano*). The iambic (∪ —, *verso tronco*) and the dactyllic (— ∪ ∪, *verso sdrucciolo*) endings (requiring respectively one syllable less and one syllable more than the *verso piano*) constitute occasional variations. We have found that these rarer lines are recognized rather as curiosities than as difficulties by the children who easily refer them to their respective normal types. They are accordingly presented in our material along with the common verses of trochaic endings. Our illustration of the five syllable line given above showed specimens of the dactyllic ending (*sdrucciolo*, — ∪ ∪). Here is another example of alternating trochaic (*piano*) and dactyllic endings:

> In címa a un álbero
> C'é un uccellíno
> Di nuóvo génere. . . .
> Che sía un bambíno?
> (L. SCHWARZ, *Uocellino.*)

(Translation: "There's a very strange little bird up in that tree! Why, it's a little child!")

In the following decasyllables, the trochaic ending alternates with the iambic (*tronco*):

> Lungi, lúngi, su l'áli del cánto
> Di qui lúngi recáre io ti vó'
> Là, ne i cámpi fioríti del sánto
> Gange, un luógo bellíssimo, io só.
>
> (CARDUCCI, *Lungi, lungi.*)

(Translation: "I will take thee far, far away on the wings of my song: there, among the flowery fields of the sacred Ganges, I know of a beautiful spot").

Some difficulty arose, however, when we came to lines with alternations of parisyllables and imparisyllables; though this new movement aroused real enthusiasm among the children, who greeted it as a new and strange music. It often happened that after the pleasurable effort of analyzing a poem with lines alternating in this way, the pupils would choose as "recreation" the study of lines of even-numbered syllables. Here is an example of the new type:

> Eran trecénto, eran gióvani e fórti,
> E sóno mórti!
> Me ne andávo al mattíno a spigoláre
> Quando ho vísto una bárca in mezzo al máre:
> Era una bárca che andáva a vapóre,
> E alzáva una bandiéra tricolóre.
> All'ísola di Pónza s'è fermáta,
> È stata un póco e pói si è ritornáta;
> S'è ritornáta ed è venúta a térra:
> Sceser con l'ármi, e a noi non fécer guérra.
>
> (PRATI, *La spigolatrice di Sapri.*)

(Translation: "There were three hundred, young and strong! And now they are dead! That morning I was gleaning in the fields; I saw a boat at sea,— a

steamer flying the white, red and green. It stopped at
Ponza, remained a while and then came back — came back
and approached the shore. They came ashore in arms,
but to us they did no harm ").

While the rhythmic accents were being studied, we
found that the discovery of the cæsura (interior pause)
formed an interesting recreative diversion. In fact this
work aroused so much enthusiasm that the children went
from exercise to exercise, continuing at study for extended periods, and far from showing signs of weariness,
actually increased their joyous application. One little
girl, in the first six minutes of her work, marked the
cæsura of seventy-six ten-syllable lines without making a
mistake. An abundant material is necessary for this exercise. Example:

> Dagli atri muscosi, | dai fori cadenti,
> Dai boschi, dall' arse | fucine stridenti,
> Dai solchi bagnati | di servo sudor,
> Un volgo disperso | repente si desta,
> Intende l'orecchio, | solleva la testa,
> Percosso da novo | crescente rumor.
>                     (MANZONI, *Italiani e Longobardi.*)

(Translation: " From the damp atria, from the ruined
squares, from the forests, from the hissing forges, from
the fields bathed with the sweat of slaves, a scattered
horde of men suddenly is roused. They listen, lift their
heads, startled at this strange increasing roar ").

The step forward to the perception of the syllabic units
of the line is a purely sensory phenomenon: it is analogous to marking the time of music without taking account
of the measure divisions. Syllabiating according to

rhythm and beating on the table with the fingers solve even the subtler difficulties such as dieresis and synalepha, in recognizing the rhythmic syllables.  Examples:

La | so | mma | sa | pi | en | za e'l | pri | mo A | mo | re

We print this verse in the above form, because it was thus divided by a child in his very first spontaneous effort at syllabiation.  As a matter of fact, we present the material normally according to graded difficulties, using over again for this purpose the materials used in the study of accents.  At this point also the accents themselves suddenly acquire a new interest, for the child is able to observe on "what syllable they fall."  Thus his metrical study approaches completion, for now he can readily acquire the nomenclature of metrics and versification: *dodecasyllable, hendecasyllable,* etc.  Then, combining his knowledge of the numbers of syllables and the location of the rhythmic accents, the child is at the point of discovering the rhythmic laws of verse construction.  We were expecting the children to begin producing definitions like the following:  " The dodecasyllable line has twelve syllables and four accents which fall on the second, fifth, eighth and eleventh syllables," etc.  The spontaneous impulse of the pupils led instead to the construction of " mirrors " or " checkerboards " like the following:

| | 1 | 2 | 3 | 4 | 5 | 6 | 7 | 8 | 9 | 10 | 11 | 12 | 13 |
|---|---|---|---|---|---|---|---|---|---|---|---|---|---|
| Decasyllable *piano* (trochaic) | | | 3d | | | 6th | | | 9th | | | | |
| " *tronco* (iambic) | | | 3d | | | 6th | | | 9th | | | | |
| Eight syllable *piano* | | | 3d | | | | 7th | | | | | | |
| " " *tronco* | | | 3d | | | | 7th | | | | | | |
| Dodecasyllable *piano* | | 2d | | | 5th | | | 8th | | | 11th | | |
| " *tronco* | | 2d | | | 5th | | | 8th | | | 11th | | |

The additional step to using the symbols of metrics was an easy one, and a graphic diagram resulted much as follows:

| Eight syllable | 1 | 2 | 3 | 4 | 5 | 6 | 7 | 8 | 9 | 10 | 11 | 12 | 13 |
|---|---|---|---|---|---|---|---|---|---|---|---|---|---|
| (Title of Poem) | ⏑ | ⏑ | ´ | ⏑ | ⏑ | ⏑ | ´ | ⏑ | | | | | |
| e. g. | ⏑ | ⏑ | ´ | ⏑ | ⏑ | ⏑ | ´ | | | | | | |
| "Il ritorno in Italia" | ⏑ | ⏑ | ´ | ⏑ | ⏑ | ⏑ | ´ | ⏑ | | | | | |
| "Return to Italy" | ⏑ | ⏑ | ´ | ⏑ | ⏑ | ⏑ | ´ | | | | | | |
| | | | | | | | | | | | | | |
| | ⏑ | ⏑ | ´ | ⏑ | ⏑ | ⏑ | ´ | ⏑ | | | | | |
| | ⏑ | ⏑ | ´ | ⏑ | ⏑ | ⏑ | ´ | | | | | | |
| "Solitude" | ⏑ | ⏑ | ´ | ⏑ | ⏑ | ⏑ | ´ | ⏑ | | | | | |
| | ⏑ | ⏑ | ´ | ⏑ | ⏑ | ⏑ | ´ | | | | | | |
| | | | | | | | | | | | | | |

| Decasyllable | 1 | 2 | 3 | 4 | 5 | 6 | 7 | 8 | 9 | 10 | 11 | 12 | 13 |
|---|---|---|---|---|---|---|---|---|---|---|---|---|---|
| (Title of Poem) | ⏑ | ⏑ | ´ | ⏑ | ⏑ | ´ | ⏑ | ⏑ | ´ | ⏑ | | | |
| "Passion" | ⏑ | ⏑ | ´ | ⏑ | ⏑ | ´ | ⏑ | ⏑ | ´ | ⏑ | | | |
| | | | | | | | | | | | | | |
| | ⏑ | ⏑ | ´ | ⏑ | ⏑ | ´ | ⏑ | ⏑ | ´ | ⏑ | | | |
| "The Oath of Pontida" | ⏑ | ⏑ | ´ | ⏑ | ⏑ | ´ | ⏑ | ⏑ | ´ | ⏑ | | | |
| | | | | | | | | | | | | | |
| "The Battle of Macloud" | ⏑ | ⏑ | ´ | ⏑ | ⏑ | ´ | ⏑ | ⏑ | ´ | ⏑ | | | |
| | ⏑ | ⏑ | ´ | ⏑ | ⏑ | ´ | ⏑ | ⏑ | ´ | ⏑ | | | |
| | | | | | | | | | | | | | |
| "Far, far away" | ⏑ | ⏑ | ´ | ⏑ | ⏑ | ´ | ⏑ | ⏑ | ´ | ⏑ | | | |
| | ⏑ | ⏑ | ´ | ⏑ | ⏑ | ´ | ⏑ | ⏑ | ´ | | | | |
| | | | | | | | | | | | | | |

The next development is a complete study of the stanza or strophe in the form of a summary; the number of lines, the rhymes, the accents, number and location of the syllables. To *distinguish* between the stanzas is also to classify them, which becomes a pleasing task for the children.

One little girl, who was making a summary study of four terzets of Dante, suddenly called the teacher to inform her with an expression of complete surprise: "See, the rhyme always begins at the last accent!" She had before her:

> Per me si va nella città dol*ente;*
> Per me si va nell'eterno dol*ore;*
> Per me si va tra la perduta *gente.*
> Giustizia mosse il mio alto fatt*ore;*
> Fecemi la divina potest*ate,*
> La somma sapienza e il primo am*ore.*
> Dinanzi a me non fur cose cre*ate.* . . .
> (Dante: Inscription over Gate of Hell.)

So in metrics also the children, following the natural inclinations of their growth, pass from sensory discipline, to intelligent cognition, and graphic representation. Then they become the "explorers of their environment," the "discoverers" of general laws.

* * *

Translator's Note: The basis of Italian verse is in the syllable count, and the rhythmic accent. In English verse, however, the question of the syllable count is dependent on a much more complex consideration: syllable length; and syllable length, in its turn, is conditioned not only by the phonetic situation in and around the syllable, but by rhetorical stress as well. It is clear that Signora

Montessori's experiments on the simpler Italian line have little direct bearing, save as an illustration of method, on the pedagogy of English Metrics. For whereas, the principal classifications of Italian lines involve merely the problem of syllabiation (complicated by dieresis and synalepha), with a numerical terminology (*quinario, ottonario, decasillabo,* etc.), the study of English versification demands an analysis of measure (feet) and of number of feet, with a terminology relative to each: trochee, iambus, dactyl, spondee, anapest, etc., hexameter, pentameter, etc., to mention only the most obvious elements of a science which, applied even to simple English verse, soon becomes extremely complicated. How much, then, of the study of English metrics, beyond the elementary concepts of stanza and rhyme, should be included in the Montessori Advanced Method, and what order of presentation of facts should be followed, still remains to be experimentally determined.

However, the most illuminating fact, as regards method, which detaches from Signora Montessori's experiments with metrical forms, is that *long parisyllables* are more readily analyzed by children than imparisyllables; and secondly that *short* imparisyllables prove easier than long imparisyllables. We might wish more explicit evidence that the hardest parisyllable is easier, therefore more *natural,* than the easiest imparisyllable — as implied in Signora Montessori's presentation of this subject. Even so, her conclusions are interesting, and from more than one point of view. It will be recalled that the most ancient and the most fortunate of the meters used in French, Spanish, and Provençal poetry is precisely the decasyllable (*Song of Roland,* the Provençal *Boecis,* etc.), whereas the favorite line of old Italian popular poetry was the octo-

syllabic verse. These are both parisyllables, though the
succession of *theses,* or rhythmic beats, is not quite analogous to that of the modern Italian verses used in this
experiment. It would seem, in fact, as though the children initiated by Signora Montessori into metrical studies,
were actually traversing the earlier experiences of their
Latin race.

Doubtless the reason why the parisyllable submits
more readily to rhythmic analysis than imparisyllables, is
that when the syllables are in even numbers, the line tends
to reduce to two simple rhythmic groups — the decasyllable to groups of 4 and 6, with two rhythmic beats in
each group; the dodecasyllable to groups of 6 and 6 (therefore of 3 and 3 and 3 and 3); the octosyllables to groups
of 4 and 4; the six syllable to groups of 3 and 3. The
imparisyllables on the contrary are rarely capable of such
division — of such *monotony,* if you wish. They lend
themselves to more complex rhythm, especially to "par-
agraphic" treatment. They are distinctly the rhythms
of erudite, "cultivated," "literary" poetry.

We should suspect, accordingly, that what appears in
the above experiments as *length* is in reality *reducibility*
to simpler forms; and that lines capable of such reduction should be given first in an adaptation of Signora
Montessori's method. It is, however, highly improbable
that in English, where the only constant element in
rhythm is the stress and not the syllable count, the line
compounded of two simpler rhythmic groups should prove
easier for the child than either of these simpler groups
themselves. We see no reason to assume, for instance,
than an eight-stress line, reducible to two four-stress lines,
should be more readily analyzed than a four-stress line;
or that a seven-stress line, reducible to a four-stress and

a three-stress line, should be easier than either one of
these. In fact, the predominance of these simpler elements in the English feeling for these longer groups is
indicated by the fact that such compound lines are commonly broken into their constituent parts when printed
(cf. *The Ancient Mariner*), even in cases where the iso-
lation of these parts is not emphasized and rendered natural by rhyme. It will be observed that in the Montessori
experiment the order of presentation was first, three-
stress (anapestic), then four-stress (iambic), then two-
stress (iambic) lines. This situation happens to correspond to that found in the commonest popular English
verse, which gives undoubted preference, as witness our
nursery rimes, to three-stress and four-stress iambics.
Two-stress lines constitute in reality four-stress lines divided by rhyme; just as, in poems of distinctly literary
savor, the two-stress line is further reducible by interior
rhyme to two one-stress lines.

### THREE-STRESS LINES (TRIMETER)

*Iambic:*

O lét the sólid grotínd
Not faíl beneáth my feét
Befóre my lífe has fotínd
What sóme have fotínd so sweét.

TENNYSON.

The motíntain sheép are sweéter,
But the válley sheép are fátter;
We thérefore deémed it meéter
To cárry óff the látter.
We máde an éxpedítion;
We mét an hóst and quélled it;
We fórced a stróng posítion,
And kílled the mén who héld it.

PEACOCK.

*Trochaic:*

Háil to theé blithe spírit!
Bírd thou néver wért,
Thát from heáven or neár it
Poúrest thý full heárt. . . .

SHELLEY.

*Anapestic:*

I am mónarch of áll I survéy;
My ríght there is nóne to dispúte;
From the céntre all roúnd to the seá
I am lórd of the fówl and the brúte.

COWPER.

*Dactyllic:*

Thís is a spráy the bird clúng to,
Máking it blóssom with pleásure,
Ére the high treé-tops she sprúng to,
Fít for her nést and her treásure.[1]

BROWNING.

## FOUR-STRESS LINES (TETRAMETER)

*Iambic:*

Examples: Byron, *The Prisoner of Chillon;* Scott, *The Lady of the Lake;* Milton, *Il pensieroso.*

We coúld not móve a síngle páce,
We coúld not seé each óther's fáce
But wíth that pále and lívid líght
They máde us stróngers ín our síght. . . .

BYRON.

*Trochaic:*

Examples: Longfellow, *Hiawatha;* George Eliot, *The Spanish Gipsy.*

Wéstward, wéstward Híawátha
Saíled intó the fíéry súnset,
Saíled intó the púrple vápors,
Saíled intó the dúsk of évening.

[1] Most of our examples of various types and combinations of verse are taken from Alden, *English Verse*, New York, Henry Holt.

This line is much more common in its catalectic form:

> Háste thee nýmph and bríng with thée
> Jést and yoúthful jóllitý,
> Quíps and cránks and wánton wíles,
> Nóds and bécks and wreáthed smíles. . .
>
> Milton, L'Allegro.

*Anapestic:*

Examples:   Goldsmith, *Retaliation;* Byron, *The Destruction of Sennacherib.*

> The smáll birds rejoíce in the greén leaves retúrning,
> The múrmuring streámlet winds cleár through the vále.
>
> Burns.

*Dactyllic:*

Examples:   Byron, *Song of Saul;* Dryden, *An Evening's Love.*

> Áfter the pángs of a désperate lóver,
> Whén day and níght I have síghed all in vaín,
> Áh what a pleásure it ís to discóver
> In her eyes píty, who caúses my paín.    Dryden.

## Two-Stress Lines

*Iambic:*

Examples:   Herrick, *To the Lark;* Shakespeare, *Midsummernight's Dream* (Bottom's song).

> The ráging rócks
> And shívering shócks
> Shall breák the lócks
> Of príson gátes.    Shakespeare.

*Trochaic:*

Examples:   George Eliot, *The Spanish Gipsy;* Campion, *Art of Poesie.*

> Coúld I cátch that
> Nímble traítor,
> Scórnful Laúra,
> Swíft-foot Laúra,
> Soón then woúld I
> Seék avéngement.    Campion.

*Anapestic:*

Examples: Shelley, *Arethusa;* Scott, *The Lady of the Lake* (Coronach).

> He is góne on the moúntain,
> He is lóst to the fórest,
> Like a súmmer-dried foúntain,
> When our neéd was the sórest.
>
> SCOTT.

*Dactyllic:*

Examples: Tennyson, *Charge of the Light Brigade;* Longfellow, *Saga of King Olaf.*

> Cánnon to ríght of them,
> Cánnon to léft of them,
> Cánnon in frónt of them,
> Volleyed and thúndered.

## ONE-STRESS LINE

*Iambic:*

Example:

> Thus Í
> Pass bý
> And díe
> As óne
> Unknówn
> And góne.
>
> HERRICK.

## SEVEN-STRESS LINES (HEPTAMETER)

*Iambic:*

Examples: Howe, *Battle Hymn of the Republic;* Byron, *Stanzas for Music;* Kipling, *Wolcott Balestier;* Coleridge, *The Ancient Mariner.*

> Mine eyés have seén the glóry óf the cóming óf the Lórd.
>
> HOWE.

*Trochaic:*

Example:  Swinburne, *Clear the Way.*

Cleár the wáy, my lórds and láckeys, yoú have hád your dáy.
Hére you háve your ánswer, Éngland's yeá agaínst your náy.

*Anapestic:*

Example:  Swinburne, *The Birds.*

Come ón then ye dwéllers by náture in dárkness and líke to the
leáves' generátions.

*Dactyllic:*

Example:  Anonymous.

Oút of the kíngdom of Chríst shall be gáthered by ángels. o'er Sátan
victórious,
All that offéndeth, that líeth, that faíleth to hónor his náme ever
glórious.


## Six-Stress Lines (Hexameter)

*Iambic* (alexandrine):

Example:  Wordsworth, *The Pet Lamb.*

The déw was fálling fást, the stárs begán to blínk;
I heárd a voíce: it saíd, " Drínk, prétty creáture, drínk! "

*Trochaic:*

Example:  Swinburne, *The Last Oracle.*

Kíng, the wáys of heáven befóre thy feét grow gólden;
Gód, the soúl of eárth is kíndled wíth thy gráce.

*Anapestic:*

Examples:  Tennyson, *Maud;* Swinburne, *The Garden of Cymodoce.*

And the rúshing báttle-bolt sáng from the threé-decker oút of the
foám.

TENNYSON.

*Dactyllic:*

Examples: Swinburne, *Hesperia;* Longfellow, *Evangeline.*

This is the fórest priméval; the múrmuring pínes and the hémlocks
Beárded with móss and with gárments greén, indistínct in the
twílight.

LONGFELLOW.

EIGHT-STRESS LINES

*Iambic:*

Example: William Webbe, *Discourse of English
Poetrie.*

Where vírtue wánts and více abóunds, there weálth is bút a
baíted hoók.

*Trochaic:*

Examples: Tennyson, *Locksley Hall;* Poe, *The
Raven.*

Open thén I flúng the shútter, whén with mány a flírt and flútter,
In there stépped a státely ráven óf the saíntly dáys of yóre.

POE.

*Anapestic:*

Example: Swinburne, *March.*

Ere fróst-flower and snów-blossom fáded and féll, and the spléndor
  of wínter had pássed out of síght,
The wáys of the woódlands were faírer and stránger than dreáms
  that fulfíl us in sleép with delíght.

*Dactyllic:*

Example: Longfellow, *Golden Legend, 4.*

Ónward and ónward the híghway rúns to the dístant cíty, im-
  pátiently beáring
Tídings of húman jóy and disáster, of lóve and háte, of dóing and
  dáring.

FIVE-STRESS LINEŚ (PENTAMETER)

*Iâmbic* (Heroic pentameter):

Examples: Milton, *Paradise Lost;* Bryant, *Thanatopsis,* etc., etc.

> Sweet Aúburn, lóveliest víllage óf the plaín
> Where heálth and beaúty cheér the láboring swaín . . .
> GOLDSMITH.

*Trochaic:*

Examples: Browning, *One word more;* Tennyson, *The Vision of Sin.*

> Thén methoúght I heárd a méllow soúnd,
> Gáthering úp from áll the lówer groúnd.

*Anapestic:*

Examples: Browning, *Saul;* Tennyson, *Maud.*

> We have próved we have heárts in a caúse: we are nóble stíll.
> TENNYSON.

*Dactyllic:*

Very rare in English.

·    ·    ·    ·    ·    ·    ·    ·

While the remainder of the exercises in syllabication and graphic transcription, as described by Dr. Montessori, would seem to follow naturally on the above exercises in the analysis of line stress, it is clear that additional attention must be given to questions of terminology. For the metrical syntheses performed in the tables at the end of the preceding section will not be possible for English poetry unless the child is able to identify the kinds of feet and the kinds of lines. We suggest accordingly two supplementary drills with the card system familiar to the child from his exercises in grammar. The first consists of a list of words, each on a separate card,

with the tonic accent marked. Each word with its accent represents a foot (iambus, trochee, anapest, dactyl),
indicated on the card in graphic transcription beneath
the word:

wóndering

$\acute{-}\;\smile\;\smile$

Corresponding to each word is another card bearing
simply the graphic transcription and the name of the
foot. The exercise, of the greatest simplicity, is to pair
off the cards, arranging the words in a column on the
table, putting after each the card that describes it. The
cards, when properly arranged, read as follows:

| | |
|---|---|
| betweén $\smile\;\acute{-}$ | $\smile\;\acute{-}$ iambus |
| móther $\acute{-}\;\smile$ | $\acute{-}\;\smile$ trochee |
| disrepúte $\smile\;\smile\;\acute{-}$ | $\smile\;\smile\;\acute{-}$ anapest |
| wónderful $\acute{-}\;\smile\;\smile$ | $\acute{-}\;\smile\;\smile$ dactyl |

A second stage of this exercise consists in offering a
similar series of cards where, however, the word-cards are
without the indication of the tonic accent and without
the graphic transcription of the measure:

| | |
|---|---|
| suggest | $\smile\;\acute{-}$ iambus |
| accent | $\acute{-}\;\smile$ trochee |
| underneath | $\smile\;\smile\;\acute{-}$ anapest |
| metrical | $\acute{-}\;\smile\;\smile$ dactyl |

An identical exercise is possible for whole lines. The
first stage consists of naming the lines accompanied by

the metrical transcription with cards containing simply the transcription and the name of the meter; in the second stage, the same lines are given but on cards without the graphic transcription: for example:

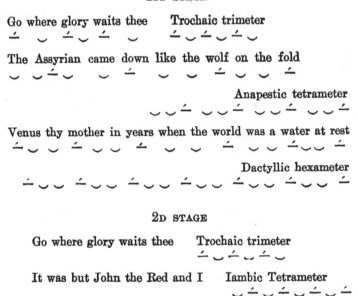

1ST STAGE

Go where glory waits thee    Trochaic trimeter

The Assyrian came down like the wolf on the fold

Anapestic tetrameter

Venus thy mother in years when the world was a water at rest

Dactyllic hexameter

2D STAGE

Go where glory waits thee    Trochaic trimeter

It was but John the Red and I    Iambic Tetrameter

etc., etc.

When these fundamental notions have been acquired the child is ready for the more difficult problems of anacrusis, catalexis, irregular feet and irregular pauses, which he can recognize in almost any poem of considerable length by comparing the transcription of a given foot with specimen transcriptions of regular lines, which are always accessible to him.

# APPENDICES

# APPENDIX I

## CHART
## FOR THE STUDY OF THE
## INDIVIDUAL CHILD

Copies of this Chart (pages 409–422) will be supplied, in convenient form, by the publishers, Frederick A. Stokes Company, 443–449 Fourth Avenue, New York, at 20 cents for the set. Diary pads are 10 cents additional.

## SCHOOL DATA

*School Year 191.* . . . . . . . . . . . . . . . . . . . . . . . . . . . . . . . . . . . . . . . . . . .

*Hours of Sessions* . . . . . . . . . . . . . . . . . . . . . . . . . . . . . . . . . . . . . . . . .

*Vacations* . . . . . . . . . . . . . . . . . . . . . . . . . . . . . . . . . . . . . . . . . . . . . . . .

*Subjects Taught* . . . . . . . . . . . . . . . . . . . . . . . . . . . . . . . . . . . . . . . . . .

. . . . . . . . . . . . . . . . . . . . . . . . . . . . . . . . . . . . . . . . . . . . . . . . . . . . . . . . . .

. . . . . . . . . . . . . . . . . . . . . . . . . . . . . . . . . . . . . . . . . . . . . . . . . . . . . . . . . .

. . . . . . . . . . . . . . . . . . . . . . . . . . . . . . . . . . . . . . . . . . . . . . . . . . . . . . . . . .

*Meals* . . . . . . . . . . . . . . . . . . . . . . . . . . . . . . . . . . . . . . . . . . . . . . . . . . .

*Teaching Staff* . . . . . . . . . . . . . . . . . . . . . . . . . . . . . . . . . . . . . . . . . . .

. . . . . . . . . . . . . . . . . . . . . . . . . . . . . . . . . . . . . . . . . . . . . . . . . . . . . . . . . .

. . . . . . . . . . . . . . . . . . . . . . . . . . . . . . . . . . . . . . . . . . . . . . . . . . . . . . . . . .

. . . . . . . . . . . . . . . . . . . . . . . . . . . . . . . . . . . . . . . . . . . . . . . . . . . . . . . . . .

*Address of School* . . . . . . . . . . . . . . . . . . . . . . . . . . . . . . . . . . . . . . .

*Rooms* . . . . . . . . . . . . . . . . . . . . . . . . . . . . . . . . . . . . . . . . . . . . . . . . . .

*Consultations with Parents and Public* . . . . . . . . . . . . . . . . . . . . . .

. . . . . . . . . . . . . . . . . . . . . . . . . . . . . . . . . . . . . . . . . . . . . . . . . . . . . . . . . .

. . . . . . . . . . . . . . . . . . . . . . . . . . . . . . . . . . . . . . . . . . . . . . . . . . . . . . . . . .

. . . . . . . . . . . . . . . . . . . . . . . . . . . . . . . . . . . . . . . . . . . . . . . . . . . . . . . . . .

. . . . . . . . . . . . . . . . . . . . . . . . . . . . . . . . . . . . . . . . . . . . . . . . . . . . . . . . . .

## DATA ON THE CHILD

*Family Name*....................*Names*......................

*Date of Birth* ...........................................

*Date of Entrance* ........................................

*Age of Parents: Father*...............*Mother*.................

*Occupations of Parents:*

        *Father* .......................................

        *Mother* ......................................

*Home Address* ............................................

*Personal History of the Child*................................

............................................................

............................................................

............................................................

............................................................

*Personal Appearance of the Child*.............................

*Notes on Child's Family*......................................

............................................................

............................................................

............................................................

............................................................

............................................................

SCHOOL YEAR 191.. 191..

*Name* ....................... *Date of Birth*....................

..........................................................................

*Date of Entering School*..............................

| ANTHROPOLOGICAL NOTES | | | NOTES ON CHILD'S PHYSICAL DEVELOPMENT |
|---|---|---|---|
| HEAD (mm.) | Cephalic Index | : : | ...................................................... |
| | Transversal diameter | : : | ...................................................... |
| | Antero-post diameter | : : | ...................................................... |
| | Circumference | : : | ...................................................... |
| Index of Weight | : : | | ...................................................... |
| Index of Stature | : : | | ...................................................... |
| Stature (sitting) (m.) | : : | | ...................................................... |
| Thoracic circum. (m.) | : : | | ...................................................... |
| Weight (Kg.) | : : | | ...................................................... |
| Stature (standing) (m.) | : : | | ...................................................... |

# SCHOOL YEAR 191..—191..

Name.....................Date of Birth.....................

.................................................................

| MONTH | STATURE IN METRES | | NOTES |
|---|---|---|---|
| | Standing | Sitting | |
| September | ......... | ......... | ............................. |
| October | ......... | ......... | ............................. |
| November | ......... | ......... | ............................. |
| December | ......... | ......... | ............................. |
| January | ......... | ......... | ............................. |
| February | ......... | ......... | ............................. |
| March | ......... | ......... | ............................. |
| April | ......... | ......... | ............................. |
| May | ......... | ......... | ............................. |
| June | ......... | ......... | ............................. |
| July | ......... | ......... | ............................. |
| August | ......... | ......... | ............................. |

*Name* ...............................................................

...............................................................

*Date of Birth* ...........................................................

...............................................................

| MONTH | WEIGHT IN KILOGRAMS | | | |
|---|---|---|---|---|
| | 1st week | 2nd week | 3rd week | 4th week |
| *September* | ............ | ............ | ............ | ............ |
| *October* | ............ | ............ | ............ | ............ |
| *November* | ............ | ............ | ............ | ............ |
| *December* | ............ | ............ | ............ | ............ |
| *January* | ............ | ............ | ............ | ............ |
| *February* | ............ | ............ | ............ | ............ |
| *March* | ............ | ............ | ............ | ............ |
| *April* | ............ | ............ | ............ | ............ |
| *May* | ............ | ............ | ............ | ............ |
| *June* | ............ | ............ | ............ | ............ |
| *July* | ............ | ............ | ............ | ............ |
| *August* | ............ | ............ | ............ | ............ |

(*Family Name*)          (*Names*)

NAME IN FULL.............................................

SCHOOL YEAR 191..–191..

# PSYCHOLOGICAL DIARY

| Diary | Name of child | | | Page Number |
|---|---|---|---|---|
| 191.. | Month | ........................ | Day...................... | |

# GUIDE FOR PSYCHOLOGICAL OBSERVATION

## WORK.

NOTE:

When a child begins to show constant application to a piece of work.

What this work is and how long he remains at it (speed or slowness he shows in completing it, the number of times he repeats the same exercise).

Individual peculiarities in application to particular tasks.

To what tasks the child successively applies himself on the same day and with how much persistency to each.

Whether he has periods of spontaneous activity at work and on how many days.

How the child's need of progress is manifested by him.

What tasks he chooses and the order in which he chooses them; the persistency he shows in each.

His power of application in spite of distractions about him that might tend to divert him from his work.

Whether after a compulsory distraction he takes up again the task that has been interrupted.

## CONDUCT.

NOTE:

Orderliness or disorderliness in the actions of the child.

The nature of his disorderliness.

Whether there are any changes in conduct as his working ability develops.

Whether, as his activities become more orderly, the child gives evidence of: accesses of joy; periods of placidity; expressions of affection.

The part the children take and the interest they show in the progress of their schoolmates.

## OBEDIENCE.

NOTE:

Whether the child answers readily when he is called.

Whether and at what times the child begins to show interest in what others are doing and to make intelligent effort to join in their work.

The progress of his obedience to *calls*.

The progress of his obedience to *commands*.

What eagerness and enthusiasm the child shows in his obedience.

The relation between the various phenomena of obedience and (a) the development of his working capacity; (b) changes in conduct.

417

PERSONAL HISTORY OF THE CHILD

SCHOOL YEAR 191—191..

## BIOLOGICAL HISTORY

**PARENTS:**

*Age of parents at marriage.....................................*

*Are the parents related to each other?..........................*

*Sickness and diseases of the parents............................*

*..............................................................*

**CHILD:**

*Were pregnancy and parturition normal?.........................*

*..............................................................*

*Was the nursing done by the mother, or artificially?............*

*..............................................................*

*The child's health during the first year:.......................*

*..............................................................*

*Subsequent sicknesses of the child:............................*

*..............................................................*

*Date of teething, learning to walk, and learning to speak:........*

*..............................................................*

*..............................................................*

420

# SCHOOL YEAR 191..–191..

## SOCIAL HISTORY

FATHER:

*Age, education and occupation:...................................*

*..............................................................*

MOTHER:

*Age, education and occupation:...................................*

*..............................................................*

---

*Are accounts kept in the family?...............................*

*..............................................................*

*Family habits (amusements, home life)..........................*

*..............................................................*

*Number of persons in the family (how many adults, how many*

*children) .....................................................*

*..............................................................*

*Does the family employ servants?...............................*

*How many wage earners are in the family?.......................*

*Does the family have income from property?.....................*

*Does the family keep roomers or boarders?......................*

*Is the housekeeping satisfactory?..............................*

421

SCHOOL YEAR 191..–191..

ETHICAL EXAMINATION

QUESTIONNAIRE FOR MORAL HISTORY

### CRITERIA OF PRAISE AND PRIDE IN THE FAMILY
NOTE:

What is commended in the family, e.g., devoutness, patriotism, or their opposites, affectionateness, honesty, modesty, neatness, generosity, kindness, independence, etc. The social relationships between husband and wife (rights, privileges or equality). Special distinctions of family members (public honors, acts of courage, etc.).

### CRITERIA OF BLAME AND EXCUSE IN THE FAMILY
NOTE:

What complaints are made in the home against members of the family, e.g., drinking, lack of affectionateness, gambling, irreligion, disorderliness, lawlessness, extravagance, laziness, etc.

### EDUCATIONAL CRITERIA IN THE FAMILY
NOTE:

What concept do the parents have of education? e.g., severity, gentleness, rewards, punishments, understanding of children, the freedom accorded the children, etc.

### MOTHER'S OPINION OF HER CHILDREN
NOTE:

What care is taken of the child and what rights are recognized by the family as belonging to him.

422

# APPENDIX II

SUMMARY OF THE LECTURES ON PEDAGOGY DE-
LIVERED IN ROME AT THE *SCUOLA MAGIS-
TRALE ORTOFRENICA* IN 1900

This appendix contains a summary of a few of my
lectures delivered in 1900 in the Scuola Magistrale Ortofrenica in Rome and published in pamphlet form for the
benefit of the teacher-students who were attending that
course. A number of distinguished physicians were at
the same time lecturing in the school on various subjects
— such as Psychology, Esthesiology, Anatomy of the
Nerve Centres, etc. I had reserved for myself the teaching, or rather the development, of a special pedagogy for
defective children, along the lines previously laid down by
Itard and Séguin.

In the summary of these old lectures of mine are included some of my experiments with certain subjects
taught in the elementary grades. They show that the
origin of my present work with older and normal children
is to be sought in my teaching of defectives.

I still possess, as documentary relics of this course, a
hundred copies of a pamphlet entitled: *Riassunte delle
lezioni di didattica della Prof*ssa *Montessori, anno 1900,
Stab. Lit. Romano, via Frattina 62, Roma.* More than
three hundred teachers followed my course, and are able
to bear witness to the work done there.

I republish the following excerpts not because I consider my work so important as to merit the preservation of

all the documents touching its origin, but to prevent the giving of undue prominence to those remnants of my earlier attempts and studies which are still to be found in the Scuola Magistrale Ortofrenica in Rome.

" The child should be led from the education of the muscular system to that of the nervous and sensory systems; from the education of the senses to concepts; from concepts to general ideas; from general ideas to morality. This is the educational method of Séguin."

However, before we begin education, we must prepare the child to receive it by another education which is to-day regarded as of the very first importance. This preparatory education is the foundation on which all subsequent education must be based, and the success we obtain in it will determine the success of our subsequent efforts. By preparatory education I here mean *hygienic education,* which in defective children sometimes includes medical treatment. That is why the educational method for defectives is sometimes described as *medico-pedagogical.*

Those who realize the importance of feeling and internal sensation in education will understand that the bodily organism must function properly in order to respond to our educational efforts. We must preserve good health where good health exists; we must restore it where it is lacking.

We are therefore under strict obligation to pay close attention to nutrition and to the condition of the vital organs. Every one is aware of the close relation existing between general sensibility and morality. Criminals and prostitutes show very scant sensitiveness to pain and to tactile stimuli. The same situation is frequently apparent in defectives; hence the necessity of restoring the tactile sense with adequate attention to hygiene.

We cannot educate the muscles to perform a given coordinate movement if they have lost their power of functioning (as in paresis, etc.). Education, properly so-called, must be preceded by a medical treatment to restore the muscles, if possible, to good health.

It will be impossible to educate, for example, the sense of hearing, if some pathological situation has produced partial deafness. We cannot educate the sense of smell if the excessive excretion of mucus prevents external stimuli from acting on the ends of the sensory nerves. Obviously, we need a medical treatment to remove these diseased conditions.

## MEDICAL EDUCATION

*General baths:* When not too prolonged they develop the sensibility of the nervous papillæ. They give tone to the cellular and muscular tissues, especially to the skin.

*Hot and cold baths* given alternately are a powerful educational instrument in attracting the attention of the child to his external environment.

*Local hot laths* may be given to areas deficient in sensibility. For instance, try bathing the hands if tactile education proves impossible, or bathe the feet if the defect in standing upright or in walking comes from the insensitiveness of the soles.

*Local cold baths:* Given to the head while the patient is entirely ·covered in warm water are a tonic to the scalp; they facilitate the knitting of the bones of the skull and the formation of wormian bones, preventing also cerebral congestion. They stimulate and regularize the cerebral circulation. Such baths are particularly useful for hydro-cephalics and micro-cephalics, but all patients are benefited by such baths, which are the most generally useful of all.

*Steam baths* develop perspiration which at times is completely absent or only partial in defectives, causing serious physical disturbances. These baths, furthermore, predispose the nerve ends to the most intense sensitiveness.

Such baths are, however, not to be used on epileptics or on children suffering from rickets, weak circulation or general debility.

In general, *local steam baths* are used especially for hands and feet, and also for the tongue.

*General cold baths* are used in cases of super-excitation, motor-hyperactivity, excessive sensitiveness to pain and touch. These baths must be accompanied by constant cold lotions on the head.

Baths may be accompanied, with goods results, by *massage* and *rubbing.*

*Rubbings* may be given either dry or with water, alcohol, aromatic creams or ointments.

Local rubbings may be applied: (a) *To the spine,* carefully avoiding the lumbar region so as not to excite the sexual sensibilities. Dry rubbings should be made with a piece of flannel and continued until the skin reddens. They are especially useful after hot baths followed by cold douches. (b) *To the chest* to stimulate respiration. (c)

*To the abdomen* to correct various internal disorders (here, however, massage is more efficacious). (d) *To the joints* (rubbings with aromatic creams and with alcohol are very effective).

A brief rubbing with alcohol or creams can be followed with good effect by massage in the case of the abdomen and joints. Massage on the abdomen stimulates circulation in the intestines and intensifies and regularizes the movements of the muscular walls.

Massage has a surprising effect on the muscles of the joints; it shocks the muscular fibers in their innermost parts and sets them in motion; it regularizes the functioning of the muscles by reducing excessive contraction and restoring deficient contractibility. Emaciated muscles are regenerated, the muscular bulk is vigorously augmented, while the fat tissue are absorbed.

The repetition several times a day of bathing, rubbing and massage has produced real miracles of physical regeneration.

### FEEDING

Intestinal disturbances have a direct influence on the functional power of the central nervous system. They merit, therefore, special consideration. For in defectives an intestinal inflammation may produce symptoms of meningitis, and a disorder in digestion even unattended by fever may occasionally give rise to convulsions.

The hygiene of feeding which is almost the same as that for normal children must therefore be rigorously observed.

The general rule is that the children should have regular meals and be allowed nothing whatever to eat between meals. It is commonly believed that a piece of candy or a bit of fruit given between meals has no bad effect. This is a common error of many mothers, who by allowing such slight irregularities in diet, become the unwitting cause of serious illnesses in their children. When we say that children should be fed at mealtimes, we mean that *nothing* should be given them *except* at meal times; nothing, not even the most innocent confection; not a crumb of bread, not a drop of milk. This severity has the additional advantage of creating regular hygienic habits in the child. It is necessary to regulate the number of meals, the quantity and quality of food allowed in each.

*Number:* For children between 2 and 7 years: 4 meals a day; for children between 8 and 14 years: 3 meals a day.

These meals should be at regular hours, and followed without exception by a period of mental rest, which must be provided for in making up the daily program of lessons.

We need special researches as to what type of activity may be allowed children during digestion and what organs may be active without damage to the child while the stomach is taxed with the labor of digestion. A few things are clear. The children should be sent out of closed rooms where their play raises more or less dust, and kept in well-ventilated places, if possible, in a garden or in a woods well supplied with aromatic trees. The best thing a child can do immediately after a meal is to take a short walk in the open air without much exertion.

*Quantity:* In the case of children between 2 and 7 years of age, there should be two full meals and two luncheons. After the age of 7 there should be one lunch and two full meals. We cannot be more specific.

*Quality:* In the case of defectives it would be useful for the doctor to order a diet day by day after having examined the diaries of the nurses as is done in hospitals. For it may be possible to introduce into the food elements which constitute an actual cure for certain diseased conditions and preventives of certain kinds of attacks. In food we should realize the distinctions between the elements which build tissues — true food substances, and others whose function is purely stimulatory — alcohol, coffee, tea, etc., which should be used only occasionally.

Among the food substances properly so-called are the albuminoids (proteins), fats, and carbo-hydrates (sugars, starches, wheat and potato flours, etc.). The fats are the least digestible foods, but they produce the greatest number of calories.

The proportion of the different elements in the food should be determined by the amount of albumin, which constitutes the real food element. Albumin is of both vegetable and animal origin. Its animal forms are more nutritious, more easily digestible, and produce more calories than the vegetable forms. The foods which produce animal-albumin are milk, eggs, and meats. Vegetables themselves furnish what is known as vegetable-albumin. Children up to 6 years of age are supplied usually with the following albuminous foods: eggs, milk and

APPENDICES

vegetables. For children between 6 and 8: eggs, milk, fish and vegetables may be provided. Older children may be given chicken, veal, and finally beef.

Though for normal children a restricted meat diet is desirable, in the case of defectives a rich supply of meat as well as of albuminoids in general is to be sought. Their treatment resembles that of weak convalescent patients whose strength is to be restored. The meats best adapted to such children are those containing large amounts of mucilaginous substances and sugar (veal, lamb and young animals in general). Vegetable *purées,* fat gravies, butter, etc., are to be recommended in these cases.

For *nervous children,* fats, oils, acids, and flours should be avoided.

For *apathetic children,* who experience difficulty in digestion, tonics and rich seasonings should be used, such as spices, which have come to be almost excluded from ordinary cooking, especially for children. Spices may well be restored to the diet of institutions for defectives, since they have the additional advantage of permitting mixture with irons, of which they neutralize the taste.

Questions of food depend largely upon the individual condition of the children. The important thing is to avoid "the school ration." This is all the more true of beverages.

*Beverages:* While stimulants are usually to be excluded from the diet of normal children of 7 or under, it is often desirable to introduce tea, coffee, etc., into the meals of defectives. This should be done, however, only in the daily diets ordered by the physician for individuals.

*Nervous children* should be restricted to milk and water for their meals with some moderately sweet drink (orange juice, weak lemonade, etc.) after eating.

*Apathetics,* showing atonic digestion, may have coffee either before eating or during their meals.

Special education is necessary to accustom the children to complete mastication. Such practice in the use of the organs of mastication assists also in the later development of speech.

Among the physiological irregularities that appear among children special importance attaches to excretions.

*Defecation:* Among defectives especially, so-called "dirty children" are often so numerous that special sections have to be made for them in institutions. Such children show involuntary losses of fæces and urine, as in the case of infants. Most frequently the defecations are of liquid consistency though sometimes the reverse is true. Our remedial effort should be in two directions: we should try to regularize the operation of the intestines by giving solidity to the excretions; secondly, we should endeavor to strengthen the sphincter muscles.

A strict observance of the diet hygiene outlined above, especially as concerns regularity of meals and mastication of food, will assist in the attainment of the first object. We should try in addition to regularize defecation by stimulating it at regular intervals (to be gradually increased in length) through light massages and hot rubbings on the abdomen.

To strengthen the sphincters general tonics (iron, strychnine), and local tonics (such as cold "sitz-baths," cold showers and electric baths) may be used. Suppositories may also be used to advantage in stimulating sphincter contractions and accustoming the muscles to constrictive action.

*Urine:* Some defectives show involuntary loss of urine, especially at night, up to very advanced ages. Epileptics are particularly predisposed to this. The treatment is analogous to that just described. Beverages should be carefully supervised. Diuretics and excessive drinking in general should be avoided.

*General recommendations:* Local baths, and rigorous cleanliness to avoid any stimulus to onanism.

Education can do much in the treatment of this situation. Urination should be regularly suggested to the child before he goes to bed and when he wakes up in the morning. In special cases it might be well to waken the child once or twice during the night for the same purpose. This defect is often associated in a child with some abnormality in the phenomena of perspiration.

*Perspiration:* The sweat has almost the same composition as

urine, and perspiration is a process supplementary to the action
of the kidneys. It has been observed that often in defective
children perspiration is either entirely lacking or limited to
certain areas (the palms of the hands, the nose, etc.). It is
absolutely necessary to stimulate and regularize perspiration
over the whole surface of the body. This may be done by hot
and steam baths, by dry rubs with flannels (long sustained if
necessary), by woolen garments constantly worn next to the
skin, and other similar mechanical devices. We must, however,
absolutely avoid the use of special diaphoretic drugs, which
often bring about a fatal weakening of the organs of perspiration. The treatments we have suggested above are, first of all,
harmless, but besides they contribute to the general toning and
sensitizing of the skin.

*Nasal mucus and tears:* Tears are often lacking in defectives. On the other hand nasal excretion is very abundant and
replaces the tears, which are often so rare that some children
reach a relatively advanced age without having wept. In such
cases there is a predisposition to certain diseases of the eyes;
and excessive nasal excretion prevents the functioning of the
olfactory organs.

For this we recommend inhaling of hot vapors and of fragrant
irritants, which correct the excessive excretion of mucus and
exercise the olfactory sense. Usually the regular secretion of
tears follows as a matter of course.

*Saliva:* One of the most unpleasant abnormalities in defectives is the continuous loss of saliva from "hanging lips."
But the effects are not only unesthetic. The continuous over-
excretion of saliva makes the inner organs of the mouth flabby
and swollen. The tongue and the organs of speech in general
gradually lose their contractive power, and articulation is ultimately rendered impossible. Taste and tactile ability often
disappear altogether. Mastication becomes difficult and deglutition irregular. The secondary effects on the digestive organs
are bad. We possess a variety of efficient curatives and educational treatments for this defect: *first,* general tonics; *second,*
local cold douches on the lip muscles, electric massage of the
lips; *third,* the use of licorice sticks, large at first but gradually
reducing in diameter, to be introduced between the lips to stim-

ulate the sucking activity and the exercise of the contractive muscles. This will ultimately give the necessary muscular tone. The lips of the child should be closed mechanically from time to time to force him to swallow the saliva and to create the habit of deglutition.

### CLOTHING AND ENVIRONMENT

The principles of hygiene must be extended to the dress of the child and to the environment in which it lives.

*Clothing:* The child's clothes should be so made as to be easily put on and off. They should not hinder the normal functioning of the body (breathing). They should afford no opportunity for dangerous vices (onanism). If the child can dress and undress without difficulty, it will learn the more readily to look after itself even in those little necessities of daily life where partial undressing is necessary. Special attention should be given to stockings, which affect the development of sensitiveness in the soles of the feet and also concern the process of learning to walk.

*Environment:* Just a few reminders: for defectives perfect ventilation of course; but the walls and furniture should be upholstered in the case of impulsive defectives or of defectives who do not know how to walk. There is danger in furniture with sharp projections and in toys which may be thrown about. A "child's room," the luxury of which consists in its hygienic location, its elastic walls, and its very emptiness, is the best gift a rich family can make to the education of a defective child.

### MUSCULAR EDUCATION

Muscular education has for its object the bringing of the individual to some labor useful for society. This labor must always be executed by means of the muscles, whether it be manual labor, speaking or writing. In a word, the intelligence must subject the muscles to its own purposes and, that the muscles may be equipped for such obedience, it is necessary to prepare them by some education which will reduce them to coordination. Muscular education in defectives accordingly has for its object the stimulation and coordination of useful movements.

It prepares: for exercise; for the activities of domestic service (washing, dressing, preparing food, setting and clearing the table, etc.); for manual labor (trades); for language (use of the vocal organs). The preparation consists in bringing the child to *tonic quiescence* in standing posture. The child must learn first to stand still with head erect and with his eyes fixed on the eyes of the teacher. From this position of *tonic quiescence* we must pass to exercises in *imitation*. We obtain *tonic quiescence* by a variety of procedures, the variation depending upon individual cases. We must stimulate the apathetic and the sluggish; we must moderate the hyperactive; we must correct paresis, tics, etc. In other words, medical education must precede pedagogy itself. It may be a question of applying medical gymnastics both for active and passive movements, alternating this treatment with massage, electric baths, etc.

Let us note one or two motor abnormalities which are easy to detect in defectives. *Atony:* the child does not move; he cannot stand; he cannot sit upright nor execute any movement whatever. *Hyperactivity:* this is characterized by almost constant *incoordinated* or disorganized movements which have no useful purpose, e.g., jumping, beating, tearing up of objects within reach and so on. Such patients are dangerous to themselves and to others.

### MECHANICAL MOVEMENTS

(A).— *Movements executed* upon the person of the child: sucking of the fingers; biting of the nails; constant stroking of some part of the body. These movements are caused by imperfectly developed sensibility; the children stroke or caress, for example, that area of the skin which possesses greatest tactile sensitiveness, etc.

(B).— *Movements executed upon surrounding objects:* rapping on tables; constant and careful tearing of pieces of paper into small bits, etc. This too is associated with some sensory pleasure on the part of the patient.

*Rocking:* (a) *with patient reclining:* the head is nodded from left to right, from right to left; (b) *with patient sitting:* the trunk is rocked backward and forward; (c) *with patient stand-*

*ing:* the whole body rocks from left to right, the whole weight
resting now on one foot and now on the other.  Difficulty and
hesitation are experienced in walking.  These motory defects
proceed from the difficulty experienced by the child in finding his
center of gravity, his equilibrium.

*Inability to perform local movements:*  (a) Inability to move
certain of the fingers, the tongue, the lips, etc.  From such defects arises the impossibility of performing certain simple manual exercises (bringing the finger tips of the two hands together; taking hold of objects, e.g., inability to button, etc.) and
the inability to pronounce certain words; (b) Inability to con-
tract the lip and sphincter muscles (loss of saliva, involuntary
defecation).

*Atony* and *hyperactivity* may be overcome by appropriate
educational remedies which we will now discuss.  Local agita-
tions disappear with the general education of the senses; while
rocking is cured by exercises in balancing.

(A).—*Stimulate active movements in the atonic child until
he is able to stand erect in tonic quiescence.*

Begin by stimulating the simple movements, gradually working up to the most complicated.  We have a sure guide for this
education in the spontaneous developments of movements in the
normal child: he begins with the easiest spontaneous movements
and gradually arrives at the harder ones.

The first movement which develops in the child is the *pre-
hensile* act (grasping).  Next comes the movements of the lower
joints used in creeping and walking; next the ability to stand;
and finally the ability to walk alone.  *Grasping:* if no external
stimulation is capable of interesting the defective of low type,
grasping cannot be stimulated merely by presenting to the child
some object or other which might seem to be interesting for
color, taste or some other quality.  In such a case we must have
recourse to the instinct of self-preservation, to that innate fear
of void which defectives almost always have.  The child feeling himself fall will instinctively grasp at some support within
his reach.  This is the simplest point of departure for our possible development of the grasping faculty in the defective child.

*Method:*  The hands of the child are mechanically fixed
around the rung of a ladder suspended to the ceiling.  Then

the child is left to himself. Since his fingers are already around the support he needs only to clench his hands to find support. He may not succeed even in this simple act the first time. The teacher must patiently repeat the exercise, always being ready, of course, to catch the child if he should fall. In this exercise the defective is very much alarmed as a rule and all his muscles are as a result more or less stimulated.

Likewise based on the instinct of self-preservation is the *swing*, where the defective must cling to some support with his hands to keep from falling.

Finally a *ball* is hung from the ceiling and swung in such a way as continually to strike the child in the face. To protect himself he must keep it away by seizing it.

In still lower types we must have recourse to the instinct for nutrition which exists even in such children.

*Standing:* Under this heading we include also the movements which precede the actual attainment of the standing posture. To overcome the sinking of the knees, which impedes standing, the *swinging chair* may be used. The seat must reach nearly to the child's feet and the knees are tied to the seat. The child's feet, as he swings, strike against a board. This exercise prepares the lower joints to hold themselves in position when resting on a plane surface. Next the child is placed on *parallel bars*. The bars pass under the arm-pits and support the child while his feet rest on the floor. In these exercises we try to stimulate the movements which appear in walking (exercises of the lower joints). Next we exercise the muscles which support the spinal column. The child is made to sit down: first the spine is upright against the back of the chair; finally it remains upright when the support is removed. Little by little walking can be produced if the child is taken away from the bars and supported with a simple *gymnastic belt*. The exercise is continued until he can be left entirely without support.

When the child has learned to walk we can *command* him to stop in the position of *tonic quiescence*.

(B).— *Moderation of hyperactivity by forced quiescence.*

In hyperactive children the arms must first be restrained by holding them tight in our hands. The movements of the lower limbs may be checked by holding the child's legs tight between our knees. Finally the child may be kept entirely quiescent with his legs held between the teacher's knees, his arms in the teacher's hands, with the trunk pushed back and held firmly against the wall. By a similar process he can be kept quiet while standing; then later in a position of *tonic quiescence*.

*General Rule:* Exercises of the limbs beginning with the arms should precede those specifically directed toward the spinal column. Séguin says "*tonic quiescence* is necessarily the first step from *atonic quiescence;* or if you wish, from a disordered activity to an activity which represents harmony between the muscular system and the mind."

We noted above that the posture of *tonic quiescence* involves a fixity of gaze on the part of the child. This is the point of departure for the development of coordinative movements and *imitation* of what the child sees the teacher do.

### EDUCATION OF THE FIXED GAZE

If the child is kept in the dark for some time and is suddenly shown a bright light he will experience the sensation of *red*.

Keeping the child in a dark room for a shorter time a sudden light will attract his gaze.

Move the light along the wall until the child's gaze follows it.

Next, in a light room, the child is shown a red cloth kept in motion; a red balloon hung from the ceiling keeps striking him in the face.

After these preparatory exercises the teacher can try to get the child to fix its eyes on his own and to maintain the fixed gaze. Here use may be made also of the sense of hearing (words of command, encouragement, etc.).

Finally to obtain complete fixity of gaze, one may use the large mirror, before which lights may be passed. There the child can gaze at his own face and at the face of the teacher, which will be kept motionless and which the child may come to imitate.

*Exercises of imitation:* (1) The child is taught to become acquainted with himself. The various parts of his body are pointed out to him and he is made to touch them. This continues up to the point of distinguishing right from left. Begin with the larger members of the body (arms, legs, trunk, head) to be named in connection with movements of the whole body. Then pass to the smaller members (the fingers, knuckles, the organs of the mouth), to be referred to respectively in the education of the hand and in the teaching of speech.

(2) The child is taught coordinative movements relating to gymnastics (walking, running, jumping, pushing, etc.).

(3) Movements relating: (a) to the simpler forms of manual labor (exercises of practical life: washing, dressing, picking up and laying down various objects, opening and closing drawers); (b) to more complex kinds of manual labor (elements of various trades; weaving, Froebel exercises, etc.).

(4) Movements relating to articulate language. For this educational process the following general rules are to be followed: first, movements of the whole body must precede movements of specific parts; second, only by analyzing complex movements in their successive stages and by working out their details point by point can we arrive at the execution of a perfect complex movement.

This latter rule applies especially to manual education and the teaching of language. When movements of the whole body have been obtained it will often be necessary, before going on to movements of particular members, to alternate the educational cure with the medical: (1) to overcome the weakness of some of the muscles (perhaps of some finger), use local electric baths, passive gymnastics, etc.; (2) for retractions, retarded development of aponeurosis of the palms, etc., use orthopedic treatment.

Gymnastics, manual labor, trades and speaking are special branches of teaching, that usually require specially trained teachers.

### EDUCATION OF THE SENSES

Outline for examination.

*Sight:* Sense of color. It is necessary to call the attention of the child several times to the same color by presenting it to him under different aspects and in different environments. The stimulus should be strong. Other senses tend to associate themselves with the chromatic sense, for example, the stereognostic and gustatory senses. Whenever the teacher gives an *idea* she should unite with it the *word,* the only word which is related to the idea. The words should be emphatically and distinctly pronounced.

(1) *Pedagogical aprons:* The colors are presented on a large moving surface, as for instance, an apron worn by the teacher; e.g., a red apron. The teacher points to it, touches it, lifting it with noticeable movements of the arms, continually calls the attention of the child to it. *"Look! See here! Attention!"* and so on; then saying in a low voice and slowly, *"This is* (and then in a louder voice), *red, red, red! ! !"* Now take two aprons, one red, the other blue; repeat the same process for the blue. There are three stages in the processs of distinguishing between colors: (a) *"This is . . . red!"* (b) *"Your apron is red!"* (c) *"What color is this?"* Then try three aprons, red, blue, and yellow, bordered with white and black.

(2) *Insets* — color and form. The red circle, the blue square. There are three stages: (a) *"This is red, red, red!"* Touch it! Do you feel? Your finger goes *all the way around, all the way around.* It is *round,* it is *round, all round.* Put it in its place!" (b) *"Give me the red one!"* (c) *"What color is this circle?"*

(3) The dark room. A Bengal red color is shown: *"It is red!"* The color appears behind a circular disc: *"It is red!"* The blue is shown behind a square window: *"It is blue, blue, blue,"* etc.

(4) The child is given a circular tablet of red sugar to eat and a square lump of blue sugar. He is made to smell a red piece of cloth strongly scented with musk; or a blue piece of cloth scented with asafetida, etc.

(5) The color chart.

(6) The first game of Froebel.

The first pedagogical material given should contain the color already taught. The notion of color should be associated with its original environment.

*Shapes: Solids, Insets:* The procedure is always in the three stages mentioned. (1) Show the object to the child. (2) Have him recognize it. (3) Have him give it its name.

*Dimensions:* Rods of the same thickness, but of graduated length. First the longest and the shortest are shown. The child is made to touch them and interchange them "Pick up the *longest!*" "Place it on the table!" etc. Repeat this exercise, adding some intermediate lengths; again finally, with all the rods. Next the rods may be disarranged; the child is to put them back in order of length. Notice whether the child makes an accurate choice in the confused pile of the graduated dimensions; or whether it is only by placing two rods together that he comes to notice the difference between them. Notice how long it is before the child makes an accurate choice in the pile and of what degrees of difference in length he is accurately aware.

Try the same exercise for *thickness:* prisms of equal length, but of graduated thickness, using the same procedure in analogous exercises. Games may be used for the estimation of distances.

*The tactile sense proper:* One board with a corrugated surface (like a grater) and one smooth. Another board with five adjacent surfaces of graduated roughness. Similar exercises may be used in the feeling of cloths (guessing games).

Games: The child is blindfolded and lightly tickled. He must seize what is tickling him, putting his hand rapidly to the irritant. ("Fly catching," a game for the localization of stimulants.)

Liquids
{
Astringents
Glues
Oils
}

*Tactile muscular sense:*

Elastic bodies
Non-resilient bodies
}
Balls
{
Rubber
Wooden

Use skins, leather gloves, and various kinds of cloths for feeling.

*The muscular sense:* Balls of the same appearance, but of graduated weights. Differentiation of coins by weight.

*The stereognostic sense:* Recognition of elementary forms, of rare objects, of coins.

*Thermal senses:* Hot liquids, iced liquids; relative warmth of linen and wool, wood, wax, metal.

*Olfactory sense:* Asafetida, oil of rose, mint, etc.,

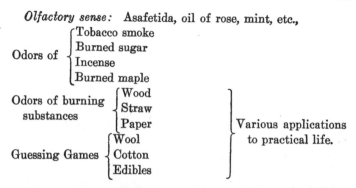

Odors of
- Tobacco smoke
- Burned sugar
- Incense
- Burned maple

Odors of burning substances
- Wood
- Straw
- Paper

Guessing Games
- Wool
- Cotton
- Edibles

Various applications to practical life.

Odors of foods (practical life): fresh milk, sour milk, fresh meat, stale meat, rancid butter, fresh butter, etc.

*Taste:* The four fundamental tastes (guessing games). Instructive applications to practise in the kitchen and at meals.

Tastes of various food substances:

Exercises of practical life
- milk gruel (milk and flour);
- diluted wine;
- sweet wine;
- turned wine (vinegar), etc.

The practise of the senses begins in the lower classes in the form of guessing games; in the higher classes the education of the senses is applied to exercises of practical life.

*Hearing:* Empirical measurement of the acuteness of the sense of hearing. Specimen game: the teacher about 35 feet away from the blindfolded children and standing where an object has been hidden, whispers the words *" Find it! "* Those who have heard her will be able to find the object. Having removed from the line the children who have heard, the teacher steps to another place about a yard nearer and repeats the experiment to the children who are left over, etc.

*Intensity of sound:*

Throw to the floor metal blocks of various sizes, coins of graduated weight.

Strike glasses one after the other according to size.

Bells of graduated size.

*Quality of sound:* Produce different sounds and noises.

Bells $\begin{cases} \text{of metal} \\ \text{of terracotta} \end{cases}$

Open Bells.
Closed Bells.
Strike with a wooden stick on tin plates, glasses, etc.
Identify various musical instruments.
Identify different human voices (of different people).
Identify the voice of a man, a woman, a child.
Recognize different people by their step, etc., etc.

*Pitch:* Intervals of an octave, of a major triad, and so on; major and minor chords. However, musical education requires a separate chapter.

*Sound projection, localization of sound in space:* The child is blindfolded. The sound is produced: (1) in front of him; behind him; to the right; to the left; above his head; (2) the blindfolded child recognizes the relative distance at which the sounds are produced; (3) the child decides from which side of the room the sounds come; he is made to follow some one who is speaking.

*The horizontal plane:* This is the first notion imparted to the child concerning his relationship to the objects about him. Almost all the objects the child may perceive around him with his senses rest on the horizontal plane: his table, his chair, and so on. The very objects on which the child sits or puts his toys are horizontal planes. If the plane were not horizontal, the objects would fall, but they would strike on the floor which, again, is a horizontal plane. Place an object on the child's table and tip one end of the table to show him that the object falls.

*Guessing game for the plane surface:* This game serves to fix the notion of the plane surface and at the same time trains the eye and the attention of the child.

1. Under one of three aluminum cups is placed a small red ball, a cherry or a piece of candy. The child must remember under which cup the object is hidden. The teacher tries herself and fails, always raising the empty cups and returning them to

their places. The child, however, finds the object immediately.

2. The teacher now begins to move the three cups about on the plane surface. The child has to keep his eye on *his* cup and never loses sight of it.

3. Repeat this exercise with six cups.

*Checkerboard game:* This serves to teach the child the limits and the various divisions of a plane. The squares are large and in black and white. The whole board should be surrounded by a border in relief. Various points are indicated on the plane: forward, backward, right, left, center, by placing a tin soldier at each point indicated. The soldiers may be moved about by the child in obedience to directions of the teacher: " The officer on horseback to *the center*": " Standard-bearer *to the right,* etc.! " Finally, make all the soldiers advance toward the center of the board over the black squares only; then over the white squares only, etc.

These notions may be applied to exercises of practical life. The children already know how to set the table without thinking of what they are doing. From now on, the teacher may say: "Put the plates on the *plane surface* of the tables!" "Put the bottle *to the left! In the center!*" etc. Have a small table set with little dishes, having the objects arranged in obedience to commands of the teacher. After this, we may proceed to the Froebel games on the plane surface with the cubes, blocks, and so on.

*Inset game as a preparation for reading, drawing, and writing:* After the child knows the different colors and shapes in the inset, the color tablets of the big inset can be put in place: (1) on a piece of cardboard where the figures have been drawn in shading in the respective colors; (2) on a cardboard where the same figures have been drawn merely in colored outline (linear abstraction of a regular figure).

*Inset of shapes where the pieces are all of the same color* (*blue*): The child recognizes the shape and puts the pieces in place: (1) on a cardboard where the figure is shaded; (2) on a cardboard where the figure is merely outlined (linear abstraction of regular geometrical figures). Meanwhile, the child has been touching the pieces: " The tablet is smooth. It turns round and round and round. It is a *circle.* Here we have a *square.* You go this way and there is a *point;* this way, and there is another point, and another, and another; there are *four points!* In the *triangle* there are *three points!*" Then the child follows with his finger the figures outlined on the cardboard. "This one is entirely round: it is a *circle!* This one has four points: it is a *square!* This one has three points: it is a *triangle!* The child runs over the same figures with a small rod of wood (skewer), etc.

### SIMULTANEOUS READING AND WRITING

At this point, we may bring in the chart with the vowels, painted red. The child sees "irregular figures outlined in color." Give the child the vowels made of red wood. He is to place them on the corresponding figures of the chart. He is made to touch the wooden vowels, running his finger around them in the way they are written. They are called by their names. The vowels are arranged according to similarity in shape (reading):

o  e  a
i  u

Then the child is commanded: "Show me the letter *o!* Put it in its place!" Then he is asked: "What letter is this?" It will be found at this point that many children make a mistake, if they merely look at the letter, but guess rightly when they touch it. It is possible accordingly to distinguish the various individual types, visual, motory, etc.

Next the child is made to touch the letter outlined on the chart, first with his forefinger only, then with the fore and middle fingers, finally with a little wooden skewer to be held like a pen. The letter must always be followed around in the way it is written.

The consonants are drawn in blue and arranged on various charts, according to similarity in shape (reading, writing). The movable alphabet in blue wood is added to this. The letters are to be superimposed on the chart as was done for the vowels. Along with the alphabet we have another series of charts, where, beside the consonant identical with the wooden letter there are painted one or more figures of objects, the names of which begin with the letter in question. Beside the longhand letter, there is also painted in the same color a smaller letter in print type. The teacher, naming the consonants in the phonic method, points to the letter, then to the chart, pronouncing the name of the objects which are painted there, and stressing the first letter: e.g., "m . . . man . . . m: Give me *M!*" "Put it where it belongs!" "Follow around it with your finger!" Here the linguistic defects of the children may be studied.

The tracing of the letters in the way they are written begins the muscular education preparatory to writing. One of our little girls of the motory type when taught by this method reproduced all the letters in pen and ink long before she could identify them. Her letters were about eight millimetres high and were written with surprising regularity. This same child was generally successful in her manual work.

The child, in looking at the letters, identifying them, and tracing them in the way they are written, is preparing himself both for reading and writing at the same time. The two processes are exactly contemporaneous. Touching them and looking at them brings several senses to bear on the fixing of the image. Later the two acts are separated: first looking (reading), then touching (writing). According to their respective type, some children learn to read first, others to write first.

*Reading:* As soon as the child has learned to identify the letters and also to write them, he is made to pronounce them. Then the alphabet is arranged in phonetic order. This order is to be varied according to individual defects made apparent while the child is pronouncing spontaneously the sounds of the consonants or vowels, or the words illustrating the consonants on the charts. We begin by showing the child and having him pronounce, first, syllables and, then, words which contain the letters he is able to pronounce well. Then we go on to the sounds he has trouble with, finally to those he cannot pronounce at all (linguistic correction). The phonomimic correction of speech requires special discussion. In primary schools speech correction should be in the hands of a specially trained teacher, like gymnastics, manual training and singing. Should no defects in speech appear in the child, the letters of the alphabet should be taught in the order of physiological phonetics.

Beside the big long-hand letters should be placed the small letters in print type. The letter is taught; then recognition is prompted by asking as each large letter is reached: "I want the little one like it." The two types of letter appear also on the illustrated charts. Next the printed letter is shown, with the request: "Give me the big letter that goes with it." Finally: "What letter is it?" The little letters are not "touched," because they are never to be written.

### DRAWING AND WRITING

The child is given a sheet on which appear a circle and a square in outline. The circle is filled in with a red pencil, the square with blue (insets). Smaller and smaller circles are next given, also circles and triangles. They are variously disposed on the page. They are to be filled in with colored pencils. Then comes the tracing. The black lines are followed around with colored pencils: the circle, the triangle, the square. This comes easily to the child who has been taught to trace with the wooden skewer the figures outlined on the inset-charts. Writing follows immediately on the exercises in tracing with the skewer on the charts of the written alphabet. Some help can be given the child by having him darken with a black pencil the letter written on the copy book by the teacher. As the child writes, his attention should be directed to the fact that he is writing on a *limited plane surface;* that he begins at the top, moving from left to right and little by little coming down the page.

Séguin's method began with shafts and curves. His copybooks for the shafts were prepared as follows: the shaft to be executed by the child was delimited by two points, connected by a very light line. In the margin of the pages appear two shafts to be executed by the teacher. Similarly for the curves: ( ( ( (. He has the printed capitals drawn as combinations of shafts and curves: B, D, etc.

## SIMULTANEOUS READING AND WRITING OF WORDS

The child, through sensory education, has acquired some notions of color, shape, surface (smooth and rough), smell, taste, etc. At the same time, he has learned to count (one, two, three, four points). Uniting all possible notions concerning a single object, we arrive at his first concrete idea of the object itself: the object lesson. To the idea thus acquired, we give the *word* which represents the object. Just as the concrete idea results from the assembling of acquired notions, so the word results from the union of known sounds, and perceived symbols.

*Reading lesson:* On the teacher's table is the large stand for the movable alphabet in black printed letters. The teacher arranges on it the vowels and a few consonants. Each child, in his own place, has the small movable alphabet in the pasteboard boxes. The children take from the box the same letters they see on the large stand, and arrange them in the same order. The teacher takes up some object which has a simple word for a name, e.g., *pane* ("bread"). She calls the attention of the child to the object, reviewing an objective lesson already learned, thus arousing the child's interest in the object. "Shall we write the word *pane?*" "*Hear* how I say it!" "*See* how I say it!" The teacher pronounces separately and distinctly the sounds of the letters which make up the word, exaggerating the movements of the vocal organs so that they are plainly visible to the children. As the pupils repeat the word they continue their education in speaking.

A child now comes to the teacher's desk to choose the letters corresponding to the sounds and tries to arrange them in the order in which they appear in the word. The children do the same with the small letters at their seats. Every mistake gives rise to a correction useful to the whole class. The teacher repeats the word in front of each one who has made a mistake, trying to get the child to correct himself. When all the children have arranged their letters properly, the teacher shows a card (visiting-card size) on which is printed (in print-type letters about a centimeter high) the word "*pane.*" All the children are made to read it. Then some child is asked to put the card where he finds the word written before him; next, on the *object* the word stands for. The process is repeated with two or three other objects, with their respective names: *pane* (bread), *lume* (lamp), *cece* (peas). Then the teacher gathers up the cards from the various objects, shuffles them and calls on some child: " Which object do you like best? " " *Lume!* " " Find me the card with the word *lume!* " When the card has been selected, all the children are asked to read it: " Is Mary right in saying that this is the word *lume?* " " Put the card back where it belongs! " (i.e., on its object). In the subsequent lessons, the old cards, with the objects they stand for removed, should be mixed with the new ones. From the entire pack the children are to select the new cards and place them on their objects. A primary reading book ought to present these words next to a picture of the object for which they stand.

In this way the children are brought to unite the individual symbol into words. When they have been taught to make the syllable, the reading lesson may be continued without the use of objects, though it is still preferable to use words which will, if possible, have a concrete meaning for the children.

*Writing:* The children are already able to use the cursive (writing) alphabet which corresponds to the small letter (print-type) that is neither " touched " nor written, but is merely *read.* They must now write in hand writing, and place close together, the little letters which they have assembled in the movable alphabet to compose words. As each word is read or written for every object lesson, for every action, printed cards are being assembled which will later be used to make clauses and sentences with movable words that may be moved about just as the individual letters were moved about in making the *words* themselves. Later on, the simple clauses or sentences should refer to actions performed by the children. The first step should be to bring two or more words together: e.g., *red-wool, sweet-candy, four-footed dog,* etc. Then we may go on to the sentence itself: *The wool is red; The soup is hot; The dog has four feet; Mary eats the candy,* etc. The children first compose the sentences with their cards; then they copy them in their writing books. To facilitate the choice of the cards, they are arranged in special boxes; for instance, one box is labeled *noun:* or its compartments are distinguished thus: *food, cloth-*

*ing, animals, people,* etc. There should be a box for *adjectives* with compartments for *colors, shapes, qualities,* etc. There should be another for *particles* with compartments for *articles, conjunctions, prepositions,* etc. A box should be reserved for *actions* with the label *verbs* above; and then in it a compartment should be reserved for the *infinitive, present, past* and *future* respectively. The children gradually learn by practice to take their cards from the boxes and put them back in their proper places. They soon learn to know their "word boxes" and they readily find the cards they want among the *colors, shapes, qualities,* etc., or among *animals, foods,* etc. Ultimately the teacher will find occasion to explain the meaning of the big words at the top of the drawers, *noun, adjective, verb,* etc., and this will be the first step into the subject of *grammar.*

### GRAMMAR

#### NOUN LESSON

We may call persons and objects by their *name* (their *noun*). People answer if we call them, so do animals. Inanimate objects, however, never answer, because they cannot; but if they could answer they would; for example, if I say *Mary,* Mary answers; if I say *peas,* the peas do not answer, because they cannot. You children *do* understand when I call an object and you bring it to me. I say for example, *book, beans, peas.* If I don't tell you the name of the object you don't understand what I am talking about; because every object has a different name. This name is the word that stands for the object. This name is a *noun.* When I mention a noun you understand immediately the object which the noun represents: *tree, chair, pen, book, lamb,* etc. If I do not give this noun, you don't know what I am talking about; for, if I say simply, *Bring me . . . at once, I want it,* you do not know what I· want, unless I tell you the name of the object. Unless I give you the *noun,* you do not understand. Thus every object is represented by a word which is its *name* and this name is a *noun.* To understand whether a word is a noun or not, you simply ask "Is it a thing?" "Would it answer if I spoke to it?" "Could I carry it to the teacher?" For instance, *bread.* Yes, *bread* is an object; *table,* yes, it is an object; *conductor*, yes, the conductor would answer, if I were to speak to him.

Let us look through our cards now. I take several cards from different boxes and shuffle them. Here is the word *sweet*. Bring me *sweet*. Is there anything to answer when I call *sweet?* But you are bringing me a piece of candy! I didn't say *candy:* I said *sweet!* And now you have given me sugar! I said *sweet.* If I say *candy, sugar,* then you understand what I want, what object I am thinking about, because the words *candy, sugar,* stand for objects. Those words are *nouns.* Now let us look through the noun cards. Let us read a couple of lines in our reading books and see whether there are any nouns there. Tell me, are there any nouns? How are we to find some nouns? Look around you! Look at yourself, your clothes, etc.! Name every object that you see! Every word you thus pronounce will be a noun: Teacher, clothing, necktie, chair, class, children, books, etc. Just look at this picture which represents so many things! The figures represent persons and objects. Name each of these figures! Every word you pronounce will be a noun!

VERB: ACTION

Mary, rise from your seat! Walk! Mary has performed a number of *actions.* She has *risen.* She has performed the *action* of rising. She has *walked. Walk* stands for an action. Now write your name on the blackboard! *Writing* is an action. Erase what you have written. *Erasing* is an action. When I spoke to Mary, I performed the action of speaking. (Just as the noun was taught with objects, here we must have actions. Objects represented in pictures will be of no use, since actions cannot be portrayed by pictures.)

The next step will be to suggest a little exercise of imagination. Look at all these objects! Try to imagine some action which each might perform! A *class,* for instance; what actions might a class perform? *Store:* what actions might take place in a store? Let us now look through our cards after we have shuffled them. Next try our reading book. Show me which of the words are verbs. Give me some words which are verbs (infinitive).

Persons, things (proper and common nouns). Singular, plural, masculine and feminine. The articles: " Choose the article that goes with this noun!" etc.

Present, past, future. I am performing an action now. Have I performed it before? Did I do it yesterday? Have I always done it in the past? When I walk now, I say I *am walking, I walk.* When I mean the action that I performed yesterday, I say: I *was walking, I walked.* The same action performed at different times is described differently. How strange that is! The word referring to an object never changes. The beads are beads to-day. They were beads yesterday. *Actions,* however, are represented by words which change according to the time in which they are performed. To-day I *walk.* Yesterday I *walked.* To-morrow I *shall walk.* It is always *I* who do the walking, *I* who perform the *action* of walking; and I walk always in the same way, putting one foot in front of the other. The objects you see perform an action always perform it. Do you see that little bird which is flying — which is performing the *action* of flying? It was flying yesterday. It flew at some time in the past. To-morrow also, that is, at some *future* time, if the little bird lives, it will fly and it will fly always in the same way, beating its wings to and fro. You see what a strange thing a verb is! It changes its words according to the *time* in which the action is performed. It is different according as it represents action in *present* time, or action in *past* time, or action in *future* time. Now, see! I am going to take out some of my cards and make up a little sentence:

Now I am going to change the word which stands for the time when the action takes place. In place of the card *now* I am going to use this one:

| yesterday |

Is this a good sentence? No! Supposing we change the time
of the verb: *Yesterday George ate an apple.* This makes good
sense. Put these cards back now in the boxes where they belong.

### ADJECTIVE

Every object possesses certain *qualities.* Tell me what you
can about this apple. It is red, it is round, it is sweet. What
qualities can you find in this chair? It is hard, it is brown,
it is wooden. What about your school-mates, the children?
Are they good, are they pretty, are they polite, are they obedient, or are they naughty, impolite, disobedient, disorderly?
Let us look through our cards to see whether we can find words
which stand for the qualities of objects. Supposing we select
some from the drawer of the adjective and some from the
drawer of the noun. Now let us place beside each noun a
card which makes sense with it: here, for instance, I have
*Charles, red, quadruped, transparent.* Does that mean anything? Well then find me some adjectives which will go well
with *Charles.* Adjectives are words which stand for qualities
of a given object. They must go well with their noun. Find
me some adjectives which fit well with the noun *dog.* They
must be words which stand for some quality of the dog. Now
put all the cards back in the compartments where they belong.
(This latter exercise is very instructive.)

In this method of teaching grammar we make use of objects
and actions directly relating to life. Such lessons may be made
more attractive with story telling, etc. The teaching of grammar at this period should be extended as far as is possible without forcing the pupil.

### OBJECT LESSONS

There should be concise and vivid descriptions of some object. The attention of the child should be sustained by changing the tone of voice, by exclamations calculated to excite the
child's curiosity, by praise, etc. Never begin with the *word,*

but always with the *object*. All the notions possessed by the child should be as far as practicable in a given case applied to his study of the object. First it should be described as to its qualities; next as to its uses, then as to its origin; for example, Here is an *object!* What color is it? What is its shape? Feel of it! Taste of it! etc. If possible, have the child *see* the use of the object and its origin in every possible way. Just as the concrete idea of the object is imparted by verbal description and by various appeals to the senses of the child, so the different uses of the object should be brought out in *describing actions* which the child *sees* performed with it before him. This, of course, is an ideal which the teacher should try to realize as far as possible. The object should be shown the child in different circumstances and under different aspects so as to give it always the appearance of something new and something to excite and hold the attention of the child. Take, for instance, a lesson on the word *hen*. Show a paper model of the hen, the live hen in the courtyard, the stereopticon slide of the hen: the print of the hen in the reading book: the hen alive among other domestic fowls; pictures of the hen among pictures of other birds, etc. Each new step should be taken on a different day and each time the word should be connected with the object. Write the word on the blackboard; make up the printed card for the card file and put it in its proper box. "Who wants to take the blackboard out-doors? We are going to write some words in the yard. Now in your reading books there is the figure of the hen. Next to it is the word *hen*. Write this word in your copy books. Who can repeat what we have said about the hen? Write down what you know about the hen." The amount of information given about a particular object will depend, of course, upon the class. The simplest description should be followed by one more minute, passing thus to speak of uses, habits, origin, etc. The writing of a simple word may be developed into a written description. But the lessons on the given object should always be short, and they should be repeated on different days. For the lessons on trees, plants, and vegetables, a garden is necessary: the children should see the seeds planted, a growing vegetable, a picture of the fruit, etc. If possible the domestic use of the garden products should be demonstrated. This applies also to flowers. The blackboard with crayon should never be lacking in the garden. For object lessons we need toys to represent furniture, dishes, various objects used in the home, tools of different trades, rooms and the furniture that goes in each, houses, trees, a church (to build villages), etc.; dolls equipped with all the necessaries for dressing. There should be a shelf for bottles containing specimens of different drinks; various kinds of cloths (for tactile exercises); the raw materials out of which they are made, demonstrations of the way they are manufactured, etc. Show also specimens of the various minerals, etc.

### HISTORY

History is taught first on a little stage with living tableaux, gradually advancing to action; second, by descriptions of large illustrations and colored pictures; third, by story-telling based on stereopticon views. The teacher should strive for brevity, conciseness, and vivacity in descriptions. Historical story telling should, as in the case of all other lessons, bring about additions of printed cards to the word boxes. Various information on the seasons, months of the year, etc., should be imparted by illustrations and pictures. Every morning the child should be asked: "What day is it? What day was yesterday? What day will to-morrow be?" and "What day of the month is it?"

### GEOGRAPHY

1. Exercises on the plane for the cardinal points, with various gymnastic and guessing games. 2. Building games out of doors. Make a lake, an island, a peninsula, a river. 3. Carry the houses and church into the yard and construct a small village. Put the church on the north; the schoolhouse on the east; the mountain on the west; in front of the school place the national flag. 4. In the classroom fit out a room with its proper furniture to be placed on a map of the room outlined on a large chart. As the furniture is removed, make a mark on the map to indicate where each article was. Make a little village in the same way, houses, church, etc. Take away the church, etc.; mark the place of each object on the map as it is

removed. Then identify each spot. " Where was the church ? "
" What was over here ? " etc. Thus we get a conception of the
geographical map. Read the map, making use of the cardinal
points. 5. Physical characteristics of regions may be shown
by clay modeling to represent hills, etc. Draw outlines around
each model, remove the clay and read the *geographical map*
resulting.

### ARITHMETIC

The children are to count: 1 nose; 1 mouth; 1, 2 hands;
1, 2 feet; 1, 2, 3, 4 points in the insets; 1, 2, 3, 4, 5, 6 soldiers
on the plane. How many blocks did they use in the building?
1, 2, 3, 4, 5, 6, 7, 8, 9. Thus for the elementary steps in counting.

### COMPUTATION

Computation should be taught practically in the store from
the very beginning. The shopkeeper sells 1 cherry for 1c. The
children have 2c and get two cherries. Next they get two nuts
for 1c. Place 1c on the counter and place 2 nuts beside it.
Then count all the nuts and there are 2 for 1c, etc. The child
wants one cherry and has a two-cent piece. The shopkeeper
must give him 1c in change $(2+2=4; 2-1=1)$. In
money changing it will be observed that at first some children
recognize the coins more easily by touch than by sight (motor
types).

### WRITTEN NUMBERS

Charts with the nine numbers: one for each number. Each
chart has pictures representing quantities of the most varied
objects arranged around the number, which is indicated by a
large design on the chart. For instance: on the *1* card there is
one cherry, one dog, one ball, etc. Yesterday the shopkeeper
sold one cherry for 1c. Is the cherry here? Yes, there is the
cherry! And what is this? *One* church! And this? *One*
cent! etc. What is this figure here? It is the number *one*.
Now bring out the wooden figure: What is this? Number
*one!* Put it on the figure on the chart! It is *one*.

Now take the charts to the store. Who has 1c? Who has

2c? etc. Let us look for the number among the charts. The shopkeeper is selling three peas for 1c. Let us look for number *3* among the charts! Numbers should be taught in the afternoon lesson in the store. The designs representing the figures should be shown the following morning. Next time the charts with the figures previously taught should be taken to the shop to be recognized again. Other numbers are brought out in the new computations. The figures for the new numbers then taught in the store should be shown the following day, etc. To make the store interesting, the topic lesson on the objects offered for sale should be frequently repeated. The child should be taught to buy only perfect objects, so that on receiving them he may examine them carefully, observing them in all their parts. He should give them back if they are not perfect or if mistakes are made by the shopkeeper in giving them out. For instance: A spoiled apple should not be accepted. " I refuse to buy it! " Beans should not be accepted for peas. Again the child refuses to buy them. He must pay only when he is sure he has been served properly (exercise in practical life).

The storekeeper will make mistakes: first, in *kinds* of objects, to sharpen the observation of *qualities* by the children who purchase; second, in the *number* of objects given, to accustom the child to purchasing proper *quantities*.

### ODD AND EVEN NUMBERS

Even numbers are red. Odd numbers are blue. There are: movable figures in wood; red and blue cubes in numbers corresponding to the figures on them; finally, charts with numbers drawn in color. Under each design are small red and blue squares arranged in such a way as to emphasize the divisibility of *even* numbers by 2 and similarly the indivisibility by 2 of *odd* numbers. In the latter case one square is always left by itself in the center.

$$1 \quad 2 \quad 3 \quad 4 \quad 5 \quad 6$$

The child places the movable numbers and the cubes on the figures on the charts. The teacher then makes two equal rows of cubes to correspond to the even numbers (red). The division is easy! But try to separate the odd numbers (blue). It is not possible! A block is always left in the middle! The child takes the figures and the blocks and arranges them on his table, imitating the design on the chart. He tries to make two equal rows of cubes for the even numbers. He succeeds. He does not succeed in doing so with the odd numbers. The numbers which can be divided thus are *even;* those which cannot be so divided are *odd*.

*Number boxes:* On these boxes are designed red and blue figures identical with those on the charts. The child puts into each box the number of ·cubes called for by the figure on the box. This exercise follows immediately the work on odd and even numbers described above. As the child transfers each series of cubes from his table to the boxes, he pronounces the number and adds *odd* or *even*.

*Exercises in attention and memory:* A chart of odd and even numbers in colors is placed on the teacher's desk in view of all the children. The red and blue cubes are piled on the teacher's desk. The teacher passes the wooden figures to the children and tells them to examine them. Immediately afterwards the children leave their seats, go to the teacher's desk, and get the numbers which correspond to their own figures. On going back to their places they fit the cubes under the corresponding figure in the arrangement just learned. The teacher is to observe

1. Whether the child has remembered the color of his figure (frequently a child with a red number takes the blue cubes).
2. Whether he has remembered his *number.*
3. Whether he remembers the proper arrangement.
4. Whether the child remembers that the chart from which he *can copy* is before him on the stand and whether he thinks of looking at it.

When mistakes are made, the teacher has the child correct himself by calling his attention to the chart.

### COUNTING BY TENS

*(For more advanced classes)*

In the store ten objects are sold for one cent, e.g.:
(10 beans), one cent for each *ten.*
One ten = ten, 10.
Two tens = twenty, 20.
Three tens = thirty, 30, etc.
From forty on (in English from sixty on) the numbers are more easily learned because their names are like simple numbers with the ending *-ty* (Italian-*anta*).

Charts should be prepared (rectangular in shape) on which nine tens appear arranged one under the other; then nine cards where each ten is repeated nine times in a column; finally, numerous cards with the unit figures 1, 2, 3, 4, 5, 6, 7, 8, 9, to be fitted on the zeros on the cards where the tens are repeated nine times.

$$10 - 10 - 20$$
$$20 - 10 - 20$$
$$30 - 10 - 20$$
$$40 - 10 - 20$$
$$50 - 10 - 20$$
$$60 - 10 - 20$$
$$70 - 10 - 20$$
$$80 - 10 - 20$$
$$90 - 10 - 20$$

Some difficulty will be experienced with the tens where the names do not correspond to the simple numbers: 11, 12, 13, etc. The other tens, however, will be very easy. When a little child is able to count to 20, he can go on to 100 without difficulty. The next step is to superimpose the little cards on the first chart of the tens series, having the resultant numbers read aloud.

*Problems:* Problems are, at first, simple memory exercises for the children. In fact the problems are solved practically in the store in the form of a game; buying, lending, sharing with their schoolmates, taking a part of what is bought and giving

it to some other child, etc. The store exercises should be repeated in the form of a problem on the following morning. The children have simply to remember what happened and reproduce it in writing. *Problems are next developed contemporaneously* with the various arithmetical operations and computations (addition, multiplication, etc.). The teacher explains the operations starting with the problem, which becomes for the children a very amusing game. The problem, finally, becomes an imaginative exercise: "Suppose you are going to the store to buy," etc., etc. We can ultimately arrive at real problems that require reasoning. In the store the teacher illustrates the various operations on the blackboard, using simple marks at first: "You have bought 2c worth of beans, at three for a cent. Let us write that down: III—III. Then let us count.
III III
1, 2, 3, 4, 5, 6. There are six. Well, then, $3+3=6$. We can also say: 2 groups of III equals 6; twice, three, six; two times three, six; $2 \times 3 = 6$. How much is $3+3$? How much is $2 \times 3$? How much is $3 \times 2$?"

The following morning, when the written problem is given, the child should have before him for reference the computation charts with all the combinations possible.

The transition to mental computation will come after this and not before.

SAMPLE CARDS

(Addition)

| | | |
|---|---|---|
| $1+1=2$ | $2+1=3$ | $3+1=4$ |
| $1+2=3$ | $2+2=4$ | $3+2=5$ |
| $1+3=4$ | $2+3=5$ | $3+3=6$ |
| $1+4=5$ | $2+4=6$ | $3+4=7$ |

(Multiplication)

| | | |
|---|---|---|
| $1 \times 1=1$ | $2 \times 1=2$ | $3 \times 1=3$ |
| $1 \times 2=2$ | $2 \times 2=4$ | $3 \times 2=6$ |
| $1 \times 3=3$ | $2 \times 3=6$ | $3 \times 3=9$ |

Subtraction in the same way. The development of these various operations followed logically on the practical exercise in the store, where multiplication proved to be a product of sums, division, a process of successive subtractions.

In our classes we have arithmetic lessons every day. The afternoon practice in the store prepares for the theoretical lesson of the following morning. Accordingly, on the day when the practical exercise occurs, there is no theoretical lesson and vice versa.

The decimal metric system applied to weights, measures and coinage is taught in the same way. The store should be equipped with scales, weights, dry and liquid measures, etc. All kinds of coins should be available, including bills up to $20 (100 francs). Work in the store should continue to be not only a help toward arithmetical computation but also toward the preparation for practical life. For instance, when cloth is sold, some attention should be given to its actual market value; its qualities should be emphasized by feeling, etc.; and the child should be taught to observe whether the storekeeper has given him the right amount and the right quality. Money changing should be made ready and easy. The money which the children spend at the store should be earned by them as a reward for their application to study and their good behavior.

GENERAL RULES

To attract the attention of defective children strong sensory stimulants are necessary. The lessons, therefore, should be eminently practical. Every lesson should begin with the presentation of the object to be illustrated by the teacher in a few words distinctly pronounced with continual modulations of the voice and accompanied by vivid imitative expression. The lessons should be made as attractive as possible and, as far as practicable, presented under the form of games, so as to arouse the curiosity of the child: guessing games, blindman's buff, storekeeping, the sleep walker, the blind store-keeper, etc. But however amusing the game may be, the lesson should always be stopped while the child is still willing to continue. His attention, which is easily fatigued, should never be exhausted. To fix ideas, lessons should be repeated many times. Each time, however, the same objects should be presented under different forms and in a different environment, so that it will always be interesting by appearing as something new: story-telling, living tableaux, large illustrations; colored pictures; stereopticon views, etc. In case individual teaching is necessary, as happens in the most elementary classes, care should be exercised to keep all the other children busy with different toys: insets, lacing-and-buttoning-frames, hooks and eyes, etc. When children refuse to take part in their lessons it is better not to use coercion, but to aim at obtaining obedience indirectly through the child's imitation of his schoolmates. Glowing praise of the pupils who are showing good will in their work almost always brings the recalcitrants to time. When a child shows he has understood the point under discussion, it is better not to ask for a repetition. His attention is easily fatigued, and the second time he may say badly what at first he gave successfully; and the failure may discourage him. It is well to be satisfied with the first good answer, bestow such praise as will afford the child a pleasant memory of what he has been doing; and go back to the subject on the following day, or, at the earliest, several hours later.

In manual training, however, the situation is different. The lesson in this subject can be a whole hour long and should take the form of serious work and not of play. The child should be set early at some useful task, even if a little hard work, not unattended with risk, be involved (wood-cutting, boring, etc.). From the outset, thus, the child will become familiar with the difficulties of bread-winning effort and will learn to overcome them.

Interest in work may be stimulated by appropriate rewards. The child may earn during work-hours the money for his purchases at the store, for his tickets to the theater and the stereopticon lecture. The child who does not work may be kept away from the more attractive lessons, such as dancing and music, which come immediately after the work hour. As a matter of fact, these children take to manual training very readily, provided the tasks assigned are adapted to the natural inclinations of the individual child in such a way that he may take in his work the greatest possible satisfaction and thus by natural bent attain a skill useful to himself and society.


MORAL EDUCATION

By the expression "moral education" we mean an education which tends to make a social being of an individual who is by nature extra- or anti-social. It presents two aspects which may be paralleled with the education thus far treated and which we call "intellectual education."

In this latter training of the mind, we began by an appropriate hygienic cure of all those physical defects which could stand in the way of successful mental education. In moral education, likewise, we try to eliminate such defects as arise from some passing physical ailment. We should carefully consider the apparently causeless "naughtiness" of children, to see whether it may not be due to some intestinal disturbance, or to the early stages of some infectious disease. The symptoms of such diseases should be known to the teacher. I have been told that English mothers use the empirical method of administering purgatives or cold shower baths to "naughty children," often with good correctional effect. I suggest that such empiricism is hardly prudent where science is able to prescribe much safer and more efficacious methods. Child hygiene must be well known to the educator and should be the pivotal point of every educational system.

In mental education, we began by reducing the child to *tonic quiescence;* here we must begin by reducing the child to *obedience.*

In mental education, to give the child his first notions of his physical person (personal imitation: touching of the parts of the body) and of his relations to environment (personal imitation: moving of objects, etc.) we had recourse to *imitation;* here, to instil in the child elementary notions of his duties, we must throw around the child an atmosphere morally correct, an environment in which, after attaining obedience, he can *imitate* persons who act properly.

In mental education we went on to the training of the senses; here we pass to the education of *feelings.* Our next step, in the one case, was to the education proper of the mind; here it is to the training of the will.

The parallel is perfect:

hygienic training: hygiene;
*tonic quiescence:* obedience;
imitation: imitation (environment);
sensory education: education of the feelings (sensibilities);
mental education proper: education of the will.

## OBEDIENCE

In a command the will of the teacher is imposed upon the defective child who is lacking in will. The will of the teacher is substituted for the child's will in impelling to action or inhibiting the child's impulses. From the very first the child must feel this will, which is imposed upon him and is irrevocably destined to overcome him. The child must understand that against this will he cannot offer any resistance. The teacher's command must be obeyed at whatever cost, even if coercive measures must be resorted to. No consideration should ever lead the teacher to desist from enforcing her command. The child *must* submit and obey. The teacher accordingly, should be careful at first to command only what she is sure to obtain. For example, she may command the child to move; since, if necessary she can *force* him to move. She may command the child to stand motionless because, if necessary, she can tie him or put him in a straight-jacket. She should never, on the other hand, command the child to " beg pardon," because the child may refuse, and in the face of this refusal the teacher may find herself helpless and lose her authority. To acquire authority in command, the teacher must possess a considerable power of suggestion; and this she can partially acquire. The teacher should be physically attractive, of an " imposing personality." She should have a clear musical voice, and some power of facial expression and gesture. These things may be in large part acquired by actual study of declamation and imitation, subjects in which the perfect teacher should be proficient. The artistic study of *command,* which the teacher may undertake, presents itself under three aspects: voice study, gesture, facial expression.

*Voice and speech:* The voice should be clear and musical, word articulation perfect. Any defect in pronunciation should effectually bar a teacher from the education of defective children. On days when the teacher has a cold and her voice is likely to assume false or ridiculous intonations, she should not think of correcting or *commanding* a defective child. The teacher's voice must be impressive and suggestive to the child. If shouting and declamatory tirades have gone out of fashion in the education of normal children, they may serve very well in the education of defectives. Whereas, in the mental education of these unfortunates, we are to pronounce a few words, but very distinctly, here there is no objection to a veritable flood of speech, provided such lectures be free from monotony, the voice passing from tones of reproof to tones of sorrow, pathos, tenderness, etc. A few words are to receive special emphasis — those which we intend shall convey to the child what we wish him to understand. The rest of all we say will constitute for the child merely modulated, musical or painful sound. It is in the music of the human voice that the elements of the education of the feelings reside; whether in the prohibition against doing something wrong, we introduce the corrective command, or, in the order to perform some action, we include encouragement, menace, or promise of reward.

Often the command is very simple. When the child is told to do something, he does not refuse. Nevertheless he is not easily persuaded. He must try to understand, first of all, what we want of him. The technique of such a simple command falls into two parts. We may call the first *incitement,* and the second *explanation.* The whole command should be repeated several times with varied intonations and with stress on different words until each word in its order has been emphasized. "James, put that book on the table." In the first instance the command will be *incitive* in character, calling the attention of the child to the action and urging him to perform it. Here the accent should fall on the name of the child and on the imperative. The tone should be that of absolute command. "*James, put* that book on the table." As we pass from the command to the explanation, the tone should be changed and somewhat softened. The first word should be clear and impelling, followed by slow, insistent words —" James, put *that book* on the table ": " James, put that book on the *table* ": " James, put that book *on* the table." Thus the voice both in commanding and in describing what was commanded, while urging the child to perform the required action and guiding him to do it, was also affording us help in its suggestive power and by explanation.

*Gesture.* The teacher must study particularly expressive gesture. She must always accompany what she says with gestures serving both to impel the child to actions and which suggest imitation and explain the command. Gesture should be expressive enough to be readily intelligible even without words; for example, if it is desirable to bring the child to perfect quiescence, as the command is given, the teacher should stop, become almost rigid, looking sharply at the child in such a way that he may be impressed by that rigid fixity which he sees before him and be brought by suggestion to imitate it. Then to keep the child motionless, the teacher may attract his attention by a slight almost continuous hypnotizing sort of whistle. To excite an apathetic child to movement the teacher should herself move, accompanying the stress of her voice with motion in her whole body.

In the *simple command,* arm gesture only should be used and as follows:

For *Incitement:* rapid movement in straight line.
For *Explanation:* slow movement in curve.
Command of *quiescence:* gesture up and down, from without toward the body.
Command of *movement:* gesture from down, up, from within, out from the body.

*Facial expression and gaze:* The gaze has a powerful effect on the child. It is the same gaze which impressed the child and brought him to the first steps in his education (see our chapter on the *Education of the Gaze*). All the expressions of the eye are useful provided the teacher employs them properly. It is not a question of scowling at the child to frighten him, as might be supposed; but rather of bringing the eye as well as the whole face to express all those emotions which the teacher must herself actually feel in the presence of an obedient or rebellious, a patient or angry child; and of giving to this expression such clearness that the child cannot possibly be mistaken as to its meaning (Séguin, page 679). The teacher's face must be expressive, mobile, hence in harmonious relationship with what is to be expressed (calmness, gaiety, effort). The expression must never vary momentarily on account of any extraneous diversion which may occur; otherwise the children will soon learn to provoke such distractions of the teacher's attention. Such commands, which demand on the teacher's part so much artistic study, will, of course, not be necessary during the whole period of the child's education.

THE END

CPSIA information can be obtained
at www.ICGtesting.com
Printed in the USA
BVHW071159010720
582722BV00001B/23